Rhinoceros/West Press

D1596435

The Modern Architectural Dictionary & Quick Reference Guide

for Architects, Interior Designers, and the Construction Trades

Edited and Illustrated by
Robert Deitch

Rhinoceros/West Press

Sherman Oaks, California

Published by: Rhinoceros/West Press
                  P.O. Box 57365
                  Sherman Oaks, CA 91413
                  www.RhinocerosWestPress.com

ISBN   0-9675345-6-9

Library of Congress Catalog Card Number: 99-091276

Front cover designed by Robert Deitch
Front cover photograph by Sharon Ackerman
Printed by Papermaster, AZ

Printed in the U.S.A.

ACKNOWLEDGMENTS

The herculean effort needed to complete this book turned out to be far greater then I ever imagined when I originally decided to write it. Clearly, without the dedication and professionalism of, in particular, M. Kate St.Clair *(my editor and proofreader)*, and my dear friend Catherine Stel *(who did a great deal of typing)*, it would probably still be a work in progress. I especially want to thank my brother, Don, for his steadfast support, and I'd also like to acknowledge my gratitude for the loving efforts of two *(long-time)* friends, Sharon Ackerman and Norma Jacobs. And finally, a special thanks to Ron Paulson at Papermaster (printing) and his staff for their outstanding efforts.

ABOUT THE AUTHOR

ROBERT DEITCH received a Bachelor of Arts degree in 3-Dimensional Design from California State University Northridge, and went on to a forty-year professional career in the fields of architecture, interior design and construction. This varied career has enabled him to develop both his manual building and artistic skills, and has included positions as a professional interior designer with ASID professional membership status, model maker, master carpenter, and *for the last 10 years*, as a computer-specialist set designer, creating the working drawings used to plan and build the sets and props used in movies and television.

FOREWORD

The rich language associated with the world of art and architecture are constantly evolving with the introduction of modern materials, techniques, and new and different styles. I have written this dictionary and reference guide from the perspective of a working designer. The role of the professional designer is becoming even more important. And even though most decisions are made by committee, the ultimately responsibility falls to the project's designers to make it all come together as expected.

TABLE OF CONTENTS

STYLE GUIDE

This guide is to help the reader better understand the methodology used to define the various architecture and design terms. The following examples will demonstrate the anatomy of a definition as used in this dictionary.

The definition style was designed for its simple, easy to find, easy to read and understand format, which all starts with an easily readable font style.

Example (1)

gimbal A device made to suspend an object on a horizontal plane between two points, allowing it to rotate laterally. Often incorporated as part of a **gyroscope. gimbaled** A.K.A. **gimbal rings**

As in the typical example above, the word or term being defined is both larger and bolder type so that it stands apart from the rest of the text and is more easily picked up by the eye when scanning for the term you are seeking. The word being defined is immediately followed by its definition. Additional definitions are labeled... **2.**, **3.**, **4.**, etc., as seen in Example (2) below. *(NOTE: "1" is always assumed and is the first definition).*

Variations of the word defined and their proper spelling immediately follow the definition (as the word **gimbaled** in the above example).

In Example (1) the last word, **gyroscope**, is also **bold** to indicate another term. Looking up these words will give the reader a better understanding of the use of the object being defined, but probably won't add to its definition.

Example (2)

segmented arch Any rounded arch that is less than a true semicircle. **2.** An arch *(less than semicircular)* embellished, on its face, with tapered segments of an arch. *NOTE: Segmented refers to that part or segment of a circle used as the radius of the arch.* See: **arches**

Example (3)

truss To tie up or bind tightly. **2.** Architecturally, the flat, rigid raftered framework that rests on the sidewalls, shaping the roof and stabilizing the walls of a structure. *NOTE: Trusses are generally used to create an unobstructed span of more than 20 ft. from wall to wall.* **truss beam, trussed beam** See: **roof truss details**

NOTE:, HISTORIC NOTE:, INVENTOR:, etc., are strictly informative and are all italicized so that these notations remain visually separate from the text of the term's actual definition. In general, italics are used to indicate a reference or to assist in an explanation.

<u>A.K.A.</u> or <u>See:</u>

A.K.A. is an abbreviation for **Also Known As**. These words are **synonyms** and have an almost identical meaning.

See: These words are also **synonyms**; they are, however, the current or preferred **synonym** for the term being defined, and indicate where a more detailed definition can be found.

- A -

abacus The slab forming the uppermost portion of the capital of a column, that divides the capital from the entablature.

abrasion A surface discontinuity caused by roughening or scratching.

abrasive A hard substance for removing material by grinding, lapping, honing, or polishing, as sandpaper. Abrasive materials are always harder than the material or finish being sanded or polished.

absorbent A material which, by contact, attracts certain liquids or gases and physically changes its form, e.g., *sponge, cloth, paper towel, etc.*

absorption The process by which liquids or gases are drawn in, filling the porous mass of the absorbing material. **2.** The increased weight of the porous material resulting from the addition of the liquid or gas. **3.** The process by which radiant energy is converted to other forms of energy. **4.** The process through which sound is suppressed. **5.** The extraction of liquids and/or gases.

abstract design An artistic expression that depends solely on intrinsic form rather than on narrative content or pictorial representation

abutment The masonry mass that supports a bridge or arch.

acacia *(Wood)* A light brown hardwood from Australia and Africa, once used for religious and sacred buildings. Primarily used for furniture and for architectural and ecclesiastical woodwork.

acceleration An increase in the speed at which cracks spread or mountains rise, fall, or move. **2.** The rate at which concrete and other materials harden.

accelerator A substance, which when added to another material like **concrete, mortar,** or **grout,** speeds the rate of hydration and/or hardening.

accent colors Contrasting colors added, in moderation, to spice up an existing color scheme.

accent lighting

accent lighting Directional lighting that emphasizes a particular object or draws attention to a particular area.

access Means of approach, e.g., *road, street, or walk.*

access control Environmental space specifically designed to encourage easy yet subliminally restricted access. In practical terms it is intended to promote the feeling that visitors are on private property and are expected to act responsibly. *NOTE:* **Access control** *is one of a series of design considerations meant to passively discourage vandalism and unauthorized entry.* See: **territorial reinforcement, surveillance and observation**

access door A door, *usually small,* provided to service or maintain mechanical equipment.

accessible Allowing physical contact through a door, panel, or easily removable cover.

accessories Refers to available options, but not essential to the use or operation of a particular device or object.

access panel Same as access door. Usually indicates a situation where only hand access is required.

access stairs Any set of stairs that provides access to a particular area. 2. A set of stairs servicing two or more floors, in addition to those stairs required by code for the safe use of the building.

accident An unexpected event.

accordion doors Any door hung from an overhead track that folds back on itself, like a bellows. 2. A hinged door consisting of a series of panels that when closed form a solid barrier and when open fold back on each other.

aceitillo *(Wood)* West Indian hardwood with a fine grain, resembling **satinwood** in color and appearance. Primarily used for furniture.

acetone A highly flammable solvent that evaporates rapidly. Used primarily in lacquers, paint removers, and thinners. Also used to dissolve various glues and adhesives.

acetylene A colorless gas used in welding, that burns above $3,500^\circ C$ when mixed with oxygen.

acetylene torch A hand-held device that controls the mix of oxygen and acetylene and directs the flame. Used to weld and cut metal.

AC generator A portable generator of *(alternating current)* electrical power. A.K.A. **generator**

acid-etching A method of cutting into metal that uses acid to eat away the surface and leave a decorative design.

acid soil Soil with a *ph* content of less than 6.6, particularly important in gardening.

acoustic Used to describe the characteristics and dimensional properties of sound waves. **acoustical**

acoustical ceiling A ceiling covered with tiles of acoustical material, often used to absorb sound and control sound pollution.

acoustical ceiling system A metal framing system designed to hold up acoustical ceiling tiles. A.K.A. **drop ceiling**

acoustical material Any material designed to absorb sound.

acre A measured unit of land equal to 43,560 sq ft or 4,046.85 sq meters (2.59 sq km).
1 sq mile = 640 acres

acropolis Any elevated group of buildings serving as a civic symbol. In ancient Greece, the fortified stronghold surrounding the temples of the gods.

acrylic fiber A synthetic fiber made of polymerizing acrylonitrile.

acrylic resin One of a group of thermoplastic resins used as a binding adhesive and in caulks and sealants.

Adirondack chair

acute angle An angle of less than 90°.

adaptation Capturing the essence or flavor of an original style.

addendum A written or graphic supplement to a contract or agreement for the purpose of changing, clarifying, correcting, or adding to the contract's original specifications.

addition New construction that expands the square footage of an existing building, including decks, porches, attached garages, etc.

additive A substance or material used to modify a specific property of another material or to improve its characteristics.

adhesive A sticky substance used to bond two surfaces together, e.g., **carpenter's glue**, **contact cement**, etc.

Adirondack chair A wooden deck chair that was developed in the 1870s as part of the leisure resort lifestyle that existed in the Adirondack mountains of northern New York.

adjustable shelving Shelves supported by clips, pegs, or other movable supports, making it possible to adjust the height of individual shelves.

adobe Spanish word for sun-dried, earthen building blocks, *not hardened by heat other than the heat of the sun.* Particularly associated with the Pueblo Indians of the southwest U.S. and Mexico. See: **vega**

adz An arched-blade cutting tool used to roughly shape wood. **adze**

aerial photograph A *bird's eye view* photograph, usually taken from an airplane, blimp, or rocket in flight.

aerosol paint Paint packaged in a pressurized container *(compressed liquefied gas)* for spray painting applications.

A-frame

A-frame A modern style developed for weekend or vacation houses, featuring a very steep dominant roof *(in the shape of the letter "A")* from the ridge to the ground. The glass panels and windows in the gable ends provided a spacious plan with a large living/dining area.

A-frame

African mahogany *(Wood)* Dense hardwood, native to the African continent. A.K.A. **Khaya**

age Making something look older. **aged, aging**

aggregate Crushed stone, gravel, or other granular materials *(sand)*, that when bound together form concrete, mortar, or plaster.

agreement A meeting of the minds. 2. A legally enforceable contract or promise that states the terms and conditions of a contract between two or more parties.

AIA *Abbr.* **American Institute of Architects**.

AIEE *Abbr.* **American Institute of Electrical Engineers**.

airbrush A *small, finger controlled,* fine-point spray paint gun used for small projects of all kinds.

air circulation The movement of fresh clean air within a confined area.

air compressor A machine that compresses air so that it can be used to power a variety of pneumatic tools and equipment. A.K.A. **compressor**

air conditioner A machine used to condition or treat the air. See: **air conditioning**

air conditioning The process of cleaning, recycling, and distributing air within an enclosed space, room, or building. Air conditioners may also control temperature, cleanliness, humidity, and odors.

air conditioning duct See: **air duct**

air conditioning system Describes all the components (air conditioner, plumbing, air ducts, fans, outlets, etc.) used to provide air conditioning to all the rooms of a building from a central source. A.K.A. **central air conditioning system**. See: **central heating and air conditioning**.

air curtain A device that delivers a downward stream of high-velocity, temperature-controlled air, across an open exterior door or loading dock, to form a barricade that prevents heat loss and makes it possible to air condition or heat the interior space.

air dried The process that takes advantage of the natural absorption of water by the sun, as with laundry hung out to dry on a laundry line or fresh paint drying on a building.

air duct A hollow, flexible tube or rectangular construction used to transfer air from one location to another. A.K.A. **airway**

air hose Used to transfer compressed air from an air compressor to pneumatic equipment and tools.

airless sprayer A device that uses hydraulics (liquids) rather than pneumatics (air) to power a spray paint gun, that both eliminates microscopic air bubbles *(associated with pneumatic sprayers)* and allows a faster application time. Especially useful on large painting projects.

air lock A space designed to isolate and control the air between rooms or compartments, to prevent the spread of airborne substances, as in a **clean room**.

air shaft A space designed for the free passage of air. A roofless area inside a large building that provides ventilation and light. A.K.A. **light well**

airtight An enclosure or barrier that does not permit the passage of air.

air vent A slotted cover plate that allows the release of trapped air, such as from an **air duct**, usually located at the highest point in the system.

airway See: **air duct**

aisle A longitudinal passageway between sections of seats in an auditorium, theatre, or church

alabaster A slightly translucent, milky white, fine-grained stone.

alarm A device that alerts the occupants of a building to a fire or an unauthorized entry.

alarm system See: **burglar alarm system, smoke detector**

alcove An architecturally separated or recessed space within a larger room.

alder *(Wood)* A variation of birch hardwood.

alignment Definitive lines that establish the position of things (such as a curved or straight beam). **2.** Lining up numerous items in a straight line.

alkaline soil Soil containing soluble salts of magnesium, sodium, or the like, and having a pH value between 7.3 and 8.5.

alley A narrow delivery or service access driveway or a secondary means of public access to a building or property. **2.** A narrow passageway between or behind buildings.

alloy Mixing two or more metals to produce a new substance. Brass is an alloy made of copper and zinc.

alteration A change in the layout or structural supports of an existing building without increasing the building's overall size. **2.** Remodeling.

aluminum A lightweight, malleable, lustrous, silver-white, nonmagnetic metal used in extrusions, castings, and sheet goods. Available in various hardnesses and shapes. Surface colored by anodizing or painting.

aluminum foil Very thin aluminum sheet goods (about 0.006 inch or 0.15 mm); used for thermal insulation, vapor barriers, wallpaper, and food wrap.

aluminum window Any window constructed principally of extruded aluminum components.

6

amaranth

amaranth *(Wood)* A dark purple, fine-grained South African hardwood. Primarily used for contemporary furniture.

ambient light The available background lighting, *natural or artificial*, in a given area.

amboyna *(Wood)* A rich brown East Indian hardwood, with yellow and red streaks. Used for modern cabinetwork and veneers.

wall anchor / engaged anchor

anchor bolt

American bond See: **common bond**

American Institute of Architects (AIA) The nationally recognized association of professional architects.

American Renaissance See: **beaux arts**

American Society of Interior Designers (ASID) The nationally recognized association of professional interior designers.

amperage The flow of electric current in a circuit, expressed in amps.

amphitheatre A circular, semicircular, or elliptical auditorium in which a central arena is surrounded by rising tiers of seats 2. Any outdoor theatre. **amphitheater**

amusement park A commercially operated park featuring entertainment, thrill rides, refreshment stands, etc.

analogous colors Colors adjacent to each other on the color wheel, e.g., blue, blue-violet, and violet. See: **color wheel**

anchor A device used to attach to or hold an object in a fixed position.

anchor bolt An expansion bolt embedded into various materials, and used to attach something to a surface -- as the **sill plate** of a wall is attached to a concrete foundation. See: **sill**

anchor line A cable or rope, attached at one end to an anchor.

angle The figure formed by the meeting of two lines. 2. The difference in direction, measured in degrees, between intersecting lines.

angle brace A strip of material connected to the corner of a frame, adding rigidity and maintaining square.

angle bracket An L-shaped, heavy metal strapping used to secure a horizontal object or structural member to a vertical member. Often used to attach individual shelves to a wall.

angle dividers An instrument used to measure and divide an existing angle.

angle iron An extruded L-shaped (normally 90°) metal bar or structural steel member.

angle rafter The primary roof rafter that defines the angle of a hip roof. See: **hip roof**

annex A subsidiary structure near or adjoining a principal building. **annexe** *(British)*

APPLIANCES
STANDARD SIZES

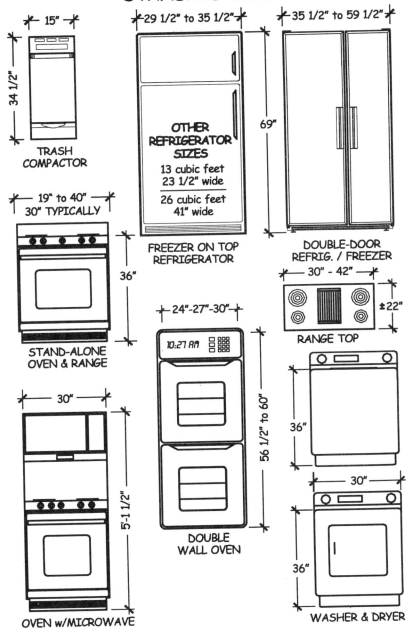

15"

34 1/2"

TRASH COMPACTOR

29 1/2" to 35 1/2"

69"

OTHER REFRIGERATOR SIZES

13 cubic feet
23 1/2" wide

26 cubic feet
41" wide

FREEZER ON TOP REFRIGERATOR

35 1/2" to 59 1/2"

DOUBLE-DOOR REFRIG. / FREEZER

19" to 40"
30" TYPICALLY

36"

STAND-ALONE OVEN & RANGE

24"-27"-30"

10:27 AM

56 1/2" to 60"

DOUBLE WALL OVEN

30" - 42"

±22"

RANGE TOP

30"

36"

5'-1 1/2"

OVEN w/MICROWAVE

36"

30"

36"

WASHER & DRYER

annual plant

annual plant A plant whose life cycle is completed in a single growing season. **annuals**

anodize A process using **electrolytes** to adhere a hard, noncorrosive oxide film to a metal surface, primarily aluminum.

antechamber A small entry room preceding an inner office or chamber. See: **anteroom** A.K.A. **waiting room, lobby, foyer, vestibule**

anteroom A room adjacent to a larger, more important room; frequently used as a waiting area, foyer, lobby, or vestibule. A.K.A. **antechamber**

antique Defined, according to U.S. law, as objects and works of art over 100 years old.

antiquing Applying a finish technique that makes the piece appear old and used.

anvil A tool on which metal is shaped.

apartment A room or group of rooms, designed as a separate dwelling. One of several similar units in a building designed as permanent housing.

anvil

apartment building A term used to describe a building containing multiple dwelling units. A.K.A. **apartment house**

apartment house See: apartment building

apex The highest point, peak, or tip of any structure.

apple (Wood) A light-colored, fine-grained hardwood used for furniture, suitable for stains or natural finishes. Also a sweet-smelling firewood.

appliances Mechanical devices made to accomplish a specific task, e.g., **refrigerators, dishwashers, laundry** See: **appliances: standard sizes Pg.#7**

applied molding Molding applied to the surface of a wall, door, or frame.

applied trim A.K.A. **applied molding**

applique (Fr) An ornament applied to a surface.

appraisal An evaluation or estimate by a qualified professional appraiser, of the market value of real property, meaning land or buildings.

approach A path or driveway leading to the entrance of a building.

approved An authorized way of doing something or a manufacturer's approved replacement parts. **2.** Acceptance or authorized permission to proceed by the owner, architect, contractor, or agents of local government with a project as designed and planned. **3.** Status granted upon successfully passing required inspections, ensuring a building or structure conforms to plans and local building codes.

approving authority In construction, an agency, board, department, or agent authorized by the state, province, county, city, or parish legislature to recommend, administer, and enforce specific requirements of the building codes.

apron Part of the trim around a window, underneath the sill. **2.** A board, molding, or combination that runs along the underside of a tabletop or along the edge of a shelf or cabinet.

aquarium A watertight rectangular vessel or tank of glass, within which an environment capable of sustaining aquatic life is created.

aqueduct A channel for supplying water. Early aqueducts depended entirely on gravity to move water from one location to another, which is why many were built atop high architectural columns and arches.

arabesque Intricate geometric pattern of stylized plants or forms of Arabic origin. **2.** An infinite variety of ornamentation *(painted, inlaid, or carved)* used to enrich flat surfaces and/or molding.

arbitration A legally binding alternative to judicial proceedings for resolving disputes. Requires the agreement of both disputing parties and the facts of the case. Guilt and innocence are decided by one or more neutral persons

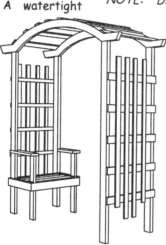

arbor

(called *arbitrators*). Usually much cheaper than going to court, in cases that exceed the average $5,000 small claims court limits.

arbor A light, open garden trellis structure used to support creeping and twisting vines. **2.** The rotating shaft of a circular saw, spindle molder, sharper, etc. *NOTE: Differs from a trellis in that an arbor has depth, where a trellis is a flat structure.*

arbor-vitae *(Wood)* An evergreen tree native to North America and eastern Asia. An excellent building and furniture wood, with similar characteristics to **thuya**. See: **thuya**

arc Any portion of the circumference of a circle.

arcade A series of arches and columns that form a corridor or passageway. **2.** A corridor lined on both sides with various shops, offices, and games of skill or chance.

arch A basic architectural structure spanning an opening and supported at both ends. Arches vary in shape from the horizontal, flat arch to semicircular and elliptical arches to bluntly or acutely pointed arches.

architect A person educated and experienced in the design of buildings and the coordination and supervision of all aspects of building construction. **2.** A legal designation reserved for a person

ARCHES

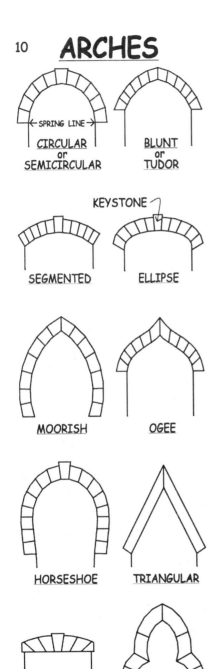

CIRCULAR
or
SEMICIRCULAR

← SPRING LINE →

BLUNT
or
TUDOR

KEYSTONE

SEGMENTED

ELLIPSE

MOORISH

OGEE

HORSESHOE

TRIANGULAR

FLAT

TREFOIL

or organization professionally qualified and licensed to perform architectural services, including analysis of project requirements, creation and development of project design, preparation of drawings, specifications, bidding requirements, and general administration of the construction contract.

architect-engineer An individual or firm offering professional services as both architect and structural engineer.

architect's scale A long, triangular-shaped measuring device, calibrated in various relationships from 1/16" = 1'-0" to 3" = 1'-0" and used to create or measure a **scaled** drawing or model. See: **scale** *NOTE: 1/4" scale (1/4"=1'-0") is the scale most used in architectural working drawings*.

architectural Pertaining to architecture, its features, characteristics, details, and materials used to build or ornament a structure.

architectural drawings One of a number of conceptual or scalable working drawings prepared by an architect or draftsman for a specific construction project. See: **conceptual drawings, rendering, color rendering, working drawings**

architectural element An object (**mantel, staircase, columns,** etc.) or detail used to add character or function to a building or structure.

architectural order See: **column details** A.K.A. **classic order, classical order**

architecture The use of art and science in the construction of buildings. 2. Refers to the style (*Victorian, Craftsman, Modern, Tudor, etc.*) incorporated in the design of buildings. 3. Building or buildings collectively.

architrave The lowest part of the lintel, which rests on the top of a column. See: **column details**

archway A passage under an arch.

arc welding The fusion of metal by use of a controlled electric arc.

arena Referred originally to the central area of a classic Roman amphitheatre or coliseum where gladiators fought and circus acts performed. Today, a large theatre-in-the-round surrounded by risers and seats, but without a raised (**proscenium**) stage. 2. Any building, indoor or outdoor, for sports events, conventions, large exhibits, etc.

armoire *(Fr)* A cabinet on top of a chest, *usually a man's chest*, or wardrobe. Originally a weapons cabinet or wardrobe for armor.

armor-plate Refers to thick **metal cladding**, as found on a military tank.

armor-plate glass See: **bulletproof glass**

armory A building used to store or manufacture military weapons. A.K.A. **arsenal**

arsenal See: **armory**

Art Deco A decorative style definitively displayed at L'Exposition Internationale des Arts Decoratifs et Industriels Modernes 1925 Paris exposition. Widely used in the architecture of the 1930s, and characterized by sharp angular or zig-zag surface forms and ornaments. A.K.A. **art moderne, skyscraper modern, modernistic, style moderne, jazz pattern** *HISTORIC NOTE: The term Art Deco was coined in the 1960s when a revitalized interest occurred.*

art director An artist hired to direct and supervise, *at some level*, the design and construction of a specific project.

artifact An object, *made or used by humans*, of great antiquity or from a given historic period, including sharpened stones used for tools, pottery, even bones.

artificial daylight Light from an artificial source, resembling natural daylight.

artificial marble A composite material made for sink tops that resembles marble.

artist A person knowledgeable and skilled in the creation of works of art.

Art Moderne *(circa 1930 - 1945)* Art and architecture characterized by its streamlined appearance.

Art Nouveau A style of art developed in France and Belgium toward the end of the 19th century; characterized by organic and dynamic forms, curving designs, and whiplash lines. The German version is called *Jugendstil*, the Austrian variant *Sezession;* in Italy *Stile Liberty*, and in Spain *Modernismo*.

Arts & Crafts

Arts & Crafts An English movement that became popular in America during the second half of the 19th century, emphasizing the importance of craftsmanship and high standards of design for everyday objects.

asbestos A fire-resistant fiber once used as insulation, floor coverings, and fire curtains. *WARNING: Asbestos has been declared a health hazard and is no longer an approved building material.*

asbestos abatement The removal of asbestos-based material. Requires special handling and must be done by a certified and licensed professional.

ash *(Wood)* A very hard, straight-grained, light brown hardwood, native to the eastern U.S. Primarily used for furniture.

ash dump A covered opening in a hearth through which fireplace ashes may be emptied into an ash pit below.

ash pit In a fireplace, an area under the firebox where ashes are temporarily stored.

ASID *Abbr.* **American Society of Interior Designers**

asphalt A dark brown or black tarlike material mixed with stones, sand, and gravel to form cementitious paving. Also used to waterproof roofs. A.K.A. **blacktop**

asphalt tile Lowcost floor tile composed of various fibers, finely ground limestone fillers, mineral pigments, and asphaltic or resinous binders. See: **asphalt**

assessed valuation The value of a property as determined by a municipality for the purpose of assessing property taxes.

assessment A tax levied on property for specific city services or improvements.

assignment The transfer of a legal right, as in a sublease.

assurance bond See: **completion bond**

astragal Molding used to cover the clearance gap left between double doors or double casement windows. See: **door styles: French doors**

atrium A principal room or central courtyard, with an open roof. *NOTE: Originally used in ancient Roman architecture.*

attached garage A garage with at least one wall (or part of a wall) in common with a building. **2.** Connected to a building, as by a covered porch.

attached pillow back Refers to upholstered furniture with permanently attached *(non-reversible)* back cushions. A.K.A. **pillow back**

attic Small interior space, between the ceiling joists and the ridge beam of a gabled roof. Often used for storage.

auditorium A building or large room , usually with theatre-style seating, designed to accommodate an audience.

auditorium seating See: **theatre seating**

automatic Anything that operates either unattended or without direct contact.

automatic door A power-operated door that is opened and closed by a remote control device.

avodire *(Wood)* A fine-textured, blond hardwood with strong, dark brown streaks. An exotic wood used for modern furniture and veneer.

awl A pointed hand tool used for piercing holes.

awning A rooflike covering, often adjustable, positioned over a window or door to protect against the sun, rain, and wind.

awning window A window consisting of a number of top-hinged horizontal sashes, one above the other, the bottom edges of which swing outward. See: **window styles**

ax A sharp-edged steel tool for splitting wood and hewing timber. **axe**

axis A straight line indicating the center of symmetry of a solid or plane figure or the spring line of an arch.

azure A heraldic term used to describe a particular shade of the color blue.

- B -

back Opposed to front. To the rear of, or behind. 2. That portion of a chair or sofa that supports the occupant's back and upper body.

backbar A work surface and display area for various kinds of liquor, located behind a bar. Usually contains cabinets for storage and refrigerated coolers. Similar to a back counter in a restaurant, or behind a lunch counter.

back counter A work surface behind the front serving counter of a restaurant, with storage below.

back door Denotes a door at a rear entrance.

backdrop A large background painting used to provide a realistic setting for theatrical (film, TV, and live theatre) stage productions and to mask the backstage area from the audience.

backfill Refers to refilling (back to grade level) a trench dug for the purpose of installing or replacing electrical or plumbing lines, from existing service to a new location. Any application, such as the building of a wall or foundation, where dirt is removed for a specific purpose and then is refilled. **backfilling**

background lighting Lighting that accentuates elements in the background.

background sound Extraneous sounds or noise, from a source other than that being listened to, recorded, or measured.

backhoe A machine, with a hydraulic arm and shovel, used for excavating and cutting trenches.

backing Any material attached or behind, used to reinforce, stiffen, or to provide a stable base for another material. 2. A theatrical term used to describe a

backsaw

painted background. A.K.A. **backdrop**

backsaw A hand saw having a stiff metal strip along its back and small teeth for fine, accurate cuts.

backsplash A protective wall panel (tile, marble, etc.) behind a **sink** or **counter**. A.K.A. **splash back, splashboard**

backsaw

backstage The entire area behind the **set** or **backdrop** on a theatre stage, including the rear of the stage, dressing rooms, and storage areas, that is not exposed to the audience.

backup Overflow or backwards flow of wastewater in a drain or piping system, due to stoppage. **2.** Supportive. **3.** Copies of computer software or documents on disk, so previous work is not lost in the event of a hard disk crash.

baffle A barrier (plate, wall, etc.) used to deflect, reduce, or regulate the flow of various substances -- liquids, gases, sound, light, etc.

bagging A version of a **rag-rolled paint finish**, that uses a plastic bag around the rag to achieve a desired painting effect. See: **rag-rolled finish** A.K.A. **ragging**

baked finish A tough, durable paint, glaze, or varnish finish, obtained by baking, usually at temperatures above 150°F (65°C).

balance A pleasing arrangement of objects, either symmetrical or asymmetrical, around an imaginary central point.

balance beam A beam attached to a **gate** or **drawbridge**, at one end and a counterbalanced weight at the other, to facilitate opening or closing the **gate**. A.K.A. **balance bar**

balconet A false balcony, used as a decorative element rather than for practical use.

balcony A projecting platform on the interior or exterior of a building, either cantilevered or supported from below, and enclosed by a railing or balustrade. **2.** A theatrical term used to describe an area of seating above or over the main floor of an auditorium or theatre.

ball A round-shaped ornament.

ball-and-claw foot The leg of a piece of furniture carved to resemble the talon or claw of a bird of prey clutching a ball.

ballast A device used to provide the voltage needed to start a fluorescent or other electric-discharge lamp.

ball-joint A rotating joint in which a ball-shaped end is held in a spherical shell, permitting the axis of one part to be set at any angle with respect to the other.

balloon framing A method, introduced in the early 1830s, of framing, utilizing long studs, which the floor joists are attached to, unlike the modern framing practice of resting the floor joists on top of stud walls. **2.** Framing of a building using relatively short boards nailed together, to create a bulge, rather than long, straight lumber.

balloon shade A type of window shade that forms fluffy fabric folds when raised.

ball peen hammer A machinist's hammer having a cylindrical, convex-faced surface at one end and a rounded, ball-shaped head on the other. Used primarily for shaping metal.

ballroom A large social hall designed expressly for dancing, but also used for other functions.

balsa wood *(Wood)* A lightweight wood of minimal density used particularly for models. Also used to create theatrical props (e.g., furniture) that easily breaks apart in a staged fight without actual injury to the actors. A.K.A. **corkwood**

baluster An upright support, traditionally turned wood, used to hold up the handrail of a staircase. Part of a **banister. 2.** A decorative element used in doors, windows, and furniture. See: **staircase details**

balustrade A series of balusters, as in a staircase or balcony railing. See: **baluster**

bamboo *(Wood)* A woody, tropical perennial plant, native to Asia, used for *(rattan)* furniture, ornaments, building material, pipes, paper, and food.

bamboo turning Wood turned *(See: turning)* on a lath to

look like bamboo, used predominantly to produce furniture.

band Any horizontal flat element or group of moldings slightly projecting from a wall plane. Used primarily to mark a division in the wall or column. A.K.A. **belly mold, band course, band molding**

banding Various materials used to cover the unsightly end grain or the unfinished edge of plywood. **2.** An accent strip, either flat or built-up, on the edge or top of a table, or around a building.

band saw A wood milling machine that turns an endless belt of flat steel, with teeth on one edge, at high speed, to cut wood.

banister An entire railing system, including the newel posts, handrail, balusters, and bottom rail (when present), of a staircase or balcony rail.

bank A mass of soil rising above a level grade. **2.** An establishment that receives, lends, and exchanges money and carries out or processes financial transactions.

banner A piece of cloth with a motto or logo of a professional organization or club. **2.** A headline spanning the width of a newspaper page.

banner

banquet hall A large room, designed to accommodate a large number of people, and often used for dining, meetings, and social gatherings.

banquette *(Fr)* Benchlike seating alongside a table.

bar

bar A counter, *usually 42 inches high*, primarily used to serve alcoholic beverages. **2.** A length of solid metal having a square, rectangular profile.

barbed A repetitive sharp projection or hook, intended to rip or cut, as in barbed wire.

barbed wire Two or more wire strands twisted together that incorporates, at regular intervals, sharp points or hooks. Used primarily for fences. **barb wire**

barcelona chair A revolutionary chair for its time, utilizing modern materials and designed by architect Mies van der Rohe. See: **chair styles**

bar clamp A device used in carpentry to hold two or more pieces of wood tightly together while glue dries. Consists of a long bar along with one permanently attached clamping jaw and one adjustable clamping jaw.

bar compass An instrument used to draw or cut large circles and arcs. The concept of using a long, straight horizontal bar with two movable points, set measurably apart, has long been used by draftsman and carpenters to draw large circles or arcs. A.K.A. **trammel points, beam compass,**

bargeboard See: **barge rafter**

barge rafter The exposed, overhanging rafter projecting beyond the face of a gable wall. Used as decorative trim to finish the edge of an overhanging roof. A.K.A. **bargeboard, lookout rafter, gable board, rake board**

bar molding

bar molding A scrolled *(rabbeted)* molding (See: **rabbet**) traditionally applied to the edge of a bar or counter. **bar mold** A.K.A. **bar rail**

barn A building to house and shelter farm animals, primarily horses, and equipment, and to store hay and other agricultural produce.

baroque The art, architecture, and decoration of the Italian Renaissance (circa 16th century), characterized by bold details, sweeping curves, and large scale. A dominant European style through the 18th century, and includes a later phase, known as Rococo, with a French influence.

barracks Permanent or temporary housing for soldiers or, less often, workmen.

bar rail See: **bar molding**

barrel A large, cylindrical, wooden container with a bulging middle, used to hold a variety of liquids, grains and other products. The staves (wood slats) are bound together by several metal hoops. **2.** Once used as a standard of measurement. For liquids, equal to 31.5 U.S. gallons or 36 *British* imperial gallons, and as dry measurement equal to just under 200 lbs of flour, fish, or pork.

barrel vault A semicircular masonry vault supported by parallel walls or arcades. A.K.A. **barrel ceiling, barrel roof,**

cradle vault, tunnel vault See: vaulted ceilings: barrel

barricade An obstruction used to prevent the passage of people and/or vehicles. A.K.A. **barrier**

barrier See: barricade

barroom A room containing a **bar** where liquor, *by the glass*, is served.

base Anything from which a start is made. 2. The lowest of the three principal parts of a column or **pier**, that rest on a **plinth, pedestal,** or **podium.** See: **column details** 3. The bottom of a wall with baseboard trim. **4.** The lowest visible part of a building, often distinctively treated. A base is distinguished from a foundation or footing in being visible rather than buried. **5.** Pertaining to paint, either the medium or the main chemical ingredient. 6. The first of several layers of paint or plaster.

baseboard A carpentry term used to describe either a single piece of molded base material or the collective pieces of boards and molding used to ease the visual transition from a vertical element *(wall)* to a horizontal element *(floor)*. 2. A rectangular board, to which **cap molding** and **base shoe** are attached to make up the base molding. A.K.A. **skirting board, mop-board, base mold, base**

baseboard heater A heating system in which the elements are installed as panels along the baseboard of a wall. *NOTE: Baseboard heaters, in some cases, eliminate the need for baseboard.*

base coat The initial application of plaster, paint, or any other similar material, used as a filler and base for a finish coat to follow. A.K.A. scratch coat, first coat.

base line A line from which measurements originate, principally used in surveying.

basement The lowest story of a building, usually partly or entirely below grade. A.K.A. **cellar**

base molding A small molding (cap) used at the top of a baseboard. A.K.A. **cap molding** See: **molding detail s: casing & base mold**

base shoe A small molding, usually quarter-round, used as trim for the bottom of the baseboard on interior walls.

base tile The lowest (**course**) row of tiles on a tiled wall.

basin A shallow vessel to hold water. 2. A shallow depression in the land, where rainwater often collects.

basket weave A textile weave that imitates the construction of reed baskets, with alternating threads or strapping.

basket weave bond A masonry term used to describe a standard bricklaying arrangement.

bas-relief An applied casting, carving, or embossing that protrudes from the surface, as opposed to cutting into the surface and removing material. A.K.A. **low relief, basso-relievo, bass-rilievo**

basswood *(Wood)* Medium low

BATHROOM DETAILS

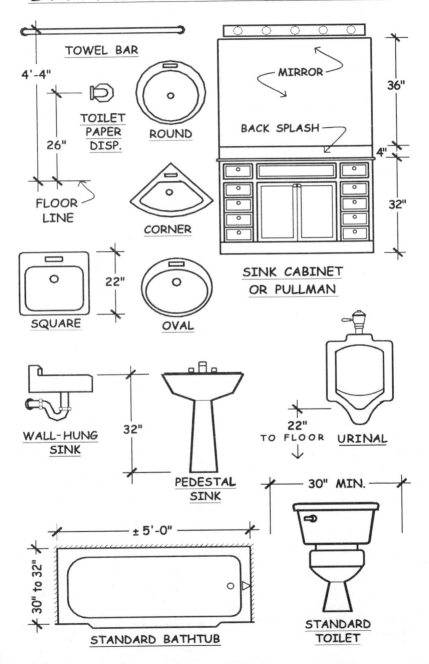

TOWEL BAR

4'-4"

TOILET
PAPER
DISP.

26"

FLOOR
LINE

ROUND

CORNER

MIRROR

BACK SPLASH

36"

4"

32"

SINK CABINET
OR PULLMAN

22"

SQUARE

OVAL

WALL-HUNG
SINK

32"

PEDESTAL
SINK

22"
TO FLOOR   URINAL

30" MIN.

± 5'-0"

30" to 32"

STANDARD BATHTUB

STANDARD
TOILET

density wood used extensively for plywood and molding. North American linden.

bastard A nonstandard item; one of irregular or abnormal size or shape or of inferior quality.

bastille The 14th century Paris tower fortress, which by the 17th century had become a prison and political target during the French Revolution. **bastile**

bastion A stronghold. 2. A projection in a perimeter wall meant to provide a defensive advantage.

bat The thin, equally spaced, vertical strips used to visually break up a flat wall and cover seams. **batten** See: **bat-and-board**

bat-and-board A style of wall cladding or siding, where equally spaced, vertical strips of wood are applied to cover joints and aesthetically break up a plain flat wall. A.K.A. **battening**

bath The act of bathing. A cleansing of the body.

bathhouse Refers primarily to a public bathing facility catering, *as in Roman times*, predominantly to men. Bathhouses have been part of human culture, worldwide, since the beginning of civilization and were popular well into the 20th century, until modern plumbing was installed in virtually every home. 2. A small structure containing dressing rooms or lockers for bathers, as at the seaside.

bathroom A room containing a water closet, lavatory, and **bathtub** or **shower**. See: **bathroom details**

bathroom cabinet A built-in cabinet containing a sink and storage. 2. A medicine cabinet built into the wall. A.K.A. **Pullman**

bathroom fixtures Tubs, sinks, and toilets, usually made of **porcelain**. A.K.A. **plumbing fixtures**

bathtub A plumbing fixture used for bathing. A.K.A. **washtub**

bathroom cabinet

batten Refers to **bat-and-board** siding. **battening** See: **bat-and-board**

batten door An unframed door constructed of vertical boards held together by Z-brace battens. See: **door styles**

battered wall A wall that is wider at the base than at the top.

battery A device that stores and supplies DC electrical power. 2. A group of two or more similar items (*i.e., cannons, toilets, etc.*) that use a common resource or disposal system.

battlement A fortified parapet wall. **embattlement**

Bauhaus A school of design established by **Walter Gropius** in Weimar, Germany (1919-1932), which emphasized the functional aesthetic in modern art and architecture of the Industrial

bay

Age. The Bauhaus had a profound impact on the world of contemporary design.

bay The space between columns or building supports. **2.** A protruding structure, as a **bay window**. **3.** The space created by the **muntins** of a sash window meant for glass.

bay window A large angled or curved window projecting outward from the surface of a wall. A.K.A. **projecting window**

baywood *(Wood)* See: Honduras mahogany

bazaar A fresh-air marketplace, usually a narrow alley, street, or series of streets consisting of small shops or stalls that sell produce, prepared food, and other consumer goods.

bead Denotes a long, semicircular or half-round detail traditionally used as trim in art and architecture. See: **bead molding 2.** As applying a bead of caulk or sealant from a caulking gun. **beading** A.K.A. **running bead 3.** A small rounded or expanded edge, strip, flange, or noising having a rounded edge.

beadboard A bead scored, about 2" apart, in 1/4" plywood, traditionally used in **wainscoting**.

bead molding A small molding that features a beadlike shape as its principal or dominant element. See: **bead. 2.** A narrow wood strip, rounded on one edge, against which a door or window sash closes. A.K.A. **stop bead**.

bead weld A welding term to denote a small, uniform running weld.

beam A structural member whose prime function is to carry a heavy load (e.g., a **joist**, **girder**, or **rafter**).

beam ceiling A ceiling featuring exposed *(either structural or applied)* **beams**.

beam compass See: **bar compass**

bearing Supporting. **2.** The vertical structural elements (walls, columns, etc.) that support **beams**, **trusses**, or other horizontal structural members.

bearing wall A wall intended to support a large amount of weight, such as additional stories and/or a roof structure.

beaux arts French for *fine arts*, as defined by the *Ecole des Beaux-Arts*, France's preeminent, turn-of-the-century school of art and architecture. **2.** Also used to describe a style of architecture known as **American Renaissance (1880-1920)** A.K.A. **The Architecture of Big Business**, that represents America's nouveau riche industrial barons' desire to bring the best of Europe home, and explains why **beaux arts** incorporates a cornucopia of architectural styles -- **Italian Renaissance**, **French baroque**, and **neoclassical revival**. Popularly used in row townhouses, office buildings, and grandiose country estates.

bed A piece of furniture that includes a comfortably soft, flat surface to sleep on. **2.** A layer or stratum of preparation to provide a stable base for the application of a second, finished layer, as in

preparation for a concrete slab or in masonry. **3.** A landscaping term used to describe an area covered by low spreading plants.
See: **bedding plants**

STANDARD BED SIZES

twin	3'3" x 6'6"
double	4'6" x 6'6"
queen	5'0" x 6'8"
Calif. king	6'0" x 7'0"
std. king	6'6" x 7'0"

bed chamber An apartment or chamber intended for a bed, or for sleeping and resting. See: **bedroom**

bedding plants Annual and subtropical plants used for their seasonal effects in landscaping.

bedrock Denotes a large, solid rock base underlying the earth's surface soil, upon which a building's foundation can be firmly established.

bedroom A room with a bed, and where clothing is kept.

beech *(Wood)* A pale, straight-grained hardwood, native to Asia and Europe, often used for flooring and furniture. Similar in characteristics to **maple** and **birch**, and used in similar applications.

beehive tomb A beehive-shaped, underground Mycenaean monumental tomb.

belfry A room at or near the top of a bell tower. **2.** A tower containing bells and their supporting timbers.

bell Refers to anything made to resemble the profile of a bell. *(i.e., a bell-shaped dome, arch, roof, or coupling that accepts two different-sized pipes).*

belly A convex swelling of any surface, element, or piece. As the rounded center of a vase; the underside of a beam.

belly course See: **belt course**

belt course A horizontal detail or molding (wood or masonry) that runs around the middle of a buil ding. A.K.A. **belly mold, belly course**

belvedere A high open terrace, usually on the top floor of a building, providing a commanding view of the countryside, the town square, or a garden. A.K.A. **lookout tower**

bench A long seat with or without a back, usually with a slatted wooden seat, and primarily, but not exclusively, intended for exterior use.

benchmark In surveying, a permanent reference point or fixed object. **2.** A measurement of speed to determine the fastest of several computer systems to do a specific task.

bench sander A stationary power tool (table mounted or on a stand) equipped with a rotating abrasive disk or belt, and used to smooth and shape the surface and edges of **numerous** materials.

bench vise A large vise, attached to a bench, that holds material or components that are being worked on.

benchwork Any work performed best by sitting at a bench rather than standing.

bentwood A technique by

which wood is steam heated and bent into shape, rather than by carving or machining.

Berber carpet A woven carpet with an angulating pattern.

Bergére chair (Fr) A style of armchair with an upholstered seat and back and an exposed wood frame.

berm A raised section of earth. **2.** A continuous bank of earth against a building, masonry wall, or along the side of the road; a shoulder. **3.** A narrow terrace or shelf built into an embankment and breaking the continuity of a slope.

Bergére chair

berth Originally, all the space allotted a sailor for his bunk, clothing, and personal items onboard ships. Now refers to more luxurious accommodation onboard ships.

bevel A slanted or chamfered edge. **beveled**

bevel square A device carpenters use to duplicate an existing angle. A.K.A. **miter square**

bias Any material applied at a 45° diagonal. **2.** Threads that run at a 45° diagonal. A.K.A. **warp threads, weft threads**

bid An offer to perform specific work, or designated portion thereof, as described or stipulated in a contract or specifications, for a specified price.

bid price The amount of money for which the bidder offers to perform the described or specified work.

bid request An invitation, notice, or advertisement to potential bidders, along with instructions, requirements, and a description of the scope of the project and conditions (including a closing date) which bids should address and conform to in order to qualify for consideration.

bin A container for storing loose materials.

binding Strips of heavy fabric sown to the edges of a carpet to prevent unraveling and to decorate the edge. A.K.A. **carpet binding**

birch (Wood) A light brown, fine-grained, high-density hardwood, native to North America and northern Europe. Takes paint and stain well, and can be stained to imitate walnut. Used extensively for cabinets, doors, trim, flooring, and furniture. Similar in characteristics to **maple** and **beech**, and used in similar applications.

birdbath Usually a garden ornament, consisting of a shallow concrete basin on a pedestal, meant to attract birds.

bird's-eye view A view from above. **2.** Known as the **plan view** in architectural drafting.

bird's mouth A notch cut near the bottom of a rafter that allows the rafter to set flat on the top plate of a supporting wall.

biscuit joinery A system of connecting flat boards together to make a wider board, as for a tabletop.

bit   A small tool, one of many similar shapes or sizes that fit into the chuck of a drill, screw gun, or router.

blackboard   A board specifically made to write on with chalk. See: **chalkboard**

black light   A fluorescent bulb that puts out an invisible ultraviolet light, used in conjunction with ultraviolet paint to create a visual effect.

blacktop   See: **asphalt**

black walnut   *(Wood)* One of the most beautiful hardwoods grown in the U.S. with a rich color and a very handsome, fine-grained appearance when highly polished. Scarce and expensive, used mainly for high-quality furniture.

blade   The cutting part of any sharp instrument; like a knife.

blank   Bare. Having little or no detail. Said of a wall without a door or a window.

blasting   Using explosives to loosen rock or other closely packed materials.

blasting cap   A device used to detonate explosives.

bldg.   *Abbr.* **building**.

bleeding   To show through or run together, as in layered paint and glazes.

blemish   A minor irregularity or defect in any material that does not affect its durability or strength.

blending   Mixing to a common consistency.

blind   A device used to obstruct vision or keep out light; a shade, screen, or series of adjustable slats known as a **Venetian blinds**. 2. Not in sight or view of.

blind door See: **dummy door** A.K.A. **sham door**,

blister   A roughly circular or elongated raised portion of any surface, often caused by pressure, as in a pipe.

blistering   Small blisters, bubbles, or bulges that form an irregular surface. 2. A chemical reaction to a painted surface, either as paint remover or used for its decorative effect.

bloated   Swollen.

block   Refers to the size of something -- a small piece of wood, a large piece of marble. 2. A large chunk of something that is intended to be cut down to a more usable or consumable size. 3. One of many or a group of equivalent items, such as building or concrete masonry blocks, or as a block of stock. 4. Part of a mechanical device, known as a block and fall, used for hoisting. 5. A plot of land that can be subdivided. 6. A segment of a street (the sidewalk) between two perpendicular crossing streets -- three blocks north means three streets or intersections north.

block-and-fall A device used in rigging to lift and move heavy objects.

block & fall

blocking

blocking Fixed pieces of wood arranged to reinforce, join, secure, or fill spaces. **2.** Small blocks of wood used for shimming. **3.** A carpentry term used to describe the stiffening of studs or joists by linking them together at regular intervals.

block plane A small hand tool with an angled cutting blade, used to take off a thin strip of wood each time the plane passes over the edge of a wooden board. Often used to slightly round off the sharp edges of shelving and countertops.

blue board A type of **drywall** made to resist moisture. Used in areas where water is present, e.g., **kitchens** and **bathrooms**.

blueprint Originally referred to a now-antiquated photographic process for reproducing large drawings, in which the background came out blue and the drawing came out white. Today it refers to any reproduction of architectural or engineering working drawings.

blunt arch An arch that rises to a slight point. See: **arches**

blushing A painting term used to describe white- or grayish-cast paint resulting from the incompatibility of water, oil, or solvent.

board A thin slab of wood cut to a uniform width, length, and thickness.

board-and-bat See: **bat-and-board**

boarded up Windows and doors covered with plywood, to secure and protect the property.

board foot The cubic measurement used in the sale of lumber, equal to 1 square foot by 1 inch thick. A.K.A. **board measure**

boarding school Any school with living accommodations for its students.

board measure See: **board foot**

board sheathing The use of boards, rather than plywood products, to cover and stiffen exterior wall studs or rafters. A.K.A. **sheathing board**

boardwalk A walkway made of long boards or planks, mimicking an old wooden pier and often found in or near oceanfront communities.

boathouse A structure built specifically for storing and repairing small boats when not in use, generally built at the water's edge; often with provisions for social activities, studios, or offices.

bodily injury A legal term describing liability for the physical injury, sickness, or disease sustained by any person, resulting from the neglect or malfeasance of the property owner.

body The principal part of a building, structure, or object.

boiler A closed vessel used to heat or vaporize liquids, usually water. Part of the plumbing system of a house or building that produces hot water.

boilerplate Thick sheets of steel used for making boilers and tanks.

boilerplate operation

boilerplate operation A systematic and repetitive assemblage process.

boiler room A utility room where a boiler and associated equipment are located.

bolster A pillow that is part of the design of an upholstered piece of furniture. A.K.A. **cushion**

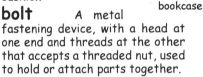

bookcase

bolt A metal fastening device, with a head at one end and threads at the other that accepts a threaded nut, used to hold or attach parts together.

bolt lock A slide bolt used on a door for extra security.

bomber hinge A spring hinge that allows a door to swing in both directions and automatically returns the door to its closed position. A.K.A. **double-action spring hinge**

bond The adhesive strength of the material or process used to hold two surfaces *(as with lamination)* or objects together. **2.** A financial guarantee. See: **completion bond 3.** A masonry term to describe the pattern layout of the bricks or blocks.

bonnet The **cap** piece on top of something. **2.** A small **roof** over a **bay window** or any similar structure.

book Assembling or preparation of material for installation. As in the preparation and folding of wallpaper, prior to hanging. **booking, booked**

bookcase A series of horizontal shelves to hold books and other objects.

bookstack Refers to the many stacks of shelved books in a library. A.K.A. **bookcase**

boom The rigging and track used to support a hoist *(lift)*. **2.** The projecting arm of a crane or derrick.

booth A small private compartment, as telephone booth or voting booth. **2.** Sectioned seating, around tables in a restaurant.

border That which defines an area or shape. The outer edges **2.** A theatrical curtain. See: **tease**

boring Drilling with the intent of extracting a sample or removing a medium-size hole.

bottom rail The lowest horizontal structural member of a door, banister or balcony safety railing.

boulder A large, naturally rounded rock.

boulevard A major thoroughfare, on which opposing traffic is often divided by a raised, curbed island with plants and grass.

boundary An area defined by its own limits.

boundary survey See: **survey**

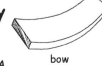

bow

bow A longitudinal curvature or bend in the surface of lumber. **bowed**

bowl

bowl A shallow basin or inverted dome shape.

bow window A bay window with a rounded shaped. See: **bay window**

box A 6-sided object, one of which is a lid or opening. Denotes that something can be put inside. A toolbox or a switch box. **2.** Something that is made to resemble the square or rectangular characteristics of a box. **3.** Prime seating in a theatre or auditorium.

boxed stairs A stairway completely enclosed by walls, and usually having a door at each floor.

box nail Standard nail with a flat head and pointed shaft. A.K.A. **common nail**

box office A room or booth where event or theatre tickets are sold.

box pleating Fabric, folded and sewn in place to cover the legs of upholstered furniture.

boxwood *(Wood)* A light-colored, fine-grained, very dense hardwood, used for marquetry and furniture.

box pleating

brace A wood or metal support (permanent or temporary) used to stiffen or keep a wall straight and square. See: **sway brace 2.** A bracket with a support bar diagonally from the two ends. **3.** A nonelectric tool *(like a drill)* used for boring holes in wood.

braced frame A frame or wall with a diagonal board, let-in to stiffen the wall against lateral forces. A.K.A. **braced framing, full frame**

bracing Stiffening or supporting structural elements used to stabilize a structure.

bracket A device that is attached to a wall or inside of a cabinet and used to support the weight of a beam, shelf, etc.

bracketed stairs

Decorative bracket-shaped ornamentation applied to the exposed end of each step. A.K.A. **bracketed string**

brad A small finishing nail, with an almost flush head.

brad pusher A tool that holds and insets a brad into the targeted wood surface.

branch A plumbing term used to describe the system of interconnecting pipes *(feeder lines)* through which water and refuse flows to or from a main or central line. **2.** An electrical term used to describe the wiring system through which electricity flows.

brass A copper and zinc alloy, traditionally used for cabinet, door, and window hardware.

braze To join two pieces of metal together, using a hard, nonferrous, metal filler rod and heat of temperature above 800° F (427°C).

Brazilian rosewood

(Wood) Wood from the **jacaranda** tree. See: **rosewood**

breadboard edge Refers to a board that runs along the end of the boards *(covering the end grain)* that make up a cutting board or tabletop. Utilizing a breadboard along the edge stiffens and ensures against the laminated boards splitting apart.

breadboard edge

break A change in continuity or direction of a surface or detail; as in referring to the path of a wall. **2.** A machine used to bend sheet metal.

breakfast bar A counter-high table in the area of the kitchen for informal meals, usually breakfast.

breakfront A large cabinet or bookcase with a protruding center section, often with glass doors.

breezeway A covered passageway, but open, connecting two buildings or two wings of a building.

brewery A building or complex of buildings, equipped to manufacture and distribute beer, but also includes other brewed products. **malt house**

bric-a-brac Interesting small objects and mementoes.

brick A rectangular-shaped, solid or hollow, building block of clay or shale, used to build walls, buildings, and paved walkways.

brickwork Building with bricks. What a mason does. All the work (**layout, construction,** etc.) involved in building masonry

(brick and mortar) structures. A.K.A. **bricklaying, brick masonry**

bridge Any structural element used to span a gap. **2.** A structure that spans a river or depression in the landscape and provides unobstructed thoroughfare for pedestrians and vehicle traffic.

bridging Refers to a system of stiffening and holding joists in place, which helps to distribute the load more evenly. A.K.A. **cross-bridging, solid** or **block bridging, blocking.**

bridle path A path, prepared and reserved for riding horses.

brightness The quality or condition of being bright. **2.** Sharp wit. **3.** The attribute of color by which the light source appears to emit more light or less light. A.K.A. **luminance**

brittle Describes something that will easily break apart.

broad knife A putty knife, but with a wider blade. Used to remove paint or wallpaper. A.K.A. **stripping knife**

broadloom Used to describe carpeting made typically in 9', 12' and 15' wide rolls. Any weave of carpet woven on a wide loom. A.K.A. **seamless carpet**

brocade A heavy fabric with a raised design.

broken pediment A classic Roman pediment characterized by a split in the center, often filled with an urn, cartouche, or other ornament. See: **pediment**

bronze

broken pediment

bronze A copper and tin alloy. Often used in the casting of sculptures. **2.** As sculpture, a process of casting in which a wax mold, buried in damp sand, is replaced with molten bronze.

bronzing Applying a bronze coating.

brownout A reduction (not a complete disruption) of electrical service, which affects the operating capabilities of electrical appliances and equipment that require electric power. *NOTE: Brownouts are the result of more demand than capacity, and usually affects a large area supplied by a single electric utility company. In particular, brownouts are the result of our massive use of air-conditioning on extraordinarily hot days.*

brownstone Refers to a style of building, *often a row house or apartment,* popular in the eastern United States during the mid- and late 19th century with a dark brown or reddish brown sandstone facade.

brush An implement made of natural or artificial bristles used to apply paint.

bucket A vessel, with a handle, to carry small objects or liquids. **2.** The large scoop attachment on an excavating machine, that digs or carries loose materials (earth, gravel, stone, concrete, etc.).

buckle A distortion in any surface, such as a bulge or wrinkle caused by unequal distribution of weight, temperature, moisture, or the result of enormous pressure or strain.

buckram A light linen canvas used to line or stiffen fabric, giving a more finished look to upholstered pieces.

buff The cleaning and polishing of a surface or object to a high luster.

buffet *(Fr)* A cabinet for holding and displaying dishes and silverware. A.K.A. **sideboard, cupboard 2.** A table from which food is served.

build To construct or erect a structure, using any material, process, method, or design deemed safe and workable.

building Any structure. Any enclosed permanent structure used or specifically built for housing, commerce, industry, etc.

building block A rectangular masonry unit, other than brick, used in the construction of buildings.

building code The rules and regulations adopted by local authorities to establish minimum standards for the construction of buildings and structures of all kinds. A record of compliance to the local building code is a prerequisite for a certificate of occupancy.

building environment

The combination of conditions

building inspector

(lighting, noise, temperature, humidity, odors, etc.) that exist within a building.

building inspector A local official, usually from the building department, who checks building plans and physically inspects construction sites at specific stages for compliance to local building code.

building main Refers to the principal branch pipe and fittings that supply the building with water, usually from the water main the city has established for the distribution of water.

building maintenance Work performed to prevent the deterioration, decline, or failure of any part of any equipment; relating to the everyday use of or function of a building.

building materials Any material used in the construction of buildings.

building paper See: felt paper, tar paper

building permit A written authorization granted by local municipality to proceed with construction, issued after the projects plans are reviewed.

building rehabilitation See: rehabilitation

building restoration See: restoration

building retrofit See: retrofit

building service chute A vertical tube or channel used to convey (by gravity) mail, laundry,

and garbage from upper floors to a collection point on a lower level.

building services Utilities and services provided as a regular part of the building's environment (heat, air-conditioning, lighting, plumbing, electrical, gas, fire protection, and security).

building stone Any stone used in building construction.

building trades Skilled specialists (carpenters, plumbers, plasterers, masons, etc.) performing various aspects of construction.

buildup A substructure or addition of layers used to adjust one surface or plane in alignment with another.

built-in Built as an integral part of a larger construction or built to fit into a predefined space.

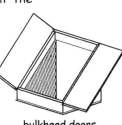
bulkhead doors

bulkhead Refers primarily to walls made of metal, as on a ship or tank.

bulkhead doors Exterior doors used to cover a cellar access. A.K.A. **storm cellar doors**

bulldozer A tractor or similar equipment used to move large amounts of earth.

bulletin board Often found in the local marketplace, a school, or in a company, a bulletin board is a place where people can post local announcements, ads, information, etc.

bulletproof glass Thick,

bull float

dense, tempered glass or plastic, capable of stopping a bullet, and used in security situations. A.K.A. **armor-plate glass, bullet-resisting glass, security glass**

bull float Generally a large, long, flat tool, operated from the parameter of a concrete pour from the end of a long wooden handle, to smooth and finish concrete. A.K.A. **leveller** See: **float**

bullnose Denotes a rounded edge or blunt corner **2.** Molding or trim used on the exposed edge of stairs, windows, tables, doors, etc. **3.** A metal bead plasterers used on exterior corners to help ensure against damage.

bumper guard A metal or rubberized mold applied to a wall or door and used to absorb potential damage from movable furniture or equipment. A.K.A. **bumper bar** or **guard bar**

bungalow A small, single-story frame house or cottage, *circa 1890-1940*, often incorporating a covered veranda. *NOTE: Bungalows were considered the first prepackaged (ready-to-build) houses, such as would be found in a Sears, Roebuck catalog.* See: **Craftsman style**

bungalow court A group of detached, single-story, single-family dwellings, arranged around a common pathway or planted area.

bunk beds Stacked narrow beds, formally used in a

bunk bed

work-camp environment in unpopulated areas. Mostly used today for small children sharing a room.

bunker A structure, often elevated, for the storage of potentially dangerous materials.

bunting Widths of striped or colored cloth *(usually the same cloth and colors used in the national flag)* used as drapery or streamers to add a sense of festivity to political and patriotic events. Origin may be from the German word *bunt*, meaning colored. **2.** Refers to the cloth used to make flags.

bunting

bureau *(Fr)* A desk or chest of drawers. **2.** A.K.A. **secretary, bureau bookcase**

burglar alarm system An electronic system, including photoelectric beams and motion detectors, designed to detect unauthorized entry. A.K.A. **security alarm system**

burl *(Wood)* Curly wood grain, taken from the root or base of a branch. A.K.A. **curl**

burlap A coarse woven fabric of jute, hemp or, less commonly, flax, used to bundle or package loose material *(gravel, pebbles, etc.)* or small objects.

burn off A controlled burning or heating for the purpose of removing something. **burning off**

burnishing Rubbing to clean and gloss a surface.

butcher block Kitchen countertop material, made from an assembly of edge-glued hardwood blocks, as would be found in butcher shops around the turn of the century. Anything made to resemble the look of butcher block. A.K.A. **chopping block**

butler's pantry A small room, *off the dining room,* used to store wine, dishes, glasses, silverware, serving pieces, etc., needed only for special events or occasions.

butt end The cut ends of lumber, or any other material.

butter A term used to describe the spreading or applying of an adhesive material, like contact cement or mortar. **buttering**

butterfly hinge A decorative hinge having the appearance of a butterfly.

butternut *(Wood)* A light, fine-grained hardwood, grown throughout the United States. Similar to **black walnut** except for color, extremely durable, easy to work, and finishes to a highly

polished, handsome appearance. Used for flooring and ceiling, interior finishes, and furniture. A.K.A. **white walnut**

buttery See: **pantry**

butt hinge Refers to the traditional hinge used to hang a standard door. *NOTE: Whether two or three butt hinges are used on a door depends on the height and weight of the door.*

butt joint Basic wood joinery, formed when boards are joined end to end, or when the end of one plank meets the side edge or end of another plank, on the same plane.

button Virtually anything that resembles a button, like the push buttons on a telephone. 2. A disk-shaped fastener, most often used on clothing, most notably mens shirts. *NOTE: Before zippers were invented, buttons were used to close the fly on men's pants, which probably lead to the expression "button it up."*

button head The hemispherical-shaped head of a bolt, rivet, screw, or bar.

buttress A structural element, usually of brick or stone, built to reinforce or support an existing wall. See: **flying buttress**

bypass Any device *(pipe, duct, switch, valve, etc.)* used to direct flow around an element instead of through it.

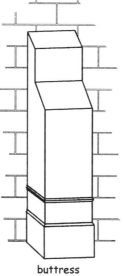

buttress

Byzantine architecture
The art and architecture of the Byzantine or eastern Roman Empire *(330 A.D. thought the 15th century)* -- the Middle Ages, characterized by its Christian theme, large domes, arches, and elaborate columns richly colored and ornamented. Widely popular, particularly in Greece, until the fall of Constantinople to the Turks *(1453).*

Byzantine revival
A mid-19th century adaptation, primarily for churches, of the Byzantine style.

- C -

cabana A tentlike structure used at the beach and at pools. 2. Originally a simple Spanish dwelling resembling a hut, cottage, or cabin.

cabin A single-story cottage, hut, or house, often of logs. 2. Any office, bedroom, or living quarters on a ship. 3. Sections of an airplane reserved for passengers.

cabinet A boxlike case consisting of shelves, doors, and drawers, often used for storing valuable items. 2. The U.S. president's primary advisors. 3. Formally a private conference room.

cabinet maker A skilled craftsman in the art of building cabinets and furniture. **cabinetmaking**

cabinet window A display window, usually projecting slightly from the front of a building.

cable Any heavy rope, chain, or wire line used for support or to exert force. 2. Any bundle of conductive wiring used to transmit electricity, communications, television, etc.

cabling Ornamental molding resembling the twisted strands of cable and rope. A.K.A. **cable molding, rope molding**

cabriole leg Designates a particular style of chair leg with an exaggerated curve, usually Queen Anne. See: **chair styles**

CAD *Abbr.* **computer-aided design**

cadmium plating A corrosion-resistant coating on metal, applied by a process known as electroplating.

cadmium yellow A sulfide pigment, used in paints, that ranges from strong lemon yellow to yellow-orange in color.

café Adapted from a French word meaning *a small restaurant open to the street.*

cage Any rigid, reinforced box or structure made of wire, bars, etc., used to confine birds and animals. 2. Any open frame structure, resembling a birdcage. 3. A fenced area used to hold prisoners of war.

caisson A watertight chamber used mainly to construct the foundations for bridges and tunnels. 2. A decorative recessed panel in a vaulted, domed, or flat ceiling. **coffer**

calendar A system of tracking time, divided into the

days, weeks, and months of the year. **2.** An ordered list of events or matters to consider, such as a court calendar.

calipers A series of instruments that measure the diameter *(interior or exterior)* or thickness of objects, such as measuring the inside diameter of a pipe.

calle Italian word for *street.*

camber A slight bend or rise, as in an arch. **2.** A natural, slight convex curvature along the edge of lumber. Carpenters always turn the camber up on floor joists and rafters to avoid sagging. **3.** The slight convex curvature of a road, enabling water to runoff.

camber window A window arched at the top.

camelback house A house that has a single-story in front with an attached two-story structure.

camelback truss A truss having a broken upper chord, like a barn. Having the humped-shape of a camel's back.

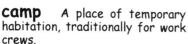

cantilever

camp A place of temporary habitation, traditionally for work crews.

campaign furniture A style of chests and desks made to resemble the kind of furniture used in the field, by the military, usually having metal corners.

canal A man-made water channel of considerable size for boats to transport cargo.

candlepower *Abbr.* **cp.** The term used to describe luminous intensity of a light source.

cane Thin, narrow wood strips woven into a seat or back for a chair.

canopy A decorative hood or roof over a door or window. **2.** Traditionally used over a bed, for privacy or to support a light fabric to repel insects. **3.** A covered path extending from a building to protect an entrance from the elements.

cant Slanted. Refers to a side, edge, or end angle other than 90°. **2.** A line or surface angled in relation to another, as a sloped wall. **3.** A log partly or fully squared. **canted** A.K.A. **splay**

cantilever A beam, girder, truss, or other structural member that projects beyond its supporting member to hold, for example, a balcony.

canvas A strong, heavy, closely woven fabric, originally made of hemp, once used for sail on ships, for tents, artist canvas, and many other applications.

cap The uppermost element of any vertical architectural structure. **2.** As molding See: **cap molding 3.** A fitting used to close the top end of a pipe.

capacity The maximum space, pressure, temperature, or velocity available or allowable.

Cape Cod cottage A simple one- or two-room house with a bedroom loft, either above or as a lean-to at the rear.

capital

Originating in colonial Cape Cod, Massachusetts, a one- or one-and-a-half-story rectangular frame house with shingled, pitched, bowed, or gable roofs, tall *(top of wall)* windows, and weathered gray clapboard siding. Built in half, three-quarter, and full Cape styles. *HISTORIC NOTE: Many of these small Cape Cod cottages were originally built as summer vacation homes, either on the beach or very close to it. They were built without foundations because the sandy soil would sometimes erode or blow away, and the houses were then dragged or floated to a new location.*

capital   The decorative crowning of a column or pilaster. **2.** The place designated as the seat of government on a federal or state level. *Example: Washington, D.C. is the nation's capital and Sacramento is the capital of the state of California.*

cap molding   A small molding used to finish off baseboard, casing, and other molding details. A.K.A. **cap trim**

cap rail   A rail fastened to the uppermost member of a railing system.

carcass   The framework of a building before the addition of sheathing or other covering. **2.** The structural body of wood cabinets and furniture. **carcase**

carding   A process of evenly spreading glue, using a stiff card of cardboard, or plywood.

carpenter's level   See: **level**

carpenter's square   See: **framing square**

carpentry   A building trade that includes cutting, framing, and joining the timbers or woodwork of a building or structure.

carpet   Any heavy, durable, fabric floor covering, usually woven, knitted, or needle-tufted.

carpet backing   The material on the underside of carpet, to which the carpet pile is attached.

carpet binding   See: **binding**

carpet pad   A padding material over which carpet is installed. Used to provide a more luxurious feeling and increase the longevity of the carpet.

carpet pile   The cut or looped tufts of yarn that stand erect from the base of the carpet and whose ends form the carpet surface. A.K.A. **pile**

carport   A covered shelter for an automobile, with sides open to the weather.

carriage   A vehicle to carry passengers. **2.** A movable platform. **3.** An inclined beam or stringer. A.K.A. **stringer 4.** As theatre and stage equipment, a counterbalanced arbor.

carriage bolt   A threaded machine bolt with a circular head covering a hexagon-shaped top to prevent turning.

carriage bolt

carriage house A small dwelling attached to, over, or converted from a garage once used to store carriages. A.K.A. **coach house**

carriage porch A roofed structure over a driveway, at a building's entrance, to protect arriving visitors from inclement weather. A.K.A. **porte cochere**

carry A carpentry term used to describe a load-bearing element.

carry up In masonry and brickwork, a term used to describe building to a specified height.

cartoon A drawing or painting with the characteristics of a comic strip or comic book characters. **2.** Slang for a quick (*explanatory*) sketch.

cartouche An ornamental shield, tablet, scroll, or medallion usually inscribed, decorated, or framed with elaborate wreaths, garlands, and scroll-like carving.

carving A design cut into various materials. Denotes the use of hand tools, such as a knife.

cascade An overlapping drop. **2.** A small stepped waterfall. **cascading**

case goods Refers to furniture used to store various objects; desks, cabinets, bookcases, etc. **case**

case hardened Producing a hard surface layer on steel, by any of a number of processes including carburizing and flame hardening.

casement window A window hinged on its vertical side, to swing in or out. See: **window styles**

casing The exposed trim or molding around doors and windows, used to produced a finished look to door and window openings. **2.** An upholstery term referring to the shell of a cushion. A.K.A. **door casing, window casing, interior casing** See: **window styles**

casing nail See: **finish nail**

casino A large room, often part of a hotel complex, equipped with various games of chance.

cast Made from a mold. See: **staff 2.** Theatrically, all the actors involved in a particular play, film, or TV series.

casters Wheels attached to furniture, particularly chairs, for easy moving. **2.** Relatively small wheels used for a variety of different purposes.

casting Intricately decorated brackets, molding and other objects, made of plaster or plastic, used to embellish the decor of a room or building. A.K.A. **staff 2.** A term used to describe molded metal parts from a **foundry**.

cast iron A carbon and silicon alloy, used extensively in the casting of metal parts.

cast-iron pipe A pipe made of cast iron and lined with a variety of other materials to reduce corrosion. A.K.A. **gray cast-iron pipe**

castle A large fortified building or stronghold, with an inner court, used by ancient nobility as a principal residence.

catacomb Architecturally, an underground cavern.

catalyst A substance, used primarily with synthetic resins, to initiate or accelerate a chemical reaction.

catch A device used to hold a door or gate closed. More elaborate than a **latch**. A.K.A. **door catch**

catch basin A reservoir, to catch and retain water drainage from the surrounding area.

cathedral arch A large, impressive arch, as would be found in a large church.

Catherine wheel window
See: **wheel window**

catwalk A fixed, narrow pedestrian bridge used in high places, such as above a stage.

caulk A variety of soft putty-like compounds used to fill, seal, or waterproof cracks and joints. **caulking**

caulking gun A tool used to extrude a variety of commercial adhesive and caulking products, which are packaged to be applied with a caulking gun.

causeway See: **highway**

cavetto (Italian) See: **cove molding**

cavity A hole or space, as between the studs of a wall where insulation is installed.

C-clamp A type of clamp, usually small, that resembles the letter C.

C-clamp

cedar (Wood) A name applied to several species of fragrant, fine-grained durable softwood used to line hope chests, clothes closets, cigar boxes, and for pencils because of its decay-resistant and insect-repelling properties. Most North American cedar is obtained from juniper trees. Similar in characteristics to West Indian cedar (part of the mahogany family) and **Persian cedar** (nanmu)

ceiling The overhead surface of a room or the finished surface covering the structural joists of the floor above.

ceiling fan A fan, with or without lights, that is attached to the ceiling.

ceiling fan

ceiling joist Any joist to which a ceiling is attached. 2. A term once used to describe a structure of joists established exclusively to hold the lath support of a plaster ceiling.

ceiling sprinkler See: **sprinkler system**

cell An entity within or part of another entity. Denotes one of many (honeycomb) or used in conjunction with others (batteries). 2. A small room, space, or cavity, as a prison cell. **cellular**

cellar A basement story having half or more of its height below grade.

celluloid The plastic cellulose material used for film in cameras and many other products.

cellulose The natural woody material *(polysaccharide glucose)* found in numerous plants, including trees, jute, flax, hemp, and ramie that is manufactured into a wide variety of everyday consumer products (paper, fuel) and building materials.

Celtic Belonging to the legacy of the people of Ireland and Scotland.

cement Any compound or a mixture of materials used to permanently fasten, fill, glue, bond, bind, or join one object to another. *NOTE: Often used incorrectly to describe concrete, which combines cement with an aggregate material and water to form a structure or object.*

cement block A block made entirely of cement. Not to be confused with **concrete block**.

cement mixer A device used to mix cement. A.K.A. **concrete mixer**.

cement mixer

cemetery Property designated a permanent burial site. A.K.A. **graveyard**

center The exact middle of a circle or half the distance between two points. **2.** The core of a laminated construction, like plywood. **centering**

centerline Generally, a broken line used in drafting to indicate the symmetrical middle of an object.

center of gravity A center point within the body of an object upon which the object can be balanced, meaning that the gravitational pull of the earth on either side of the balanced object are exactly the same. **center of mass**

centerpiece An object or ornament placed in the middle of something, as a floral arrangement for the center of a table.

center punch A tool used to punch a small hole at the center of a circle. Most prevalently used to mark the centers of predrilled holes in metal hardware, such as butt hinges.

center-to-center Refers to the distance between the center of one object (like a stud, joist, or rafter) to the center of an another similar object. A.K.A. **on center**

centimeter *Abbr.* cm; A unit of length measurement within the metric system, equal to 1/100 of a meter, or 0.3937+ inches. An inch equals 2.54 cm.

central heating and air-conditioning A.K.A. **central air-conditioning**, but incorporates a heating element.

ceramic glaze The process of fusing, by baking, an opaque, colored, satin, or gloss finish coating to clay.

CHAIR STYLES

WINDSOR

LOOP-BACK   FAN-BACK
Circa 1770

CHIPPENDALE

DUNCAN PHYFE

LYRE BACK

QUEEN ANNE

HEPPLEWHITE

LADDER-BACK   STRAIGHT-BACK   CABRIOLE LEG   SHIELD

CAPTAIN'S CHAIR   BENTWOOD   VENETIAN   NEOCLASSIC

PETITT   BREUER   BERTOLA

CHAIR STYLES

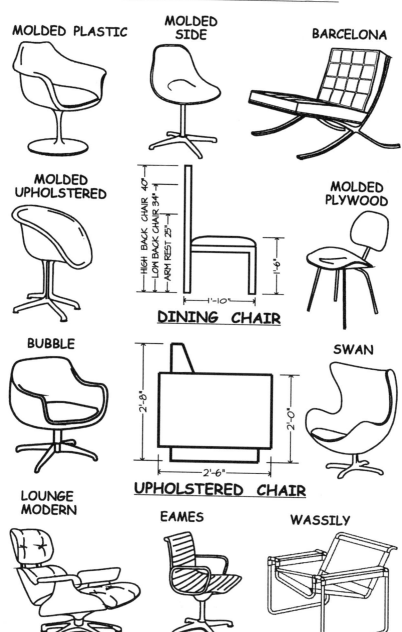

MOLDED PLASTIC

MOLDED SIDE

BARCELONA

MOLDED UPHOLSTERED

MOLDED PLYWOOD

HIGH BACK CHAIR 40"
LOW BACK CHAIR 34"
ARM REST 25"

1'-6"

1'-10"

DINING CHAIR

BUBBLE

SWAN

2'-8"

2'-0"

2'-6"

UPHOLSTERED CHAIR

LOUNGE MODERN

EAMES

WASSILY

ceramics The art of molding, modeling, baking, and glazing clay into various forms, including porcelain plumbing fixtures, lamps, tile, etc.

ceramic tile Porcelain or natural clay tiles.

certificate of insurance A document issued by an insurance company designating the beneficiary, types, amounts, and effective dates of an insurance policy.

certificate of occupancy A document issued by the local municipality stipulating the designated use of a building, confirms its construction complied with existing building codes, and permits occupancy.

certification A declaration in writing that a particular product or service complies with a specification or stated standard.

cesspool See: **septic system**

chain-link fence A fence made of heavy interwoven steel wire, providing a continuous mesh barrier, and supported by regularly spaced metal posts.

chain saw A power-driven saw, with teeth, affixed around a revolving, endless metal-chain of protruding teeth, used primarily to cut down and cut up trees, but also used to rough cut and even to sculpt wood.

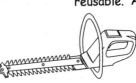
chain saw

chain switch An electrical switch that operates by pulling a chain or cord. **pull switch**

chair Furniture used for sitting.

chair rail A horizontal molding applied to the wall to shield it from nicks and damage caused by chair backs. A.K.A. **dado, dado rail, dado cap**

chaise lounge (Fr) (shaz long) A long, upholstered bedroom chair, used for reading and reclining.

chaise lounge

chalet A style of house found predominantly in the French and Swiss Alps. Characterized by exposed and decorative structural elements -- balconies, stairs, and extended eves. **2.** Any building of a similar design.

chalk A soft limestone, usually white, used in a solid stick form to write on a blackboard, and in a powdered form in a carpenter's chalk box to strike straight lines. See: **chalk line**

chalkboard A marking surface, primarily for use with chalk, which is cleanable and reusable. A.K.A. **blackboard**

chalk box A container with a reel of string and powered chalk, which carpenters stretch between two points to strike a straight line.

chalk line A light cord with chalk stretched between two points on a flat surface, and snapped, to leave a straight line of chalk.

chamber A room or suite of rooms for the private use of a person or group of people. Applies to private living quarters and formal meeting rooms, such as the senate chambers. **2.** A space equipped or designed for a special mechanical or technological function, e.g., combustion chamber or torture chamber

chamfer See: **bevel**

chancery A room, set of rooms, or house designated for use by an official with the title chancellor. 2. An area designated for the business use of visiting dignitaries.

chandelier A hanging light fixture with branches to hold small light bulbs. Originally designed to hold candles.

chandelier

change An authorized alteration or deviation in the scope or design of a project. Changes occur in virtually every phase of a project, and are part of the ongoing process of constantly reevaluating and accommodating various situations and decisions made. *NOTE: Nothing is drawn as imagined and nothing is built exactly as it is drawn.*

checks

channel In profile the shape of the letter *U* which when **extruded** resembles a long straight track or groove. **channeling** See: **extrusion**

chapel A room or small building designated for private prayer within the complex of a school, college, hospital, or other institution.

chase To follow a specific path or shape. 2. A continuous recess built into a wall to receive pipes, ducts, etc., as molding runs around the many turns in a room. **channel, groove**

chateau *(Fr)* A French castle or imposing country estate.

chateauesque *(Fr)* The most grandiose of the late Victorian styles, epitomizing all the excesses of the Gilded Age. A castle with steeply pitched hipped roofs, elaborate dormers, and gable parapets, towers, spires, and complete with gargoyles and griffins. Interiors featured enormous reception halls, conservatories, and picture galleries.

chattel A legal term referring to any article of property not affixed to land; movable property.

check A series of small cracks, fissures, or gouges, in any surface, usually the result of shrinkage during the drying process. **checking**

checkerboard A pattern of alternating light and dark squares, as in gingham fabric.

checkroom A.K.A. **cloakroom**

cheek A narrow, upright face or side of an opening. The two sides of the tongue and the two sides of the groove in tongue-and-groove construction or in mortise-and-tendon construction.

cheek cut

cheek cut An angular cut across the side of a board, which creates a new surface, such as cutting off the sides of a board to form a tendon; or the compound angular cut at the end of a jack rafter, so that it can fit tightly against a hip rafter or valley rafter. A.K.A. **side cut**

chemical bond An interlocking bond created by the cohesion of two or more materials into one.

chemical staining Treating wood with chemicals to change color or enhance grain contrast. See: **wood stain**

chequer See: **checkerboard**

cherry *(Wood)* A reddish brown, durable, high-density hardwood native to eastern Canada and the U.S. Used extensively for highly polished furniture, cabinets, and paneling and marquetry. Similar to **mahogany** in appearance. *NOTE: Cherry trees naturally grow too small to be used as dimensioned lumber and is usually sold in planks of various lengths.*

cherry picker A movable and adjustable platform at the end of a hydraulically controlled mechanical arm or extendable boom, used to position workers and materials to perform work in high places, such as the top of a telephone pole. A modern alternative to scaffolding.

chest A piece of furniture with

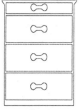

chest

drawers or shelves, often used to store clothes.

chestnut *(Wood)* A white or light brown coarse-grained hardwood, of the beech family, resembling **oak**, but with a coarser grain. Used primarily for fences, molding, and ornaments.

chest-on-chest A traditional furniture design, that falsely gives the impression of being two separate cabinets, usually with different-size drawers, stacked, opposed to a long, low dresser, for storing clothes. A.K.A. **highboy**

chevron A V-shaped shield.

chevron

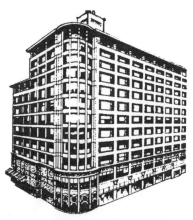

Carson, Pirie and Scott Building – Chicago School

Chicago School of Architecture
A style of steel-framed skyscraper that developed in the midwest around the turn-of-the-century, heavily influenced by **Louis Sullivan**

chicken wire A light-weight,

galvanized wire netting with a hexagonal mesh.

chiffonier *(Fr)* A narrow, high chest of drawers. A.K.A. **highboy, bureau**

chimney A vertical structure, containing one or more flues, that provides a draft and allows combustible gaseous residue, from a fireplace, to escape outside. A.K.A. **chimney stack, smokestack**

wood chisel

chimney breast
A projecting wall, in a room behind or above a fireplace, that encloses the fireplace and the flue.

china The European word used to describe porcelain dinnerware when it was first imported from China.

Chinese architecture
The traditional architecture of China, characterized by low-silhouette, simple, rectangular, wooden post-and-beam buildings with nonbearing curtain or screen walls. Prominent features include high-pitched, tile-covered gabled roofs with upward-curving overhanging eaves resting on multiple brackets, and separate roofs over porches surrounding the main buildings.

chink A crack or fissure of greater length than width.

chinking In log cabin construction, refers to filling cracks between the logs.

chinoiserie Artistic objects inspired by Chinese design.

chintz Printed cotton fabric.

chip A broken segment of material, as a chip on the edge of a fine porcelain tea cup.

chipboard See: **particleboard**

Chippendale
Elegant furniture designed by Thomas Chippendale, *circa 18th century.* See: **chair styles**

chisel A hand tool with a steel cutting edge used in woodworking and masonry to cut away or shape material.

chock A wedge or block used to prevent an object from moving.

chopping block
See: **butcher block**

chord A horizontal element in a truss. 2. The straight line between two points on a curve or the span of an arch. A.K.A. **spring line**

chroma A term used to describe the intensity or brilliance of color. See: **color wheel**

chrome A hard, mirrorlike finish applied, usually to steel, but also painted on plastic to give a chromelike appearance. Used extensively for trim on automobiles and hardware. Available in brushed and polished finishes.

chuck A device with adjustable jaws, used to hold a drill or cutting bit.

church A building designed for Christian worship.

chute A steep slide, used to convey, by gravity, material *(laundry, mail, garbage)* to a lower story. Often used in demolition work.

cinder block

cinder block A hollow, lightweight masonry block.

Circassian walnut *(Wood)* A handsome brown hardwood with curly grain *(expensive)*, from the area around the Black Sea. Used primarily for furniture and paneling.

circle A perfectly round continuous line.

circuit An electrical term used to describe the path through which electricity flows.

circuit breaker An electrical switch designed to automatically close either when the circuit is overloaded or an abnormally high current is detected.

circular saw A power-operated hand saw with a circular steel blade and perimeter teeth for cutting through wood.

circular stairs See: **spiral stairs** ·

cistern A receptacle for collecting or storing clean water *(rainwater or spring water)*.

citadel The strongest part of a fortress or castle in or near a city. Denotes military use.

city A large town.

city hall A building that houses the offices of various departments of city government.

city plan A large-scale, comprehensive map or model of a city's building and street landscape, that designates the usage *(residential, commercial, etc.)* of property within a specific area.

city planning Planning the future development and expansion of a city or urban area. A.K.A. **town planning, urban planning**

civic center An area of a city where municipal buildings (city hall, court house, public library, etc.) are grouped.

civil engineering A branch of engineering concerned with building highways, tunnels, bridges, aqueducts, etc.

circular saw

clad The outermost cover or structural material, as in iron clad. **cladding** A.K.A. **siding, sheathing**

clamp A wooden or metal device designed to hold components firmly together while gluing, cutting, shaping, etc.

clapboards The decorative use of overlapping horizontal wood planks, used as siding to repel inclement weather. **bevel siding, lap siding**

classic Refers to works of art long acknowledged as a standard of excellence.

classical order See: **classic order**

classic order A term used to describe the five dominant architectural details of classic Greek and Roman columns (**Doric, Ionic, Corinthian, Tuscan, and Composite**). See: **column details** A.K.A. **architectural order, classical order**

classic revival An early 19th century architectural movement utilizing pure classic Roman and Greek style.

classic style Reminiscent of classic Greek and Roman art and architecture.

clause A legal term describing a subdivision or subparagraph, in any legal document.

claw-and-ball foot A traditional leg or foot detail used in furniture, depicting a ball in a bird's claw.

claw foot tub
A classic style of bathtub with feet sculpted to look like an animal's claw.

claw hammer A standard carpenter's hammer with both a hammer head and a curved (for leverage), split head for gripping and pulling nails (the claw).

claw hammer

clay A natural mineral aggregate, mostly *hydrous aluminum silicates*. Deposits of fine-grained rock particles in water, malleable when moist and rigid when dry. A basic raw material in the manufacture of bricks, pottery, and ceramics.

clean room A room sealed off from the dust and debris often associated with a manufacturing operation. 2. A room made free of dust, lint, and other airborne particles that can negatively affect equipment or the products being manufactured.

clean-up mold A general carpentry term referring to any small molding used to cap the edge of a board.

clear A term used to describe lumber free of knots and other naturally occurring blemishes.

clearance The space between two objects or elements. A carpentry term allowing for the unobstructed fitting or movement of parts.

clearing Removing vegetation and debris.

clearstory An upper row of windows that provides light and a means for rising heat to escape. **clerestory**

cleat A small block or strip of wood nailed to a surface to temporarily support or hold something in place.

clinic A medical facility, or part of a hospital, specializing in specific types of care *(pediatric, physical therapy, etc.)*.

clip A special fastener, made of wire, plastic, or light-gauge sheet metal, usually supplied by the manufacturer and designed to meet the installation needs of their products.

clipped A general carpentry term used to describe something that is foreshortened, as a **clipped ceiling** or **clipped roof** - due to the slope of the roof.

cloak rail See: **coatrack**

cloakroom See: **coatroom**

cloche A glass dome that protects the objects within from the elements.

clock tower A tower whose purpose is to house a publicly viewable clock.

cloissoné

cloissoné   A technique used to create enamel decorations in which the various colors are separated by narrow metal strips. *(cloisons)*

clone   One or more identical replications.

close   To shut or shut off.

closed-circuit TV   A limited-broadcast visual surveillance and security system, utilizing TV cameras and monitors connected by a coaxial cable.

closet   A small enclosed space used for storage, particularly clothing. See: **closet pole heights**

closing costs   Additional costs *(legal and recording fees and title insurance)* associated with the legal transfer of title of real property.

closure   A device that automatically returns a door to its closed position each time it is opened.

clustered columns
Columns used in groups or in close proximity to form a support element.

clutch   A mechanical device that engages or disengages the primary source of power, as when the motor of a car or truck is engaged and disengaged every time the gears change.

coach lamp

coach lamp   A wall lamp applied near an exterior door.

coal tar   A dark brown to black petroleum product used to waterproof roofs. **tar, pitch**

coarse   Rough

coat   A single layer of plaster, paint, or any type of material applied to a surface.

coated nail   A nail treated with a glue that affixes itself to the wood as the nail is embedded, so that the nail won't work itself loose over time. A.K.A. **screechier**

coating   A layer of any material applied to a surface.

coatrack   A board with hooks attached for hanging hats and coats. A.K.A. **hat rack, cloak rail**

coatroom   A room, in a public place, to deposit or check outer garments. A.K.A. **cloakroom**

coaxial cable
An insulated cable that carries high-speed electronic data and/or video signals. The cable in cable TV.

cobblestone
Naturally flat rocks of similar size, used for paving, walls, and foundations.

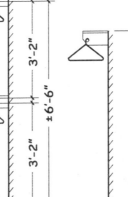

closet pole heights

3'-2"

±6'-6"

3'-2"

5'-6" STANDARD

cock See: **faucet** A.K.A. **spigot**

cocobolo *(Wood)* A dark brown hardwood with a violet cast. Used predominately for highly polished modern furniture.

code Rules and regulations adopted by a municipality describing the minimum acceptable requirements for constructing a building.

coffeehouse A small, limited-menu café specializing in coffee.

coffered ceiling A ceiling with deeply recessed panels. **coffering** A.K.A. **caisson**

cohesion The holding power of an adhesive or sealant.

coin stone coins See: **quoins**

cold-air return An air duct in an air-conditioning system that directs the flow of cold air.

cold cellar Part of a cellar that stays cold *(almost freezing)* in the winter, where root crops are stored.

cold chisel A chisel with a tempered steel cutting edge, used to cut metal and stone.

cold chisel

cold room A room that is refrigerated and used to store perishables.

coliseum A large amphitheatre reminiscent of the

Roman coliseum

ancient Romans. **2.** Today, any large sports arena, open or roofed.

collage A unique form of art made from a collection of various objects, memorabilia, trinkets, and pictures. A.K.A. **montage**

collar A flange or flashing that fits around an object.

collar beam A horizontal board used to tie together and stiffen two opposite rafters. A.K.A. **collar tie**

college A university of higher learning.

colonette A small decorative column.

colonial revival A rendition of **New England colonial** style, as exemplified in the historically restored Williamsburg, Virginia township *(the state's colonial capital)*. Mostly single-story houses with almost floor-to-ceiling windows and characteristically low-pitched roofs, and dormer attic. A.K.A. **traditional style**

colonnade A row of evenly spaced columns. The distance between the columns is known as intercolumniation.

color Our perception of color described by name, such as yellow, red, blue, etc., or a combination of such names.

color coded A system of using colors to identify specific pipes, cables, wiring, or the like, that need to be connected.

COLOR WHEEL

CHARACTERISTICS OF COLOR

HUE: Navy blue is a hue of the color blue.
CHROMA: The intensity, brilliance, or saturation of a color.
VALUE: Gradation of color from black to white.
FINISH: The presence or absence of gloss, luster, or sheen. (gloss or matte finish)

COMPLEMENTARY COLORS ARE OPPOSITES

RELATIONSHIP OF 24 BASIC COLORS

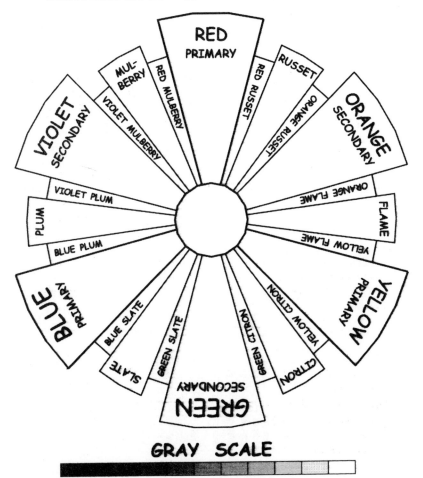

RED PRIMARY
MULBERRY
RED MULBERRY
RUSSET
RED RUSSET
ORANGE RUSSET
VIOLET MULBERRY
VIOLET SECONDARY
ORANGE SECONDARY
ORANGE FLAME
FLAME
VIOLET PLUM
PLUM
BLUE PLUM
YELLOW FLAME
YELLOW PRIMARY
BLUE PRIMARY
BLUE SLATE
SLATE
GREEN SLATE
GREEN CITRON
YELLOW CITRON
CITRON
GREEN SECONDARY

GRAY SCALE

color pigment   A insoluble powder *(iron or chromium oxides)* of various colors, that are mixed with oil, water, or synthetic liquids to make paint and stains.
A.K.A. **pigment**

TYPICALLY MANUFACTURED COLORS

RED
Alizarin crimson (rose/violet)
Carmine   (brilliant red)
English vermilion   (yellowish)
Indian red   (brownish)
BLUE
Cerulean   (greenish)
Cobalt   (reddish)
Prussian   (greenish)
Ultramarine   (reddish)
(French blue)
YELLOW
Cadmium
Chrome
Yellow ochre
GREEN
Emerald   (blueish)
Viridian   (yellowish)
BROWN
Burnt sienna   (reddish)
Raw sienna   (yellowish)
Burnt umber   (blueish)
Raw umber   (greenish)
Van Dyke   (purplish)
BLACK
Ivory black
Lamp black
WHITE
Titanium
White lead   (yellows w/age)
Zinc white

color reflection   Refers to the light-reflecting property of color, where light colors reflect light and dark colors absorb it.

color pigment

REFLECTIVE VALUE OF COLOR

white	85%
ivory	75%
light gray	65%
tan	60%
yellow	60%
light green	55%
dark gray	15%
dark brow	10%
dark green	10%
dark blue	5%
black	5%

color rendering   An elevation or perspective drawing, in color, conceptualizing what is expected to be built. A snapshot in the midst of the design process, indicating the look (style, color, etc.) or direction the project is attempting to achieve.   *NOTE: With the advent of CAD and 3D computer modeling, it is possible to produce a photorealistic perspective drawing using the exact colors, fabrics, cabinets, moldings, etc., being selected.*

color symbolism A feeling or psychological emotion associated with particular colors.

COLOR SYMBOLISM

BLACK
darkness, mourning, despair
BLUE
coolness, restfulness, truth, tranquility, constancy, sky
GOLD
wealth, luxury, power, royalty
GRAY
humility, gloomy, dismal
GREEN
hope, springtime, envy
PALE BLUE
male child

color wheel

PINK
  female child
PURPLE
  royalty, justice, depression, suffering
RED
  passion, revolution, anger, warmth, martyrdom, gaiety
WHITE
  purity, faith, cleanliness, peace, joy
YELLOW
  cheerfulness, warmth, jealousy, fruitful

color wheel A chart that shows the relationship between colors. See: **color wheel 2.** A wheel of cards illustrating the array of thousands of color variations available from a particular paint manufacturer. Each color is assigned a number, to specify and/or order, ensuring the color ordered is the color received. **color chart**

colossal column A column that rises more than one story in height.

column A vertical supporting element. May be isolated or attached to a wall. **post, pillar,** or **strut** 2. In classic Greek and Roman architecture, a cylindrical support consisting of a base, shaft, and capital that supports the entablature or roof. **3.** A pillar or monolith standing alone as a monument.

column capital A mushroomlike enlargement of reinforced concrete, at the upper end of a column, designed and built to act as an integral unit with the column and the floor slab above, to increase shear resistance.

comb-back Refers to chairs with a number of spindles used to make up the chair back, resembling the teeth of a comb. See: **chair styles** *(Windsor)* **fan-back, loop-back**

combination pliers Slip-jointed pliers that can open wide and grip larger objects.

combination square An adjustable carpenter's tool consisting of a steel ruler with an adjustable head, to check or mark either a 45° or 90° angle. Also contains a level and straightedge, and can be set to use as a marking gauge. **tri-square**

combustible Susceptible to igniting or exploding during a fire.

combustion A chemical reaction producing heat and fire.

come-along A racheted tool used to pull heavy or stubborn objects together. Consists of a wire cable on a spooled rachet suspended between two hooks. The ratchet draws in the cable and applies pulling power.

comfort zone A level at which people generally feel comfortable in their environment, whether that be temperature, the height of a workbench or desk, or any other factors.

commission The sum paid for professional services -- *painters, sculpture, architect, designers, etc.* Uusually figured as a percentage of the project's cost. 2. A panel of officials authorized to investigate and oversee a particular problem or concern of the community.

COLUMN DETAILS

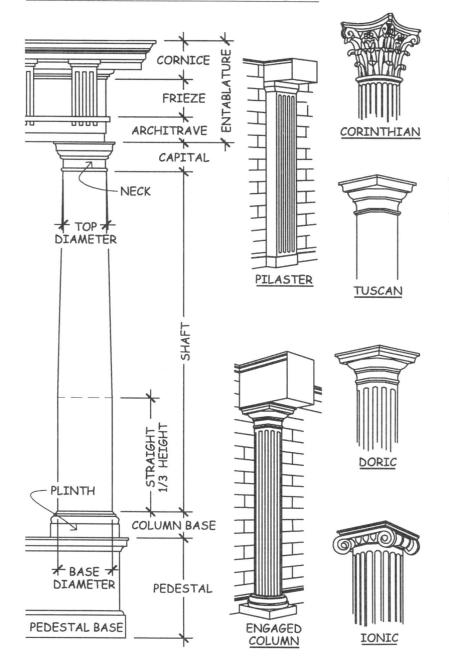

CORNICE
FRIEZE
ARCHITRAVE
ENTABLATURE
CAPITAL
NECK
TOP DIAMETER
SHAFT
STRAIGHT 1/3 HEIGHT
PLINTH
COLUMN BASE
BASE DIAMETER
PEDESTAL
PEDESTAL BASE

PILASTER

ENGAGED COLUMN

CORINTHIAN

TUSCAN

DORIC

IONIC

commode

commode *(Fr)* A low chest. **2.** A night stand once used to conceal a chamber pot.

common area Any area or convenience shared by the tenants of a commercial or residential building or complex, including things like staircases, laundry rooms, landscaping, gymnasiums, recreation rooms, etc. Denotes areas that are commonly used by tenants, but not necessarily open to the public.

common bond In masonry, a pattern in which after every fifth or sixth course, there is a run of bricks placed with their short side showing instead of the traditional long side showing. A.K.A. **American bond**

common brick A standard clay brick common to the area.

common nail A nail with a flat head. *(The kind of nail everyone imagines when they think of a typical nail.)*

common rafter A typical or full rafter, not cut to meet an intersecting slope. A.K.A. **rafter, spar rafter**

common wall A wall that is shared by two separate dwellings. A wall that separates two apartments or two attached townhouses.

community A group of people having common rights, privileges, or interests, or living in the same place under the same laws and regulations. A.K.A. village, neighborhood

community center A building or group of public buildings for social, cultural, and educational activities of a neighborhood or entire community.

compactor A machine that uses a combination of weight and vibration to compact soil. **2.** A kitchen trash compactor, that crushes waste materials into a removable container.

compartment A small space within a larger enclosed area.

compass An instrument with two adjustable points, used to measure or draw circles, arches, and distances between two points.

compass roof A roof containing a circular element. A.K.A. **turret roof**

compensation Payment for services rendered or materials furnished. **2.** Payment made to satisfy claims of damage suffered.

complementary colors Colors opposite one another on a standard color wheel. See: **color wheel**

completion bond A guarantee issued by a bonding or surety company that a contractor will perform and complete the work, as stipulated and contracted for, free of all encumbrances and liens. **construction bond, contract bond**

completion date A date, *contractually agreed to,* by which the contractor has committed to complete or substantially complete the work, so that specific equipment can be installed or so that owner / tenants can move in.

component One of several necessary parts, electrical or structural.

composite A mixture of two or more materials. **2.** A mixing of two or more attributes of the classic orders of Greek and Roman architecture, such as incorporating an Ionic volute on a Corinthian column. See: **column details**

composite order In classical architecture, the incorporation of large volutes *(spirals)* of the Ionic capital with the lush foliage of the Corinthian capital.

composition A design term describing the relationship of various elements (color, objects, lighting, etc,) used to create a finished appearance.

composition board See: **particleboard**

compound angle The plane of an element that travels in two distinct angles.

compound angle

compound arch An arch, formed by a series of concentric and progressively smaller arches set within one another. See: **pendentive arch**

compression coupling A coupling to connect sections of pipe that uses the pressure of the water within the pipe to seal the connection.

compression valve A water shut-off valve that uses water pressure to seal off the water supply.

compressor See: **air compressor**

concave A shallow curved depression. See: **convex**

concave

concealed Hidden intentionally. **2.** Said of materials, components, controls, etc., not normally within view, as behind or under something.

conceptual drawings A drawing that reflects a vision of what something should or will look. See: **architectural drawings** A.K.A. **rendering**

concert hall A theatre designed specifically for musical performances.

concourse An open space where several roads or paths meet. **2.** An open space to accommodate large crowds, as at an airport terminal or in a shopping mall.

concrete Any structure, object, or masonry block made of cement *(generically known as portland cement)*, sand, or crushed stone *(aggregate)*, and water that solidifies into a solid mass. See: **portland cement**

concrete block A building or masonry block, either solid or hollow, made of concrete and used to construct buildings and walls.

concrete floor A floor made of concrete. A.K.A. **slab floor**

concrete form A structure built to hold wet concrete to the desired shape and form while it dries.

concrete mixer A device designed specifically to mix the ingredients of concrete. See: **cement mixer**

concrete nail A hardened-steel nail used for nailing into concrete.

concrete enforcement Refers to a steel rod *(rebar)* substructure built within a form before the concrete is poured.

concrete saw A large power-operated circular saw with a diamond-tipped blade, used to groove or cut concrete slabs.

concrete slab A flat, rectangular block of concrete, used commonly as a floor or footpath.

condemned Property or building deemed unfit for use by the local municipality.

condensation The transformation of a substance from one form (a vapor) into another (a liquid), as with steam.

condominium Refers primarily to individual ownership of apartments and an interest in the common areas and elements (landscaping, hallways, elevators, laundry rooms, etc.) within a multifamily residential dwelling, such as an apartment complex or building. In addition to the cost of the apartment or unit, there is usually a monthly maintenance fee to cover the cost of maintaining and repairing common areas. A.K.A. **cooperative**

conductivity The property of transmitting heat or the flow of electricity.

conductor A material or device that transmits, or offers low resistance to the flow of electric current. 2. A material that transmits heat readily.

conduit A flexible metal tubing used to protect electric wiring. 2. A pipe or channel used to carry liquids.

configuration An arrangement of how something is set up to operate.

conical roof A tapered, round roof, usually built for a cupola or a turret.

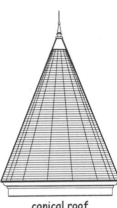
conical roof

conservation The preservation of historic buildings.

conservatory A school of higher learning that specializes in music, drama, or other fine arts. 2. A greenhouse or glass-enclosed room of a house used to cultivate and display plants.

consistency The quality of relative sameness, or the desire to achieve almost identical physical characteristics. 2. Conforms or enhances a preexisting appearance or condition.

console *(Fr)* A control panel (desk or cabinet) containing dials, meters, switches, and other

console

apparatus used to control a specific piece of equipment or instrument.

console table A narrow rectangular table, as along a wall. A.K.A. **library table**

consolidation The act of reducing in size and/or number or reshaping the form of something.

construction All the work involved in building a new or altering an existing structure. **2.** The manner in which something is built.

construction budget A document to estimate and track the actual cost of constructing an object or structure. **2.** The amount of money allocated for the construction of a specific project, often contractually stipulated. **3.** That part of the construction budget allocated for a particular purpose (framing, plumbing, painting, furnishing, etc.).

construction costs The actual cost of constructing a project, based on paid material bills and wages, and separate from the entire cost of a project, which also includes the cost of land, right-of-way(s), the preparation of architectural working drawings, specifications, or contracts.

construction documents The working drawings and specifications used to estimate and build a particular structure.

Tatlin's Project

construction management Those persons and/or companies designated by the owner to manage, supervise, and direct the construction phase of a project. This is often done by the architect and contractor, but can and does, on large projects, involve a third party.

construction paper Any paper product use in construction. Usually, a thick grade of paper, available in large sheets or rolls, used for a variety of purposes, particularly to protect a finished surface during construction. A.K.A. **felt paper, tar paper**

constructivism An art and architectural movement, originating in Moscow (early 1920s), that emphasized functional machine parts and expressed the influence of the **Industrial Age**. The illustration, Tatlin's Project, is the most widely recognized example of constructivism.

contact A part or place, usually by design, where two objects touch or are connected. **2.** A person (intermediary or representative) through whom you communicate with another entity.

contact cement An adhesive used to bond two surfaces together. NOTE: Adheres instantaneously upon contact when dry. A.K.A. **contact adhesive**

contamination The addition of sewage,

contemporary

waste, and/or chemicals (or other material) into the water supply, rendering it unfit for its intended purpose.

contemporary Buildings and structures utilizing the trends, technology, and styling of today. A.K.A. **modern**

contingency allowance A sum designated to cover unpredictable or unforeseen events or changes instigated by the owner or their representatives.

continuous beam A beam extending over several supporting elements, and used to displace the load.

continuous hinge A hinge that runs the length of the door, lid, or part to which it is applied. A.K.A. **piano hinge**

contour line A line representing the shape, curve, or profile of an object.

contour map A topographic map (**plan view**) with contour lines and elevation markers to indicate the height, widths, and location of the various (*mountainous, valley, water, etc.*) elements of the land.

contract A legally enforceable agreement between two or more persons or companies to supply specific goods and/or services for a specified amount of compensation.

contract documents The various documents that detail the aspects, terms, conditions, modifications, and changes relating to the completion of a contract.

contractor The person or company that undertakes the legal responsibility for completing the construction of a building or structure, according to the terms of a contract. The contractor can also sometimes acts as the owner's representative in hiring and scheduling carpenters, laborers, subcontractors and purchasing materials, in accordance with plans and specifications of the contract. See: **contractual conditions**

contractual conditions Legal language written into a contract establishing certain criteria, such as having to meet certain standards or pass a particular test.

contractual liability Liability assumed by **the parties of** a contract, as expressed in the language of the contract as to each party's area of responsibility or implied obligation.

control Any device that regulates (*manually or automatically*) the operation of a machine, system, or component.

control room A room that houses the control panels, technicians, and decision makers required to manage an operation or to operate a machine, system or component. **2.** Theatrically, a room with a view of the stage, from which curtains, lights, and sound are controlled.

control valve Any valve used to regulate the flow of liquids.

convalescent home A facility for the care of long-term recovering medical patients or for the elderly who require long-term custodial care.

convection   A method of cooking and heating utilizing a fan to circulate hot air.

convenience outlet   An electrical outlet conveniently placed for use at a counter or on a wall to supply electricity for large and small appliances.   A.K.A. **convenience receptacle**   See: **duplex receptacle**

conventional design Utilizing a traditional and widely accepted element of design.

conversation chair An S-shaped chair, designed to seat two people face-to-face and side-by-side for intimate conversations. Popular during the 18th and early 19th centuries.

conversation piece   An interesting object or piece of art that tends to stimulate conversation, at least about the object.

conversion To change the use of a room or building.

convex A shallow bulge in a surface, as opposed to **concave**. See: **concave**

conveyance Something that transfers. 2. A legal document or instrument used to transfer property from one person to another.

conveyor   A moving surface or series of rollers, used for moving material or packages from one location to another, such as along an assembly line. A.K.A. **conveyer belt**

convex

coolant A fluid that conducts heat, as used in automobile radiators.

cool colors   Colors that create a sense of cold, light blue in particular and its various hues from blue-green to violet-blue.

cooperative   See: **condominium**

cope To cut or shape the end of a piece of molding to fit into the contour of a perpendicular piece. **coping** *NOTE: A practice made somewhat obsolete with the advent of electric miter boxes.*

coping saw   A light, narrow-bladed hand saw used for cutting small curves in wood.

copper fitting   Various connections and angles used with copper tubing to create a water delivery plumbing system.

copper plating   A coating of copper applied to the surface of another metal by dipping or by a method known as electrolytic, which uses electricity to adhere a thin copper coating.

copper tubing   A seamless tube made from almost pure copper (99.9 percent) extensively used in plumbing to deliver water to the various sinks, plumbing fixtures, and appliances in residential and commercial applications.

corbel A shoulder or bracket attached to a wall, used both as a structural element and decoration.

cord   A heavy twine or thin rope. 2. See: **tie beam**

core The material in the middle or inside an object. As the core of a apple, or a hollow or solid core door. 2. The basic material

core drill

something is laminated to. **3.** The central part of a multistory building, containing various services and utility functions (elevators, stairwells, etc.), around which offices or apartments on each floor are designed.

core drill   A drill used to retrieve a deep sample of earth or rock at a particular site.

Corinthian order   The most ornate of the Greek and Roman architectural orders, characterized by a bell-shaped capital, acanthus leaves, and volutes.

cork   The lightweight bark of the cork oak tree, used for a variety of applications, including **bulletin boards, insulation,** and **gaskets.**

corkboard   Cork granules, glued and compressed into sheet form of various thickness. Often used as bulletin boards and gaskets.

corner   The point at which two perpendicular surfaces intersect, as two adjoining walls of a room or adjoining sides of a box.

corner bead   Any vertical molding used to protect the external edge of two intersecting surfaces. Applies primarily to the metal lath, used to reinforce external drywall corners before plastering.   A.K.A. **angle bead, corner guard, corner molding, plaster bead**

corner block   A block of wood or plaster, usually a rosette, used at the upper corners of door and window casing, as a decorative element.   **2.** A common carpentry technique to stiffen cabinetry corners using blocks or lengths of wood.

corner board   Two boards, nailed at right angle to one another, used to cover the external corners of a building, and to cover the ends of siding or into which siding is butted.

corner brace   A diagonal brace to reinforce or keep square the corners of a wood-frame structure.

corner bracket   A bracket made to be used in a corner.

corner clamp   A clamp especially made to hold frame corners tightly in place while glue dries.

corner post   Any upright supporting element made to work in a corner of an object or structure.   **2.** A framing term referring to how the corners of exterior walls are built and attached.   A.K.A. **California corners**

cornerstone   The base stone establishing a corner or angle in a structure, which often carries a dedication plaque or a historic reference.   A.K.A. **foundation stone**

cornice   The top or uppermost part, as the top face of a mountain. **2.** Refers to molding at the top of a building or just below the ceiling in a room. A.K.A. **crown molding 3.** Part of the entablature in classic Greek and Roman architecture.   See: **column details**

coromandel   *(Wood)* Refers

specifically to Macassar ebony See: **Macassar ebony** A.K.A. **calamander, coromandel ebony, striped ebony**

corona A projecting shelflike element at the top of a classic building.

coronet An ornamented crown, pediment, or band above a window or door.

corridor An interior passageway providing access to several offices, apartments, or rooms.

corrosion The deterioration, principally of metal, resulting from its exposure to weather, moisture, chemicals, or other environmental agents.

corrugated fastener A steel fastening device of corrugated metal used to join corners of a flat frame where nails and screws would not be appropriate. Used primarily where appearance is not important. A.K.A. **joint fastener**

corrugated glass Glass with corrugated ribbing that provides a visual obstruction and diffuses light.

corrugated metal Sheet metal stamped with parallel ridges and furrows to provide additional ridged strength.

cosmetic Refers to something that is entirely for decoration, and not expected to provide structural support.

cottage A small country- or village-style house. **2.** A small vacation house.

cotter pin A metal pin with split ends, used for fastening a bolt (with a pinhole in its shaft) in place. Once in place, the split ends of the pin are bent back so the bolt cannot work itself free.

cotter pin

cottonwood (*Wood*) See: **poplar**

couch A.K.A. **sofa, divan**

counter A narrow horizontal cabinet with a top surface at a comfortable height to conduct business or work at while standing.

counterbalance See: **counterweight**

counter bore See: **countersink**

COUNTER HEIGHTS

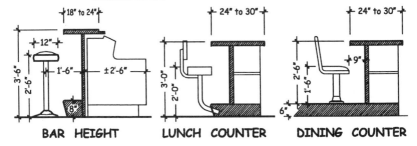

BAR HEIGHT   LUNCH COUNTER   DINING COUNTER

countersink

countersink A cone-shaped bit used to make a depression to receive the head of a screw or bolt so that it does not protrude above the surface. A.K.A. **counter bore**

countersink

counterweight A weight equal to that of an object being balanced for easy movement. 2. Used theatrically to quickly and easily move *(or fly)* suspended scenery, drapery, and props. A.K.A. **counterbalance**

couple Any pair.

coupled columns Columns used in pairs.

coupled windows Two closely spaced windows that visually form a pair of windows.

coupler A metal hardware device used to join frames and braces of tubular metal scaffolding. **coupling**

course A layer of masonry running horizontally from one end to the other, on a building, wall, or curved over an arch, as in a **soldier course**. 2. A path or channel, as a race course or golf course. 3. A regular course of action or the natural course of things.

court A courtroom. 2. A semiprivate yard. See: **courtyard**

courthouse A municipal building specifically built to house one or more courtrooms, judges' chambers, offices of the court clerks, holding cells, and offices for other court-related business and officials.

courtroom A room designed and equipped to conduct a trial.

courtyard A semiprivate, open landscaped area partially or fully enclosed with walls or adjacent buildings. A.K.A. **court**

cove molding A concave or canted surface often used as crown molding, making the transition from walls to ceilings. **coving** A.K.A. **cavett**

cover A lid or cap to hide or protect the contents of a vessel from view, the elements, or from spilling. 2. A term used in painting to describe the ability of paint to visually block out the surface below. 3. An instruction to put something over a particular surface, as with wallpaper or paneling.

coverage The area being covered or the area a particular roll of wallpaper, gallon of paint, or package of flooring or roof shingles will cover.

cover coat A coating of paint or glaze applied to a raw surface.

cover plate Refers primarily to a flush-mounted access panel.

cowl A hood to protect vertical pipe (such as soil stack or vent pipe) from rainwater and snow.

crack A partial fracture, break, or split usually without complete separation. 2. A condition in plaster and masonry walls that occurs as a structure settles or because of an earthquake. **cracking**

cracker house   Native to central Florida and the panhandle, because of its tropical climates. Symmetrical (saddlebag) shaped log cabins with hipped tin roofs with a cupola for ventilation and large, cool shed porches that deflect the heat of the sun. Kitchens were often in an attached but separate building. Unique to the cracker house style is a open pass through (dogtrot) or dominant corridor running between the front and rear porch, for ventilation. *NOTE: The term "cracker" is believed to have originated in nearby southern Georgia, where cracked corn was a dietary staple.*

crackle   A painting technique that uses paint or laquer over a softer undercoat to produce a network of fine cracks.

cradle   Refers primarily to an object supported from above, as a window washers platform, which is suspended by cables from the roof of a building.

Craftsman style   *(1890-1940)* A widely popular style of western U.S. architecture, exemplified by the work of architects and craftsmen *(brothers)* Greene and Greene *(Pasadena, CA);* spawned by the English Arts and Crafts movement, which rejected mass production and mediocre design associated with the Industrial Revolution in favor of the beauty and honesty of craftsmanship and natural materials. Characterized by low-pitched gable roofs, widely overhanging eaves, projecting balconies and porches, wood or shingle siding, and lavish gardens. Also featured hand-polished interior wood details, trim, and built-ins. A.K.A. **western stick** *NOTE: The name western stick is partly due to "Craftsman Magazine" (1901-1916) published by furniture maker and designer Gustav Stickley (1848-1942).* See: **bungalow** A.K.A. **craftsman bungalow**

crane   A hoisting machine, with a boom, to lift, lower, and move a load horizontally.

crawl space   An unfinished interior space of limited height, but sufficient to permit access. Typically, an attic space or the space under a single-story house, when it rests on piers rather than directly on a foundation.

credenza   A long low cabinet. 2. Refers to a piece of office furniture, behind a desk, that serves as storage and general work space.

creeping   Slowly moving. 2. The imperceptible shifting and settling, the stresses and strains, even the effects of the weather, that occur over time in any structure.

creole house   Typical townhouse of the 19th century New Orleans streetscape. Commonly throughout Louisiana and the Gulf Coast. Narrow one- or two-story hipped or gabled roof houses with clapboard siding and an upper-floor open gallery with French doors at both the front and rear of the building. Often containing secluded gardens and covered porches.

crescent

crescent The concave arc shape of a quarter moon.

crescent truss A truss, in profile, that takes on the appearance of a crescent, facing either up or down. See: **crescent**

crest A shield shape traditionally used in decorative and ornamented carvings. **2.** The top of anything, or the line along the summit, ridge, or wave.

crib A bed with side rails for infants. **2.** A box or structure, without enclosure -- meant to be left open.

cricket A small structure built between a sloping roof and a chimney to divert water away from the chimney.

crimp A bend, wrinkle, fold, or crease.

crinkling A.K.A. **wrinkling**

cripple In framing, a structural element, normally a short **stud**, used above and below windows and over a door opening.

crisscross The crossing of two diagonal lines.

criteria A standard used as the bases for a decision or judgment; acceptable limits established by code, the norm, or rule of thumb.

crook A bend on the surface plane of lumber.

cross An object consisting primarily of two straight pieces forming right angles with one another. **2.** The symbol of the Christian faith.

cross banding Any decorative band whose grain is perpendicular to the principal surface.

cross brace Any system of bracing that incorporates a diagonal intersection. **cross bracing** A.K.A. **X-bracing, scissor brace**

crosscut saw A saw with the teeth of its blade set to cut across the grain of wood rather than with the grain. See: **handsaw**

cross-grain A carpentry term used to describe the direction of a cut, across the grain of the wood, indicating that the board is being cut to length, as grain normally runs parallel to the long edge of a plank. **2.** The alternating of grain direction on adjoining layers of plywood for greater strength.

crosshairs Very thin wires or etched lines on the focal plane of a surveyor's telescope.

crosshatch pane window A traditional window pane detail adapted to many architectural styles, particularly **Craftsman** and **Prairie**.

cross-lap joint A joint connecting two pieces of wood together at right

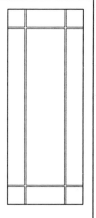

crosshatch pane window

crook

crosspiece 63

angle, where half the thickness of boards by its width is cut away from each, so that they overlap on the same plane. A.K.A. **lap joint**

crosspiece Any piece of timber or beam crossing from wall to wall or running from one part to another.

crowbar A slightly bent steel bar, with a flattened end, used for prying *(using leverage)* to lift and move heavy objects. A.K.A. **wrecking bar, pinch bar, pry bar**

crowbar

crown The head (top) of anything, particularly an arch. **2.** Any upper finishing molding or architectural element. **3.** The high point at the center of a cross section of a road, intentionally made slightly higher for water runoff. **4.** The leafy top of a tree or shrub.
crowing

crown course The top course, as the finishing course of tile or a tile ridge cap on a roof.

crown molding Any molding that serves to form a crowning or finishing element, as at the top of a door or window or at the top of a wall or building.

crystal Cut glass or molded glass, made to look like cut glass.

Crystal Palace A mostly iron and glass exhibition hall, constructed in Hyde Park, London, for the great exhibition of 1851. **2.** Any exhibition hall similarly constructed.

cube Geometrically, a solid with six equally square sides.

cubicle A small enclosed space. **2.** A partitioned space, designated as a workstation in a larger room.

cubism Painting or sculpture based on abstract design. Famous cubists include Picasso and Braque.

cupboard A small room (closet or pantry) or enclosed storage space (cabinet) with shelves for dishes, glassware, silverware, etc.

cupola A small structure, often a dome on the ridge of a roof, primarily for light, ventilation, and decoration, but formerly used as a lookout and defensive post. A.K.A. **lantern**

cupped A hollowed defect on the face or surface of a plank of wood.

cupped

curb A concrete step that separates the road from the sidewalk or planted area.
curbing

cure A metamorphic change of physical properties resulting from hydration or a chemical reaction, as in the solidification (hardening) of concrete or plaster. **curing**

curf cut A series of grooves or cuts, particularly across the width of a board or molding to facilitate bending.

curl cut See: **burl**

current Of its own time, contemporary. **2.** The flow of electricity in a circuit.

CURTAIN STYLES

curtain drop Refers to the desired length of a drape, from top to bottom.

curtains Lightweight fabric, hung over window and door openings. **curtain** See: **drapery**

curtain step The first step of a staircase, often embellished.

curtain wall A nonbearing exterior *(glass)* wall of a building.

curve A line having no straight parts.

curvilinear arch
A decorative style of arch.

curvilinear arch

cushion A pillowlike decorative pad. **2.** The reversible seat and back cushions on an upholstered sofa or chair. **3.** Padding, as around glass, to reduce the effects of vibration and abrasion.

cusp The intersection of two arcs. **2.** The figure formed by the intersection of tracery arcs.

custom-built Constructed to meet a specific dimensions or design, opposed to **factory-built**. Not prefabricated.

custom-made See: custom-built

custom millwork See: millwork

customs house An obsolete

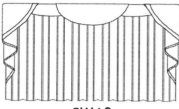

SWAG

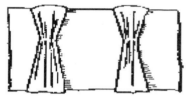

FRENCH FOLD

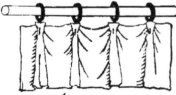

CAFÉ CURTAINS

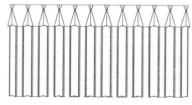

VALANCE

GATHERED

term, used to describe a historic building where customs duties were collected.

cut To slice into parts with a sharp-edged instrument (knife or saw). **2.** The void resulting from the excavation of material. **3.** The depth to which earth is excavated to create a level surface at a predetermined grade. **4.** Theatrically, a long slot or channel across the stage floor, used to introduce or remove scenery.

cutaway corner The corner of a building that appears cut off, since it is not a square corner, but is clipped off at usually a 45° angle. A.K.A. **clipped corner**

cut brick A roughly shaped brick.

cut glass Highly polished glass objects that were ground to form figures or patterns on their surface.

cut in A painting term used to indicate the careful use of a brush in painting the trim around windows, doors, baseboard, and in corners.

cutaway corner

cut line A line that marks where the material is to be cut.

cut list A list of the sizes of wooden pieces or timbers required for a particular job.

cut nail A nail cut or stamped from sheet metal.

cutoff A.K.A. **falloff**

cut-off saw See: **radial-arm saw**

cutout Any opening in any surface, such as a door or window opening in a wall. **2.** A part cut or stamped out of a sheet of material.

cut roof A truncated pitched roof that forms a flat top instead of continuing to the ridge. A.K.A. **terrace roof**

cyclone cellar A safe, covered area below grade, built in the event of a dangerous windstorm. A.K.A. **storm cellar**

- D -

dado A wide cut or groove, used as a track or to accept another piece of lumber *(shelf)* or another material. **2.** A general carpentry term use to describe a change in material surface, as a wall painted below a picture molding or chair rail and wallpapered above. A.K.A. **chair rail 3.** In classic Greek and Roman architecture, the central part of a pedestal between the base and the cornice. A.K.A. **die**

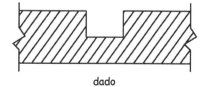
dado

dado cap See: **chair rail**

dado head A router bit or wide, circular saw blade used to cut a flat-bottomed groove in lumber. There are two types of dado saw blades: **(1)** two blades separated by chipper blades to a desired width, and (2) a blade that can be set to a specific angle, which determines the width of the cut.

dais A raised platform on one side of a large dining room where honored guests and speakers are seated, and where the evenings event is focused. A.K.A. **head table**

damper A device on a vent used to control the flow of air. **2.** An adjustable lever at the top of a firebox to regulate the drift.

dap A notch made to receive another piece of lumber.

dart The pointed object in traditional **egg-and-dart** ornamental molding.

daybed A bed that is stored under another bed during the day and rolled out at night for use. A.K.A. **trundle bed**

dead Refers to an electrical circuit that is disconnected from a source of power. **2.** Color described as lacking luster and gloss.

dead air space An unventilated space, as in a shaft, attic, or hollow wall.

dead bolt A door lock that runs a slide bolt *(embedded in the door stile)* into the doorjamb to prevent the door from being opened.

deaden To make less bright, lively, or less likely to grab attention.

dead end A false path, or anything similar. **2.** A section of pipe that is terminated with a cap.

dead light A window not intended to open.

deadman An anchor securely fastened to a horizontal surface, meant to take the strain of weight, as when used to secure the line of a **block-and-fall** while lifting something heavy.

deadwood A dead tree or branches. **2.** Something useless or burdensome.

deal *(Wood)* Of British origin, a term applied to common dimensional construction grade lumber, **southern yellow pine** and **Douglas fir** in the United States. Sometimes used incorrectly to describe pine wood alone.

decay See: **rot**

deciduous Describes trees or shrubs that shed their leaves annually, characteristic of most hardwoods.

deck A flat, open platform or the floor of a building, balcony, or other structure.

decking The material or planking used as structural flooring. *NOTE: More and more, planking used on exterior decks is made of recycled plastics.*

decor The atmosphere or style created by the combination of materials, furnishings, and objects in a room or building.

decorate To make appealing and interesting to the eye.

decorative art Objects that are more than merely useful; they delight the eye and interest the mind because of their unique shapes, color, or arrangement of its parts.

decorative block Masonry, tile, or wood block, distinctively different from common blocks *(in color, style, or type -- many with figures)*, placed in a row or randomly for a decorative effect.

découpage *(Fr)* An artistic technique for decorating a surface with paper cutouts and other materials, which is then varnished for a permanent finish.

deed A certified legal document used to transfer title *(ownership)* of real *(land)* property from one party to another.

deed restriction A limitation on the use of land, specified in a deed as restricted.

defect A flaw in material, construction, or finish, that negatively effects its durability, usefulness, or strength.

defective work Work not complying with contract specifications.

deficiencies Lacking, not to expectations.

deformity A distortion in the form, shape, or dimensions of an object due to stress or force.

degree Mathematically, a unit of measurement for angles, arches, and circles. A circle equaling 360° and a right angle equaling 90° **2.** Any successive steps or stages in a series or process.

dehumidify To remove moisture *(water vapor)* from the air, within an enclosed environment.

dehumidifier A device or apparatus, usually part of a modern air-conditioning system, used to remove moisture from air. **dehumidification**

dehydration The process of removing water vapor from an object, by drying.

delamination The failure of an adhesive to maintain a bond or separation between the layer(s) of a lamination, such as plywood or laminated timbers.

demand The usage or requirements, such as the amount of electricity or water the occupants of a building or residence require on a daily basis.

demolition The systematic destruction and removal of all, or part of a building or structure.

den A small room designated as retreat, used for work, study, or leisure. A.K.A. **chamber**

density A measure of compactness.

denticulated Embellished with dentil or dentil-like ornamentation. **denticular**

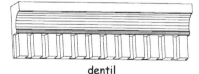

dentil

dentil A series of small tooth-like *(square or rectangular)* projecting blocks, usually found in crown molding.

depot A storehouse or warehouse. **2.** A railroad station to accommodate and shelter passengers and handle freight.

depth gauge

depth gauge A device used to measure the depth of a hole or recess.

derrick A machine used to lift *(hoist)* heavy loads, as used on an oil derrick. No boom arm, as with a crane.

design The process of developing and documenting plans for the construction of an object, building, or structure.

design documents See: **working drawings**

detached dwelling A stand-alone house, a residence.

detail The particulars of how things are to look. **2.** An elaborate *(more fully illustrated)* drawing, in a larger scale, describing a part of the whole architectural design or concept.

detail drawing A drawing that explains the specific details of a specific object.

deterioration A breakdown or erosion.

developer Individual(s) or corporation engaged in the business of planning, financing, and establishing a large residential, commercial, or combination project in a particular area.

development Previously undeveloped land improved with all the utilities (roads, water, electricity, sewers, etc.) needed to support a tract of houses or commercial buildings.

device Mechanical or electrical components or machines that do a particular thing.

dew point The temperature at which the water vapor in the air condenses and forms a liquid (**dew**).

dhurrie A traditional woven carpet from India. A.K.A. **durry, dhurry**

diagonal A line or object on an incline. Any line not perpendicular to a horizontal line. **2.** In framing, a structural element, *temporary or permanent*, running from the bottom plate of a wall to an end stud, to stiffen or keep square a wall section or truss.

diagonal bond A common bricklaying arrangement, often done in a color accent.

diagonal brace A board embedded into the studs of a wall for stability, which runs, on angle, from the bottom plate to the top plate.

diagonal buttress A support element protruding from the corner of a wall or building. See: **buttress**

diagonal flooring Any flooring material laid diagonally to the walls.

diameter A straight line through the center of a circle.

diamond drill Actual pieces of diamonds embedded into hardened steel drill bits and used to drill through extremely hard materials, like marble and glass.

diamond mesh A common type of expanded metal sheeting used as security screens and as a base for mortar and plaster.

diamond pattern Similar

dictionary stand

to a checkerboard pattern, but turned 45°, but not necessarily comprised of a perfect squares.

dictionary stand A slanted stand that rests on a table or stands on the floor to support a large, open dictionary.

die A tool for cutting threads on pipes, metal rods, etc.

die-cast Casting an object by forcing molten metal into a mold.

dies A common carpentry term to describe the termination of one object, usually into another, as baseboard dies into a **plinth block**. See: **plinth block**

diffused light The spread or reflection of light through or off an irregular surface.

diffuser Any material used to shatter or deflect air, light, or sound waves from its source.

dike A long, low dam. **2.** An earthen embankment that acts as a dam, to contain or control the flow of water. **dyke**

dilute To reduce, thin, or weaken, as with water or other liquids. **diluent, dilution**

dimension A measurement in terms of length, breath, thickness, angle, or magnitude (scope).

dimensional lumber
Refers to standard sizes that lumber is cut, stocked, and sold for common wooden construction. The size of lumber is described by a measurement of its thickness, by its width, by its length (always in that order), such as 2x4x10, originally meaning 2"x4"x10'.

Today, it means... $1\frac{1}{2}$"x$3\frac{1}{2}$"x10'.
STANDARD THICKNESSES
$1x = 3/4$"   *$6x = 5\frac{1}{2}$"
$2x = 1\frac{1}{2}$"   *$8x = 7\frac{1}{2}$"
$4x = 3\frac{1}{2}$"
  * referred to as **timber**
STANDARD WIDTHS
$x3 = 2\frac{1}{2}$" $x8 = 7\frac{1}{2}$"
$x6 = 5\frac{1}{2}$" $x10 = 9\frac{1}{2}$"
$x4 = 3\frac{1}{2}$" $x12 = 11 1/4$"
The lengths of boards are cut at 2-foot increments; 8 ft, 10 ft, etc., to a maximum of 22 ft., depending on the tree it is cut from.

diminish To make smaller.

dimmer A device (switch) used to control the intensity of a light, by varying the flow of current to the lamp or light source. A.K.A. **dimmer switch**

dining room The principal room, in a home or hotel, where people eat various meals of the day.

dip coat A paint or plaster coating that is applied by completely immersing an article in a tank of the coating; usually applied as a finish or waterproof coating.

dip-dyeing A process of dyeing textiles by dipping whole pieces into the dye. A.K.A. **piece-dyeing**

direct current An electrical term referring to the flow of current in one direction only, as opposed to alternating current. The DC in AC/DC.

directional lighting
Lighting designed to be adjusted to illuminate any work surface or object.

director's chair
A folding chair with a canvas seat and back, used predominantly by the motion picture and television industry.

director's chair

discharge pipe
Any pipe that conveys wastewater or sewage from plumbing fixtures or appliances.

dish A depression in a surface, generally for the purpose of retaining water. 2. Refers to a satellite dish capable of receiving both picture and data communications.

disk sander
A power sander that spins a circular abrasive (usually sandpaper) disk, usually used for rough finishing or set up with a buffing wheel for polishing surfaces.

dispensary
An in-house medical facility that provides basic medical and nursing care for an organization's employees. A.K.A. **infirmary, nurse's office, first-aid office,**

dividers

distant colors
Colors that exude a feeling of space and openness, as light blues and purples that represent sky.

distemper
Opaque watercolor pigment.

distillation
A water purification process that converts unpurified boiling water into cool, clean *(purified)* water.

distributed load
Weight evenly spread over a surface or structure used to support it.

distressed Made to appear as worn and old.

ditch A channel dug into the ground, for a drainage, electrical wires, water pipes, etc., are buried.

divan A large, low couch or sofa usually *(but not necessarily)* without arms or a back. 2. A coffee room (café) or smoking room. 3. In Muslim countries, a council room, customhouse, or courtroom.

diversity
Many differences, variety.

dividers Refers primarily to a carpenter's compass, used to scribe or transfer a contour line. 2. A drafting instrument with multipoints used to divide a line (*of limited length*) in up to 9 equal parts. 3. See: **angle dividers**

dock A platform at an appropriate height used to load and unload people or cargo on, into, or out of a vehicle, such as a boat or loading dock. 2. A storage area, as a **scenery dock**.

dog-eared The folded corner of a sheet of material. 2. Tattered.

dogleg stair
A staircase, of two or more flights, that makes an abrupt turn on itself, leaving no space for a stairwell between the flights of stairs. A.K.A. **doglegged stair**

DOOR STYLES

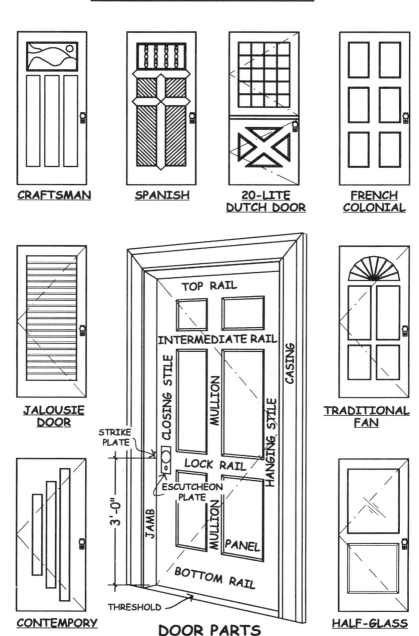

CRAFTSMAN

SPANISH

20-LITE DUTCH DOOR

FRENCH COLONIAL

JALOUSIE DOOR

TRADITIONAL FAN

CONTEMPORY

HALF-GLASS

TOP RAIL

INTERMEDIATE RAIL

CLOSING STILE

MULLION

HANGING STILE

CASING

STRIKE PLATE

LOCK RAIL

ESCUTCHEON PLATE

3'-0"

JAMB

MULLION

PANEL

BOTTOM RAIL

THRESHOLD

DOOR PARTS

DOOR STYLES

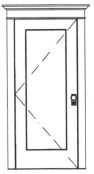

PANEL DOOR

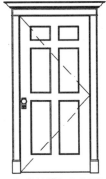

6-PANEL DOOR

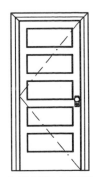

LADDER DOOR

ASTRAGAL

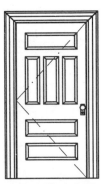

6-PANEL DOOR

FRENCH DOORS

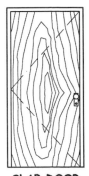

SLAB DOOR

TRANSOM WINDOW

TRANSOM BAR

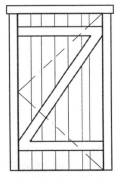

Z-BRACE DOOR

9-LITE HALF DOOR

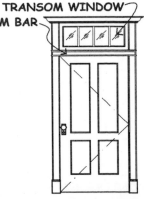

TRANSOM DOOR

dolly A *(4-wheeled)* low cart or truck used for transporting heavy or bulky equipment.

dolomite A mineral *(calcium-magnesium carbonate)* used as paving material. A.K.A. **limestone**

dome A hemispherical-shaped roof or vaulted ceiling structure.

domicile A **residence, home,** or **dwelling**.

door A hinged barrier used to keep out the weather and to control access into a building, room, or cabinet. To provide privacy and security. Doors come in a variety of sizes and styles (swinging, sliding, folding etc.) and are used for a variety of purposes.

doorbell A device to signal the occupants of a house that there is someone seeking entrance.

door casing The finished molding surrounding a door. A.K.A. **doorcase** See: **casing**

door catch See: **catch, latch**

door closer See: **door closure**

door closure A device that automatically returns a door to the closed position.

doorframe See: **doorjamb**

doorjamb The vertical inside members on each side of a door opening to which a door is hinged. *NOTE: Because of the ease of installation and a trend toward elaborate front doors and French doors, manufacturers include the finished jamb (often including a threshold) and pre-hang door(s).*

doorknob A handle on a door that also operates the locking mechanism.

door schedule A detailed list *(style, finish, size, locations, and special requirements)* of all the doors required for a particular building.

doorstep A landing or platform leading to an entrance of a house or building.

doorstop A strip of molding against which a door shuts.

door swing Refers primarily to the area that a door uses to open and close.

doorway An opening in a wall, with a door.

Doric order The oldest and simplest style of Greek architecture; adopted and refined by the Romans. One of the principal divisions of classic Greek and Roman architecture. See: **column details**

dormer A structure projecting from the plane of a sloping roof. Used to light and ventilate an attic space, or to increase (by adding **headroom**) the usable space therein. See: **dormers** A.K.A. **dormer windows**

dormer wall A dormer that is flush with the face of a building. A.K.A. **wall dormer**

dormer window See: **dormer**

dormitory A building or room used as sleeping quarters for multiple occupants.

double Flemish bond See: **Flemish bond** double glazing Two layers of glass separated by

DORMERS

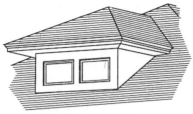

HIPPED DORMER

SHED DORMER

GABLE or PITCHED DORMER

EYEBROW DORMER

an airtight space, *or a space filled with argon gas*, to insulate and prevent the exchange or escape of treated air (either heated or cooled).

double-headed nail A nail with two stacked heads, used to temporarily attach something; easily removed when it is no longer needed or wanted. A.K.A. **double-head**

double-hung sash A standard window, with two sashes, opening both top and bottom for ventilation.

Douglas fir *(Wood)* The most often used construction grade, softwood structural lumber in North America, because it grows relatively fast, with tall, straight tree trunks. Strong and durable, works easily, and fairly inexpensive; grown in abundance because it adapts easily to modern tree-farming techniques. Extensively used in construction and plywood sheets.

dovetail A very strong method of joinery, using an interlocking wedge-shaped tenon and mortise system. Used primarily for attaching drawer fronts to the sides of a drawer. Also used to secure structural members in timber-frame construction.

dovetail

dowel A length of perfectly rounded wood.

doweling

pins Short lengths of dowel used to secure two pieces of wood together. *NOTE: The practice of using doweling pins is quickly being replaced with the use of wooden biscuits.*

down   The feathers of geese or ducks, considered the most luxurious filling for seat cushions and bed pillows.

downlight   A usually recessed light fixture, that floods a wall with a downward cast of light.

downspout   A pipe that carries rainwater from roof gutters to the ground or to a sewer connection.   A.K.A. **downpipe or rainspout**

drafting   See: **working drawings**

drafting room   A room devoted to those producing drawings.

draftsman   A person skilled in producing measurable working drawings.   *NOTE: With the advent of CAD, most planning and design projects are drawn on computers, with sophisticated software, and printed out on large format plotters.*

drain   The open end of a drain pipe, such as in a sink or bathtub into which water flows.

drainage   Diverting water away from a building.

drainpipe   A pipe used to drain away wastewater and refuse.

drain spout   A drainpipe that leads directly to an exit.   A.K.A. **rain spout, gutter spout**

drapery   Fabric, hung or swagged from **curtain rods** in front of a window for privacy. See: **curtains**

drawbridge   A bridge that can be raised and lowered. Typically used over narrow rivers where the bridge can be raised to permit a tall ship to pass, then lowered to resume normal motor vehicle traffic.

draw curtains   Curtains that are placed on a curtain rod (known as a **travertine rod**), which uses a cord and pulley system to open and close the curtains.

drawings See: **architectural drawings, working drawings**

drawing board   A large table an artist or draftsman uses to draw on.

dress   To prepare, shape, or polish to a finished state.

dressed & matched boards   Planks of lumber, chosen because of their matching color and grain, that are milled to an equal thickness with straight, square edges for **joining** together to make, for example, a tabletop or cabinet doors. *NOTE: It is a common practice when assembling a tabletop to alternate the direction of the end grain of the planks, which tends to keep the top flat and avoids cupping.*

dressed lumber   Lumber having one or more of its faces planed smooth. A.K.A. **surfaced lumber, s4s**

dressed stone See: **stone dressing**

dresser   A cabinet with drawers or shelves. Lower and wider than a chest.

dressing room A room used by actors for changing clothes. **2.** Theatrically, a room used by one or more performers and actors to prepare *(costume and makeup)* for their performance.

drill A hand- or motor-driven tool used to spin a drill bit for boring holes in material. A.K.A. **drill motor**

drill bit A small machined tool, *available in various sizes*, with a sharp spiral edge that bores holes through material when turned at high-speed in a drill motor or drill press.

drill motor A motor-driven tool used to spin a drill bit for boring holes in material See: **drill**

drill press A vertically mounted drilling machine used to drill perpendicular holes in all kinds of material.

drinking fountain A public drinking fountain *(a plumbing fixture)* that delivers cool clean water.

drip edge A noncorrosive strip of material used over doors, windows, arches, and on roofs to direct rainwater away from a building and its openings. A.K.A. **drip cap, drip mold, weather mold, hood mold, head mold, weatherboard**

drive-in A term used to describe retail business, primarily restaurants and motion-picture theatres, of the late 1940s - early 1990s, that permitted patrons to eat or watch a movie from the comfort of their own automobiles.

drive-through A term used to describe the practice of

drill press

drinking fountain

conducting business (banking, fast food restaurants, etc.) without customers having to leave their automobiles.

driveway A private road or section thereof, which leads from the public street to the front door or parking area of a residence or building.

drop The vertical descent of a pipe, path, or surface. **2.** The vertical distance between two or more horizontal levels. **3.** The drop opposed to the rise, of a stair when moving downstairs.

drop ceiling See: **suspended ceiling system** A.K.A. **dropped ceiling**

drop cloth A large sheet of plastic, paper, or cloth used to protect floors, furniture, etc., against paint drippings and splatters.

drop-lid A table or desk with a hinged top or front. A.K.A. **gate leg table, gateway table, tilt top**

drop-lid desk A desk with a hinged work surface, that folds closed. A.K.A. **secretary**

drop-lid table A table with a 3-piece folding (hinged) top, so that it can be folded out of the way when not in use. A.K.A. **gateway table**

drum A barrel-like metal container. **2.** The round wall, often pierced with windows, that directly supports a dome. **3.** A spool or cylinder around which rope and cable are wound, or any similar shaped object. **4.** The rounded segments of a column. **5.** A musical instrument, as found in the *percussion* section of an band.

dryer Primarily refers to a machine that dries laundered clothing (*as in washer and dryer*). **2.** Anything that aids in the drying process.

drying A physical change in the property of a material as a result of the evaporation of water, a chemical reaction, or a combination of both, as paint transforms into a relatively hard protective surface.

dry rot Decayed wood, caused by moisture, a fungus, or an infestation capable of destroying or weakening wood fibers.

drywall A material, usually gypsum board, used as a finished surface on interior walls. **2.** In masonry, a wall built without mortar, where stones are stacked in a manner supporting and sustaining a structure. A.K.A. **wallboard, plasterboard, gypsum board,. sheetrock, dry masonry,**

drywall contractor An individual or company that specializes in the installing and finishing preparation of drywall on the interior walls of a building. One of the many subcontractors *(tradespeople)* found on a construction site.

duct See: **air duct 2.** A tube, either underground or embedded in, or through a concrete wall or floor,

duplex
receptacle

through which electric wires or cables run or are housed.

duct tape A strong, fabric adhesive tape with a non-porous surface to prevent liquids or air to pass-through.

duct work A series of channels (including connectors, dampers, fans, etc.) through which heated, ventilated, or air-conditioned air is sent to various rooms of a house or building. A.K.A. **duct system**

dumbwaiter A vertical channel in a multistoried building within which a relatively small car or box travels up and down, predominantly for delivering hot food and other articles *(laundry)* or materials.

dummy Something which is only decorative, not functional, as a dummy door.

dummy door A fake door intended as part of the decor to create symmetry, rather than a functioning door. A.K.A. **sham door, blind door**

dump truck Any type of truck whose body can be tilted to discharge its load.

duplex One building with two separate residences.

duplex receptacle A standard 2-plug electrical wall outlet. A.K.A. **electrical outlet**

durability Resistance to the ordinary wear and tear of everyday use. A noncorrosive surface, resistant to weather,

dust collector

chemical attack, abrasion, and other conditions of service.

dust collector An area or object *(perhaps a shelf)* susceptible to attracting dust. **2.** A mechanical device (vacuum) used to capture dust-laden particles in the air of an enclosed environment.

Dutch colonial architecture A predominant architectural style in North America *(particularly New York, Albany, and the area surrounding the Hudson Valley)*, which was settled principally by the Dutch in the 17th century, and lasting long after the British took control in 1664. Characterized by gambrel roof and front door entrance facing the street. Often included storefronts and lofts for storage. Mostly made of brick or stone veneer *(for fire safety)* over timber framing and overhanging eaves.

Dutch door A door consisting of two separate sections *(called leaves)*, one above the other. Originally designed to allow ventilation while keeping infant children in and farm animals out. See: **door styles**

Dutch gable Characterized by ornamental stepped barge rafter. See: **barge rafter**

Dutchman A small piece of wood specifically shaped to fill an opening, replace a section of defective material, or hide a poorly made joint.

ears

easel

dwarf Lacking in the required or customary height.

dwarf rafter A.K.A. **jack rafter**

dwelling A residence or home.

- E -

eagle finial As a traditional icon of the United State, the eagle has been used in numerous applications, particularly as a crowning or cap element. See: **finial**

Eames chair A modern lounge chair and ottoman made of molded plywood and fitted with down-filled leather cushions, first designed by Charles Eames. See: **chair styles**

ears Any small, symmetrical earlike, decorative projections, as often found in traditional door and window casing treatments.

earth Terra firma. The planet, or the natural material that makes up the planet.

earthenware Coarse clay pottery. A.K.A. **stoneware**

easel A stand to hold an artist's canvas or a cardboard presentation.

easement A right-of-way through land owned by someone else for a specific purpose, such as access. **2.** The curve in a staircase handrail where it meets the newel post.

eastern red cedar An aromatic cedar of moderately high-density, with a distinctive red color. Widely used for fence posts, outdoor furniture, and closet linings.

eastern stick See: **stick style architecture**

eaves That part of a sloping roof that projects beyond the walls, protecting them from rainwater and providing an aesthetic quality. See: **rafter tails**

ebony *(Wood)* A dense, heavy, handsomely dark *(almost black)* hardwood from the heart of several species of tropical African trees. Used extensively for highly polished modern furniture and inlaid tabletops. Ebony sometimes has a very dark red or green color, or as in the case of **Macassar ebony**, a coffee-brown with black streaks. A.K.A. **black ebony, gabon** See: **Macassar ebony**

echinus A term describing shell-like details or molding.

echo Reflected sound waves against an obstructing surface.

eclectic A harmonious mixing of art objects and forms from a variety of periods and styles in a contemporary setting. **eclecticism**

edging Any material or molding used to cover the edge of a board, table, cabinet, countertop, etc.

egg-and-dart A decorative arrangement of alternating egg- and dartlike shapes, used as molding -- available in various forms.

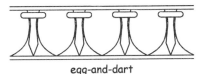

egg-and-dart

egg crate One of a series of small compartments. **2.** A construction technique that mimics the way eggs were once packaged, where a series of cuts were made half across the width of a piece of cardboard to accept a series of interlocking perpendicular pieces of cardboard, producing a series of small boxes (**pigeonholes**), and into each an egg was placed.

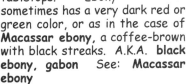

egg crate

A.K.A. **pigeonhole**

eggshell An off-white color with a semimatte finish, like the white shell of a chicken egg.

Egyptian architecture
Reminiscent of the art and architecture of Egypt *(3,000 B.C.)* to the Roman era. Simple post-and-beam construction, without arches or vaulted ceilings, and massive stone temples and pyramids.

elasticity The ability of a material to return to its original shape after being twisted, bent, stretched, or compressed *(causing tension)*, or deformed in any way.

elbow Refers to short segments of piping made specifically to join another segment or to turn a corner. A.K.A. **pipe elbow**

electric Refers to our everyday use of electricity. **electrical**

electrical appliances See: **appliances**

electrical codes The adoption, by local municipalities as part of their local building codes, of industry standards established by electrical engineers and professional organizations.

electrical contractor A licensed individual or company specializing in the installation of wiring and electrical circuits. One of the many subcontractors **(tradespeople)** found on a construction site.

electrical outlet See: **duplex receptacle A.K.A. outlet**

electrical tape A black plastic, nonconductive tape. Any tape made specifically for use with electric wiring. A.K.A. **black plastic tape**

electric arc welding See: **arc welding**

electric drill A hand-held electrically powered drill.

elephantine column A broad square column that tapers toward the top. Characteristic of bungalow-style homes. A.K.A. **tapered column**

elevations A scaled measured drawing (without perspective) showing the vertical elements, either exterior or interior, of a wall or building. Elevations work in conjunction with a floor plan, detailed drawings, and schedules - - to describe the construction of a building or structure. An essential part of the **working drawings**.

elevator A passenger cab that operates within a vertical channel *(shaft)*, to quickly transport people and equipment from one floor to another in multistory buildings. The elevator made possible the skyscraper, and is said to have built the vertical mega-metropolitan cities we enjoy today. *Inventor: Elisha Graves Otis 1852*

elevator car The passenger or load-carrying unit of an elevator, including its platform, walls, door(s), and ceiling.

elevator landing That portion of a floor, adjacent to the elevator shaft, used to receive and discharge passengers or freight.

elevator shaft The channel within which the elevator car travels.

Elizabethan architecture A very popular style of English architecture, *circa 1558-1603*, named after Elizabeth I. A step down from the traditional English castle and more reflective of a wealthy merchant or professional's country home. Characterized by large mullioned windows and board strapping. A transitional style between Gothic and Renaissance. A.K.A. **Tudor**

elliptical arch An arch having the form of a semi-ellipse.

elliptical arch

81

elliptical stairs A set of stairs with an elliptically shaped well.

elm *(Wood)* A strong, tough, durable, high-density hardwood, characterized as brown in color with a twisted and interlocked grain. Used extensively for decorative veneers, furniture, and cabinets. Stains and polishes well but is said to have a less interesting appearance than many other hardwoods.

e-mail Electronic messages transmitted over the Internet.

embankment A raised earthen structure, of rocks and gravel, used for a variety of environmental reasons, such as to retain water or carry a roadway.

embellishment To add detail or call attention to by adding decorative adornments.

embossing Impressing an image onto a variety of materials. Unlike engraving, no material is removed, instead the material is shaped.

emergency exit An exit designated for use in case of an emergency, such as a fire or earthquake.

emery A granular form of Carborundum, used for grinding and polishing glass, stone, and metal surfaces.

emery cloth Similar to sandpaper, but not used on wood, other than in the finishing process. Consists of powdered emery on a cloth backing. It can be used both wet or dry, for fine smoothing or polishing.

eminent domain The power of government to take private (real) property for public use. Actually, it is the forced sale of real property, to the government, at a price equal to its fair market value.

emission A discharge of some kind, as radiation emits from a television or computer monitor, or as heat, light, or sound are emitted from a house.

empire style Refers to the elaborate neoclassic art and architecture of the French First Empire (1804-1815).

emporium A marketplace or place of commerce. The modern department store. 2. A large building with a wide variety of merchandise. 3. In ancient Rome, a place where imported foreign merchandise was stored as it was sold off.

enamel A hard, colored glaze used in ceramics. 2. An oil-based paint made of finely ground pigments and a resin binder. Dries to form a hard, smooth, glassy finish with little surface texture.

encased Said of anything completely surrounded *(all sides)* by another material or in a case made to display it, as encased in plastic or encased in concrete.

enclosed stairs See: **boxed stairs**

encroachment The unauthorized use of land owned by someone else *(a neighbor)*.

encumbrance A restriction on the use of real property, despite a change in ownership.

end

end A general term meaning conclusion, as opposed to the beginning. **2.** The two ends of a line or board.

end butt joint See: **butt joint** A.K.A. **end joint**

end grain The grain pattern exposed when a cut across the grain is made in a piece of wood.

end lap joint See: **lap joint**

energy The capacity to do work. **2.** The electrical power a device uses during the course of operation.

engaged Attached, or made to appear attached or partly embedded into a wall or bonded to it, as an **engaged column. 2.** Fitted into or upon, as with egg crate construction.

engaged column A column partially built into a wall, not free-standing. **attached column** A.K.A. **engaged pier, pillar**

engaged pier See: **engaged column**

engineer A person trained, experienced, and licensed (or certified) to practice an engineering speciality, such as a **structural, mechanical, electrical** or **civil engineer. 2.** A person specially trained to operate a engine.

engineered beam See: **glued-laminated beam**

engineer's scale A ruler divided into multiples of 10 divisions per inch, so that measurable drawings can be produced in terms of a decimal value.

engine house A fire station where **fire engines (fire trucks)** are kept ready for action. **2.** Any building built to house an engine.

engine room A room in a building or ship where an engine is installed and operated.

English colonial

English bond A standard bricklaying pattern.

English colonial The first of three phases of English Gothic architecture, heavily influenced by French Norman decorative styles, *circa 1180-1280*, but decidedly English. Characterized by **lancet windows**. See: **New England Colonial** A.K.A. **saltbox style**

English sycamore See: **harewood**

English Tudor See: Tudor architecture, Tudor revival

entablature Formal name of the ceiling structure that is supported by columns in the Classical order of architecture. Includes the architrave, frieze, and cornice. See: **column details**

entrance The point of entry into a building.

entrance hall A corridor or passageway of a building into which visitors enter from outside.

entry An interior entrance, passage, lobby, small hall, or vestibule adjacent to an exterior door. **entryway**

environment The area *(both interior and exterior)* in which we live and work, including the ecosystems that operate within and affect that environment.

environmental designer People skilled and certified in planning and design with particular emphasis on environmental and ergonomic considerations and compatibility.

environmental impact report A detailed analysis of the probable environmental impact, *positive and negative*, of a large-scale development in a particular area. Required under the National Environmental Policy Act of 1989 (42 U.S.C. 4321 et seq.) when federal funds are involved.

epoxy A synthetic resin used to adhere or seal something.

equilateral arch An arch consisting of two equal arcs that come to a point.

equity The value of an owner's interest in property, calculated by subtracting the amount of outstanding debt *(mortgages and/or liens)* from the current value of the property.

escalator A continuously moving staircase, that carries passengers from one floor to another. Particularly used in department stores and shopping malls.

escape Any accommodation *(pipe, duct, etc.)* made to allow gas, water, heat, odor, or anything else to freely exit the confines of a building.

escape stair An interior or exterior stair, required by law, for use during an emergency, as in the event of fire.

escutcheon plate A decorative and protective hardware trim that surrounds door handles, knobs, and locking devices. 2. A flange on a pipe used to cover a hole in a wall or floor through which the pipe passes. 3.

esplanade

A protective cover at the top or end of a post, picket, or rail against a tread, floor, or wall.

esplanade A level open space for walking or driving, usually established because of an expansive view.

estate The property of a deceased person, at the time of their death. 2. An interest in real property (land).

estimate A detailed estimate of the cost of constructing a particular building or structure. **estimating**

etagere *(Fr)* An open-shelved high case for displaying decorative objects.

etch To cut away the surface of *primarily but not exclusively metal*, with a strong acid or by abrasive action, usually to re-create a logo, character, or decorative pattern. **etching**

Etruscan architecture The architecture of the Etruscan people in western central Italy, *circa 8th century B.C. to 281 B.C., when conquered by the Romans.* The Etruscan arch became an important influence on Roman classic architecture.

eucalyptus *(Wood)* The pale reddish-yellow wood of the eucalyptus tree, native to Australia and Tasmania, grown worldwide. Physical characteristics and properties vary considerably with species.

Used in shipbuilding and various decorative items. A.K.A. **oriental wood, oriental walnut, gumwood**

evaporation The vaporization of moisture, as with sun-dried paint or **kiln** baked pottery.

even-textured A texture that is evenly distributed over a surface. 2. Descriptive of wood of uniform texture and appearance.

evergreen Said of a plant or tree that remains green year round *(pine and other coniferous trees, holly, rhododendron, etc.).*

eviction The lawful removal of a tenant from property.

executive desk chair

excavation A cavity resulting from the removal of earth from its natural position.

excavator Any motorized machines used to dig or move earth, gravel, etc.

executive desk chair A chair for an executive.

exhaust fan A fan that draws air from and out of a room or building, which can also be recycled into the building's central air-conditioning system.

exhibition hall A large building where manufacturers display their products, either to the general public or to individuals and representatives of a particular industry.

existing building In regulations and in codes, a building which is already built.

exoskeleton A structure supported by an outer shell, rather than a central skeleton.

exotic plant A nonnative plant that may require some additional care or environmental considerations for it to thrive.

exotic revival A style of architecture, *circa 1835-1930*, that incorporated many of the decorative elements associated with the Egyptian, Moorish, and Turkish styles.

expanded metal A metal mesh, formed by slitting and stretching a large metal sheet. Used for a variety of applications, particularly security, and available in various gages (thicknesses).

expansion To grow in size, usually as affected by heat or cold.

expansion bolt
See: anchor bolt

expansion joint A joint or gap that permits relative movement, due to temperature changes (or other conditions), without rupture or damage. Used primarily in concrete construction.

expert witness A legal term used to describe an individual who, by virtue of his experience, training, skill, and knowledge of a particular field or subject, is qualified to testify in a court case or other legal proceeding, or to render an informed opinion on matters relating to that field or subject.

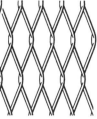

expanded metal

exploration To investigate into, or to see or discover for the first time.

explosive Any chemical compound, mixture *(dynamite or nitroglycerin)*, or device whose primary function is to detonate or explode. **WARNING: Considered extremely hazardous materials.**

exposed masonry Any masonry surface with no other finish than paint.

exposure Subjected to the effects of weather.

extension A structure added to an existing building. **2.** An accessory tool that increases the distance or length of operating parameters, as an electrical extension cord.

extension ladder A ladder with two sections that extend for use and slide together (shorter) for easy movement.

exterior door A door on an exterior wall of a building, which enables people to enter or exit the building.

exterior stair A staircase on the exterior of a building, legally required as an emergency exit in some areas.

exterior trim Any wood trim and molding used on the exterior of a building, including around doors and windows, at the cornices, gables, etc.

exterior plywood Plywood bonded with a waterproof glue.

exterior wall

exterior wall Refers to the exterior face of a perimeter wall of a building.

extra Equipment, materials or work desired by the owner, which exceed specifications and involve additional cost.

extrusion The process of forming lengths of metal channels, angle iron, and other shapes, by forcing (under pressure) hot metal through an opening of specific size and shape. **extrude, extruded**

eye Any object resembling the shape of the human eye, such as the eye of a needle.

eyebolt A bolt with a head in the form of a loop or eye.

eyebrow Applied to pediments, dormers, and other decorative and structural elements with the swooping shape of a human eyebrow, such as an eyebrow window. See: **dormers**

- F -

fabric An all-inclusive term used to describe cloth of all kinds, weights, colors, and design used as drapes and to cover upholstered furniture, etc. **2.** The carcass or basic elements of a building, without finish or decoration.

facade The front elevation or exterior face of a building.

face The finished, exposed surface of a wall, masonry, or sheet of material. **2.** The striking surface of a hammer. **3.** Applying a surface layer of one material (plaster) over another surface, as a concrete block wall. **facing**

face frame A flat frame on the front of a cabinet, that defines the cabinet's openings, to which the doors are attached, and that the draws close against.

faceplate Any protective plate, as an escutcheon plate or kick plate.

facet One of many small, flat surfaces, as the facets of a diamond.

facia See: **fascia**

factored load A structural engineering term used to describe the ultimate weight a structure is calculated to carry.

factory A building within which something is manufactured or assembled.

factory edge The edge of a sheet of material, machined straight by the manufacturer. A.K.A. **raw edge**

fading The loss of color through exposure to sunlight and weather.

Fahrenheit scale A thermometric scale based on the freezing temperature of water *(32°F above zero)* and its boiling temperature *(212°F)* at sea level and under normal atmospheric conditions.

FAIA *Abbr.* **Fellow of the American Institute of Architects.** An honor bestowed on a member / architect, by **AIA** members, acknowledging a distinguished career.

failure A structural engineering term to describe structural elements or materials that have proved incapable of carrying a specific load, or of performing a specific task for which it was designed.

fall The slope of a pipe, conduit, or channel. 2. One of the four seasons, occurring between **summer** and **winter**.

falloff That part of a board left over, and available for other uses.

fallout shelter A structure (or room therein), *built at the height of the Cold War (1960s)*, to protect against the radioactive fallout of a nuclear blast.

fan A device with blades that rotates to circulate the air within a room.

fanlight

fanlight A semicircular or semi-elliptic, fixed transom window *(light)* resembling an open fan, usually over a front door. A.K.A. **fan window**

fantail Any structure having a shape resembling a fan or positioned over a fan-shaped object, as the tail end of a ship.

fan window A.K.A. **fanlight**

farm A large expanse of land used commercially to cultivate all kinds of fruits and vegetables.

farm building Any of the structures, used for a variety of purposes that are found on a farm.

farmers market A place where local farmers gather to sell their produce. See: **produce stand**

farm house A house on a farm in which the farm family lives.

farmstead Same as a homestead, but relating to a farm and its adjacent building and service areas.

fascia Any broad, flat, horizontal structural element that is projected, cantilevered, or supported on columns or walls below. **facia**

fascia board A board that runs across the face of a building or structure. 2. A board used to cover the ends of roof rafters.

fastener A mechanical device used to connect two or more pieces of material together, such as a nail, screw, rivet, staple, etc.

fast track A project that must be completed quickly, as time is a major important consideration.

fatigue The progressive decline of a structural member that occurs because of continuous or repeated stresses and strains.

fat mix See: **rich mix**

faucet A water outlet valve, particularly interior use, as in kitchens and baths. A.K.A. **spigot, bibcock, water tap, tap**

fault line A sudden shift in the earth's surface, where the earth's plates move horizontally or vertically to one another.

fauteuil *(Fr)* An upholstered chair with open padded arms.

faux

faux *(Fr)* Refers to something simulated to look like something it is not. **2.** Often applied to various wall painting techniques that simulate **marble, reeds**, etc.

faux bois *(Fr)* A painting term meaning *simulated wood*.

feasibility study A detailed analysis conducted to determine the economic, technical, or other considerations of a proposed project.

feathered edge A tapered or eased edge.

federal style An Americanized version of the Classic British Revival style, *circa 1790-1830*. Predominantly brick with refined decoration and elongated doors and windows. Simplified symmetrical facades often concealed elegant rooms of round or oval shapes.

fee Remuneration for professional services.

feeder line Refers to a branch within a distribution or transportation system of pipes, tubes, or any other medium that empties or flows into another branch.

felt An unwoven fabric, consisting of fibers that are matted together under pressure and/or heat.

felt paper Heavy-duty construction paper used primarily as an underlayment for roofing tiles, to protect the plywood or plank sheathing *(beneath)* from the weather. A.K.A. **tar paper, building paper**

female coupling One end of a connection that accepts (within) the projecting counterpart of a male coupling.

fence An enclosing or dividing framework *(wall)* for land, yards, or gardens. It is said that good fences make good neighbors.

feng shui An ancient Chinese philosophy, for living harmoniously with the energy of the surrounding environment, that directly affects the proper arrangement and placement of buildings, architecture elements, and furnishing.

fertilizer Organic or chemical material that provides nutrients to plants and vegetables.

ferro-concrete See: **reinforced concrete**

festoon Festive decorations, including wreaths, garlands, loosely swagged fabric (like bunting), and decorated lighting fixtures.

FHA *Abbr.* **Federal Housing Administration**, an agency of the federal government that insures loans made by private lending institutions for the purchase, rehabilitation, or construction of housing on private property.

fiberboard Sheets *(usually 4'x8' or 4'x10')* of building material, composed of a variety of wood, cane, or other vegetable fibers and an adhesive binder, that is compressed to various thicknesses and densities depending on the applications requirements. *NOTE: High tech fiberboard is fast replacing exterior grade plywood in* residential and small building construction.

fiberboard insulation A thick, dense, thermal-resistant, solid insulation material sandwiched between a foil or plastic barrier material, and used primarily for exterior applications.

fiberglass Filaments of glass, formed by spinning molten glass, and processed into fabric and cords. Used for a variety of applications, including insulation for electric wiring. Used extensively with plastic resins to make molds or molded parts, which are seamed together to form things like speed boats and automobile bodies (the Chevrolet Corvette body has always been made from fiberglass rather than sheet metal).

fiber optics A medium for transmitting light through **fiber-optic cable** to numerous locations from a single light source. A.K.A. **fiber-optic cable** **2.** Telecommunications technology that uses pulsating light, through glass or plastic filament, to transmit both voice and data.

fiddle-back chair An early American version of a Queen Anne-style chair with the back support in the shape of a fiddle or vase. See: **chair styles: Queen Anne**

field Refers to a middle section, as the depressed area between evenly spaced upright stiles in paneling.

field engineer A term used to describe a designated corporate or governmental agency representative at a project site.

field house A building adjacent to an athletic field that serves a variety of related functions, such as storing equipment and/or dressing facilities, etc.

field of vision The angular extent of space which can be perceived when the head and eyes are kept fixed. A.K.A. **vision field**

fieldstone Large rocks and stones commonly found on the earth's surface.

figure The outline, likeness, illustration, representation, or shape of something, particularly the human body. **2.** Refers to the shape, color, and prominence of wood grain.

filament A slender thread of fiber or wire, as the wire within an incandescent lightbulb that glows.

file A (usually metal) tool with a rough, ridged surface used to grind away and smooth a variety of materials, including wood, metal, plastics, etc.

file cabinet A wood or metal cabinet with drawers to hold important papers.

filigree A delicate lacelike (openwork) pattern of ornamental metal art. Used extensively in metal gates and fences.

fill Soil, crushed stone, or waste materials used to raise an existing grade.

file cabinet

filler   A material use to fill a crack, hole, divot, or defect on a surface or object. Cabinetmakers and carpenters often use sawdust mixed with glue to fill unwanted defects, but there are a variety of commercially made products *(fillers)* for specific applications.

filler coat   A light coat of paint is allowed to dry, before the final (color) coat is applied, which fills microscopic depressions in the surface and provides a smooth surface for the finish coat. A.K.A. **primer coat**

fillet   A term loosely applied to almost any narrow flat band or rectangular mold that separates other molding or ornamental elements. **2.** An angled strip cut to fill a space.

film   A very thin layer, as a coat of paint or varnish on an object or surface.

filter   Any device that separates one substance from all others, such as dust from air or solids from liquids.

filtration   Filtering by passing through a sieve, filter bed, or similar device to remove foreign or unwanted material.

fin   A thin, extended structure or outward projecting flange, functional or decorative, most often used on ships and planes to reduce resistance, or any similarly shaped object.

final acceptance   A legal document reflecting the owner's acceptance of a completed project from the contractor.   Such documentation is usually accompanied by the architect's certification that the project was constructed in accordance with specifications and contract requirements.   **2.** An act of acceptance, unless otherwise stipulated, confirming acceptance, such as making a final payment.

final inspection   The final review of the project by the architect prior to his issuance of the final certificate for payment.

final payment   Payment in full, made by the owner to the contractor, upon issuance of the architect's certification of completion.

finger joint   An interlocking fingerlike projections joint used to connect short (unusable) pieces of wood, to make a long, usable piece of material. This is an extremely strong joint because of the vast amount of gluing surface.

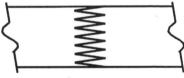

finger joint

finial   An ornamental cap, of many shapes, as at the top of a flagpole or the top of a post.

finish   The completed appearance, including texture, color, smoothness, or other properties of a surface.

finish carpentry   The production and installation of interior trim, cabinetry, bannisters and railings, etc., that requires a considerable amount of skill and knowledge.

finish coat The final coat of paint, plaster, varnish, etc. applied to any surface or application. **finishing coat**

finish nail A small nail with a slightly flared head, used for finishing work. A.K.A. **casing nail**

fir *(Wood)* Any of the softwood from the fir family of trees, including **Douglas fir, white fir, silver fir, balsam fir.** See: **Douglas fir**

fire alarm box A small box, usually red, with a push-button that sets off an alarm to alert the building's occupants and the fire department of a fire.

fire alarm system A system installed in a building to sound an alarm in the event of a fire.

firebox That part of a fireplace that contains the fire. 2. A small metal box, within which valuables are kept, that is made to withstand fire damage.

firebreak An open area or space between buildings to prevent the spread of fire.

fire door A manufactured door, tested and rated *(by the Underwriters Laboratories, Inc.)* for fire-resistance. A.K.A. **fire-rated door**

fire escape A device designed to facilitate the evacuation of people from the upper floors of a burning building. 2. An unobstructed path or escape route from a building in the event of a fire.

fire extinguisher A device specifically designed to put out a particular type of fire. Extinguishers are selected and strategically located according to the type of materials, generally, in the area where a fire could break out. "Class A" extinguishers are for ordinary combustible fires (wood, cloth, paper, rubber, and many plastics), "Class B" is for kitchen grease or gas fires, and "Class C" is for electrical fires.

fire hazard An assessment that, because of one or more factors *(environmental conditions, hazardous materials, gases)*, the potential danger of a fire starting and spreading exists, threatening the lives and safety of people and/or property.

firehouse A building where fire fighting equipment and on duty firemen are st ationed. A.K.A. **fire station**

fire hydrant An outlet device *(part of a city's water system)* that provides the fire department access to water anywhere in the city. A.K.A. **hydrant, fireplug**

fireplace Traditionally, a masonry structure that housed a firebox. Today, modern *zero clearance* firebox systems that don't require a masonry structure and can be installed at any point in time, virtually anywhere in a room.

fireproof Describes something made of materials that won't burn, and therefore don't feed a fire. A.K.A. **flameproof**

fireproofing Making something fireproof.

fire resistance The

fire-resistance rating

capacity of a material to resist, confine, or withstand fire. **2.** Material applied to existing structural elements or systems to increase their ability to resist or delay destruction by fire.

fire-resistance rating
As compared to generally accepted standards. Usually expressed in terms of time *(in hours)* that any material or construction can withstand exposure to fire, as determined by or from confirmable, impartial, standard scientific tests. A.K.A. **fire rated**

fire screen
A metal screen across the opening of a firebox, to prevent flying sparks or embers from escaping.

fire sprinkler system
An integrated, overhead system *(sprinkler heads stragically placed and supported by water pipes)* designed to automatically detect and extinguish a fire in a building.

fire stop
Any mass of incombustible material used to prevent the spread or passage of fire from one part of a structure to another.

fire wall
A wall built of non-combustible material and equipped with self-closing, fire-rated doors, to stop or at least seriously delay the spread of fire into an adjoining area.

firing
A term to describe the process of hardening, by heating, clay pottery in kilns.

first-aid office
See: **dispensary** A.K.A. **infirmary, nurse's office**

first coat
See: **base coat** A.K.A. **scratch coat**

first floor
Generally, the floor of a building at or closest to grade or ground level. A.K.A. **ground floor, first story**

first mortgage
An interest in property, which, legally, must be paid off first.

first story
See: **first floor**

fishplate
See: **scab**

fix
To make useful again. **2.** A glazing term used to describe installed panes of glass, particularly the large sheets used in commercial storefronts and curtain walls. **fixing**

fixed sash
A stationary window, not intended to open.

fixture
Any item that is semipermanently attached to a building, such as plumbing or lighting fixtures. **2.** A term used to describe a setup used to make the same cut, in the same place on a part. A.K.A. **setup, jig**

flagpole
A pole on which a flag, banner, or emblem may be raised and displayed.

flagstaff
A large flagpole. A.K.A. **flagpole**

flagstone
A thin flat stone, traditionally used as stepping-stones on paths, patios, or for terrace paving.

flamboyant
Ostentatious, showy, brilliant dazzling colors, clearly unconventional.

flamboyant style
The last phase of french Gothic architecture, *late 15th century*, characterized by flowing and flamelike tracery.

flame

flame A hot (usually luminous) zone of gas undergoing combustion.

flame resistant As opposed to fireproof. A.K.A. **fire resistant** See: **flame retardant**

flame retardant A chemical applied or added to combustible material to delay ignition and reduce spreading a fire.

flammable The ability to burn or support combustion. Subject to easy ignition and fiery combustion.

flange Any projecting collar or ring used, *decoratively or practically*, to connect a pipe or shaftlike object to any surface.

flank A lateral face, end, or side of an object or structure.

flared joint Refers primarily to electrical or plumbing connections, where the end of a piece of tubing is heated and expanded out just enough to accept an unaltered end of another piece of the same tubing.

flashing Short lengths of bent *(noncorrosive)* sheet metal, installed along the top and sloping edges of a chimney or skylights to divert rainwater and prevent water damage.

flash point The temperature at which any material will ignite and burn. The flash point for paper is 451°F.

flat Refers to paint having little or no gloss. 2. Descriptive of

a traditional, *all on one floor*, residential apartment. 3. A piece of stage scenery, such as a wall.

flat roof A roof with virtually no slope.

flecks Descriptive of many small spots or marks on a surface.

Flemish bond A standard bricklaying pattern in which each course consists of alternating **headers** and **stretchers**. See: **patterns**

fleur-de-lis *(Fr)* The ionized iris flower, associated with the former kings of France, symbolic of royalty.

fleur-de-lis

flexibility The quality of a material to bend, stretch, twist, or otherwise deform or adjust, without affecting its function.

flexible conduit See: **conduit**

flexible connector Any connection device or part that provides a degree of flexibility. Especially handy when installing a new connection to an existing service or condition.

flexible mounting Similar to a **flexible connector** with the exception that **mounting** means it is semipermanently attached to a particular surface.

flight of stairs A single straight run of stairs, as between floors or between a floor and a landing.

float A flat hand tool used to shape and smooth newly applied mortar, cement, or plaster surfaces. **floating** See: **bull float, sponge float**

floating laminated

floor A type of manufactured flooring material that is glued together on its tongue-and-groove edges, and floats on top of the floor rather than being nailed or screwed down.

float valve A valve that opens and closes depending on the vertical position of a float that rides on the surface of water in a tank, as in a water closet.

flocked paper A velvetlike wallpaper. Designs are achieved by applying sprinkling powdered wool or other material onto varnish that has been decoratively applied to paper.

flooding Any situation where water overflows its normal constraints, such as when excessive rain causes a river to rise and overflow its banks.

flood level The level at which river water begins to overflow its banks.

floodlight Lighting designed to illuminate a large area, stage, or object to a level considerably greater than its surroundings.

floor The surface in a building or structure upon which we walk and on which furniture sets. **2.** The various stories of a building. **3.** Any similar object, such as the ocean floor.

floorboards Boards or planks, usually wooden, used to form a walking surface.

flooring Any material, *structural or decorative*, used to create or cover *(lay)* a floor.

floor joists Large planks of lumber, laid on edge, to make up the support of a floor.

floor lamp A freestanding lamp.

floor line A drafting term used to identify the height of various objects or elements, when measured off the finished floor.

floor lamp

floor plan A scale *detailed* (bird's-eye view) drawing of the interior space *(including doors, windows, etc.)* of one floor of a building.

floor slab A reinforced concrete slab serving as a floor.

floor tile Any material, in modular tilelike units, used to cover a floor.

floral Any decorative flower design or pattern.

Florentine arch A semicircular arch that springs directly from the top of a column, pilaster, or pier.

Florentine arch

flow The speed at which something travels within a channel or path. **2.** Describes a desired characteristic of paint when it dries to a smooth, uniform surface, without brush marks or other undesirable evidence of the method of application.

flowchart As defined in terms of construction, a graphical representation of the various projects and subcontractors *(plumbing, electrical, drywall, etc.)*, and the time frame needed to complete their assigned work. This information enables the contractor to better schedule work, material deliveries, and to make other decisions necessary for the speedy completion of the building or structure. See: **slew** A.K.A. **shoot, flow trough**

flower box

flower box A box that hangs just outside a window, in which plants and flowers are grown.

flue A pipe, used in conjunction with a fireplace, furnace or boiler, to carry smoke, hot air, and gases up and away from a house or structure. A.K.A. **chimney flue**

fluid plan A type of office plan that emphasizes the use of large open spaces rather than individual, walled-in offices.

fluorescence The emission of visible light from a substance (such as a phosphor), resulting from the absorption of *(shorter wavelength)* ultraviolet light.

fluorescent lamp A glass tube coated, *on the inside*, with a phosphor that attracts ultraviolet light and converts it into visible light. *Different concept from the incandescent lightbulb invented by Edison.* A.K.A. **fluorescent bulb, fluorescent tube**

fluorescent light fixture A device attached or installed into a ceiling and plugged into an electrical outlet, that utilizes replaceable lamps *(an electrical term for the bulb)* to provide light.

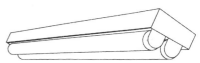
fluorescent light fixture

fluorescent paint Exceptionally brilliant colored pigment, when subjected to ultraviolet light.

fluorescent strip A lamp using fluorescent technology.

fluorescent tube See: **fluorescent lamp**

flush A term used to indicate that two or more pieces share a common surface plane. Being on the same surface plane.

flush door A flat smooth-surfaced door. A.K.A. **slab door**

flush joint Any joint finished flush with the surface.

flush plate

flush plate A flat cover that only slightly, if at all, raises above the surface it is being used on.

flush valve A valve at the bottom of a water closet (tank) that opens *(allowing the water flow into the bowl)* when the toilet is flushed.

flute One of the vertical parallel grooves or channels in the shaft of a column or furniture. **fluted**

fluting A series of parallel concave grooves, commonly used to decorate columns, pilasters, and furniture.

flux A substance used in the process of soldering metal together, as with copper tubing, that when heated, attracts solder into the connecting joint.

fly gallery In theatre, that space above the stage where scenery and props are hung and managed. A.K.A. **fly, flyer**

flying buttress A supportive element that supports lateral weight, such as an arch or ceiling piece. See: **buttress**

foam rubber Refers to latex foam rubber, which is produced from sap retrieved from rubber plants. Not made from synthetic materials. **foil** Refers to a shiny metallic material *(Mylar)* used extensively in wallpaper.

folding door Two or more doors hinged together so that when attached to a track, can be folded open. A.K.A. **accordion doors, bifold, folding, multifold doors**

folding partition A partition wall that folds away, as an accordion door. A.K.A. **accordion wall, folding wall, folding screen**

folding screen See: **screen**

foot candle The amount of light the bulb or lamp produces at a distance of one foot.

footing That portion of the foundation that directs the force of a load directly down to the ground, or into the piers sunk deep into the ground.

footlights A row of lights at the edge of a theatre stage.

footpath A narrow walkway, occasionally paved. A.K.A. **path**

footprint The area of land reflecting the perimeter shape of a building, structure, or piece of equipment upon which it sets.

forced-air The movement of air, either warm or cool, through a series of ducts by fans controlled by a central heating and air-conditioning system.

foreclosure The legal transfer of title of property to a **mortgage lender** because "the owner" failed in their contractual obligations to keep mortgage payments current.

foreclosure sale The "optional right" of the mortgagee to force the sale of property, rather than take possession of property the owner has failed to make payments on.

forecourt An outer court leading to the entrance of a large building or series of buildings.

foreman A title referring to the person in charge of a crew of carpenters or other tradespeople, and responsible for assigning them work. Reports to the **general foreman**. See: **general foreman**

foreshorten In drawing, a line representing an object, that is shorter than the actual object because of the perspective from which it is viewed. **foreshortened**

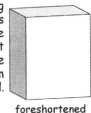
foreshortened cube

forging The working and shaping of metal parts, as did a blacksmith of the 19th century. A somewhat antiquated way of making metal parts.

forklift A power-operated vehicle with heavy-duty steel prongs to lift and move pallets loaded with various materials. Often made part of a truck delivering materials to job sites.

form Temporary construction, used to give desired shape to poured concrete, or other moldable materials. A.K.A. **concrete forms**

format A standard arrangement.

fort A military fortification or stronghold. **fortress**

fortress A stronghold, protecting a town or small city.

forum A platform or vehicle *(newspaper)* for public speaking. **2.** In ancient times, a marketplace or public square.

foul water See: **gray water**

foundation Supportive. Architecturally, refers primarily to the masonry substructure (a concrete slab, footing, or piers) upon which a structure rests and to which it is secured.

foundry A building where metal castings are made, and where furnaces used to melt metals are housed.

fountain A general term to describe a device that delivers a stream(s) of water, i.e., a **drinking fountain**, **water sculpture**, or **soda fountain**. A.K.A. **water fountain**

four-poster bed A bed frame that has a tall, usually turned, post at each of its four corners. *NOTE: With a canopy supported by the posts, it is called a **tester bed**.*

foyer A transitional passageway, as between the lobby and an auditorium or meeting room, or between the actual building entrance (the front door) and a formal lobby. A.K.A. **lobby**

frame A structural element that supports or encloses another object. **2.** Architecturally, the rough framing that encloses or supports door and window openings (door frame, window frame, etc.) of a building.

frame construction See: **framing** A.K.A. **wood-frame construction, stick framing**

framing Refers primarily to a method of construction, using dimensional lumber, that connects a series of frames (stud walls,

framing square

floor joists, roof segments, etc.) together to form the skeleton of a building. A.K.A. **stick framing, platform framing, balloon framing**

framing square An L-shaped flat, steel square commonly used in carpentry, to calculate stair and rafter cuts. A.K.A. **carpenter's square**

Franklin stove A metal, freestanding, open fireplace, resembling a stove.

freestanding An object or structure, not dependent on any other element for support.

framing square

FRAMING DETAILS

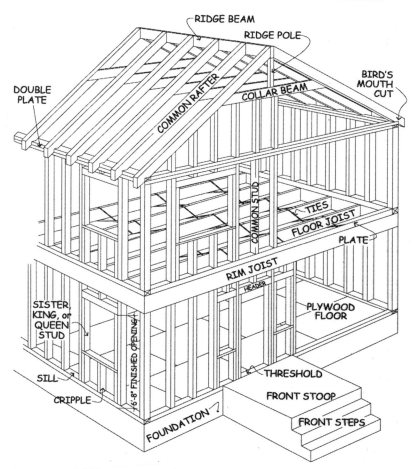

RIDGE BEAM
RIDGE POLE
BIRD'S MOUTH CUT
DOUBLE PLATE
COMMON RAFTER
COLLAR BEAM
COMMON STUD
TIES
FLOOR JOIST
PLATE
RIM JOIST
HEADER
SISTER, KING, or QUEEN STUD
PLYWOOD FLOOR
6'-8" FINISHED OPENING
SILL
THRESHOLD
FRONT STOOP
CRIPPLE
FRONT STEPS
FOUNDATION

freezer A mechanically refrigerated cabinet or room for storing frozen foods at a temperature of about 10°F (approx. - 12°C).

freight elevator An elevator used primarily for carrying freight, as opposed to a elevator car dedicated to passenger service.

French burl *(Wood)* A term applied to walnut, from Persia, with small warts or knots that give the lumber an interesting curly grain *(Hardwood)*. Used primarily in furniture and cabinetry.

French colonial An architectural style *(circa 1700-1830)* featuring two rooms and central fireplace with steeply **pitched, hipped Norman pavilion** or **gable** roof, stuccolike covered walls with narrow **French doors** pairs of casement windows, and exterior shutters opening directly onto a raised porch.

French doors

French curve A drafting tool used to create a flowing curve.

French doors Refers to a pair of doors with divided fixed glass windows running the entire length of each door. See: **door styles**

French fold A drapery term to describe the repeating trifold gathering of material at the top of drapes or valances. See: **curtain styles**

French provincial A term use to describe formal French furnishings of the 17th and 18th centuries.

French revival A stylistic, broad, picturesque representation of French architecture spanning several centuries. Characteristics include a high, steeply pitched pavilion roof, conical towers, and French doors.

French roof A Mansard roof, with nearly perpendicular sloping sides. See: **Mansard roof**

fresco The art of painting wet plaster with tempera watercolors. The color pigment is absorbed into the plaster as it drys and hardens.

fresh air Air taken into a building from outdoors.

fresh-air inlet A vent connection to a house air-conditioning system. A.K.A. **fresh-air intake**

fretwork Ornate ornamental trim, using small balusters, particularly used in the Victorian and Queen Anne styles.

friction The rubbing of two surfaces as they slide or roll against each.

frieze A horizontal transitional element, for example, the top of the siding with the soffit of the cornice. 2. A horizontally flat surface decorated with carvings

frieze panel

or ornaments. **3.** The middle *(between the architrave and the cornice)* part of the classic Greek and Roman entablature. See: **column details**

frieze panel The topmost panel in a multipanel door.

frieze rail A horizontal rail, just below the frieze panel.

front The side of a building containing the main entrance, usually the most prominent, facing the street.

front door The main entrance to a building or apartment.

front-end loader A machine with hydraulic cylinders, that manipulates a **bucket** at the end of a lift assembly, used to dig trenches and load trucks.

front yard An area between the sidewalk and a house, across the width of the property. Usually landscaped with a lawn, plants, and pathway and/or driveway leading to the front door.

frost The frozen water vapor that forms on horizontal surfaces *(i.e., the ground, roof, or on automobiles)* when the temperature gets colder than 32°F *(0°C).*

frosted glass Glass that has been surface-treated, appears semi-opaque white or frosted instead of clear. Common on lighting fixtures, because frosted glass defuses light.

frost line An imaginary line indicating how deep frost penetrates the surface or ground.

fulcrum The support point on which a lever turns to raise or move an object of considerable weight. A.K.A. **pivot point, fulcrum point**

full Cut slightly larger than needed.

full glass door A.K.A. **French doors** See: **door styles**

full-size dimension A drawing reflecting the actual size of an object. Often referred to as **F.S.D.** on architectural drawings.

full tone Describes a color, whose hue is near its full chromatic value.

functionalism A 20th century philosophy of art and architecture, that asserts that form should follow function. The aesthetic exposure of the structural elements and materials of a building, rather than covering those elements with decorative ornamentation.

furnace That part of a boiler or heater in which combustion takes place.

furnish To fill a space with furnishings, which includes furniture, wall and window coverings, and accessories.

furniture Items of comfort and convenience *(upholstered pieces, cabinets, tables, and chairs*, used to furnish interior habitable spaces.

furniture pad A heavy, blanketlike padding manufactured expressly to cover and protect furnishings when in transit. A.K.A. **pad**

furring strips   Spacers, wooden strips, used to level a finished surface.

fuse   An antiquated protective device to prevent circuit overload. Fuses have been replaced by the use of circuit breakers.

fuse box   A metal box containing circuit breakers for a building's electric system.

fusion A welding term referring to the melting together of filler metal and base metal.

futon   The Japanese version of hide-a-bed. A multipurpose piece of furniture used for either seating *(folded)* or flat *(unfolded)* for sleeping.

futuristic   Buildings and structures shaped in unconventional forms, reflective of an imagined vision of the future, such as exemplified by the work of architect **Eero Saarinen**. See: **Saarinen, Eero**

- G -

gable   The vertical triangular end of a building having a double-sloping roof.   See: **roof styles gable, roof & pitches**

gable board   A.K.A. **barge board**

gable dormer See: **dormers**

gable end   A exterior wall, that in elevation, reflects the shape of a gable roof.

gable roof   A roof having a gable at one or both ends.   A.K.A. **saddleback roof**

gablet   A miniature decorative gable.

gable wall A.K.A. **gable end wall**

gable window   A window within or shaped like ∩ gable.

gage   See: **gauge**

gallery An interior or exterior covered corridor. 2. An elevated, *perhaps uppermost*, section of seating in an auditorium. 3. A room or areas within a building set apart for special uses, such as a place to display paintings and sculpture. 4. A service passageway, lighting gallery, or an area within a building, where visitors and sightseers can observe whatever is taking place below.

gallery rail   A small railing used along the edge of a shelf.

galvanized   A **zinc** coating applied to steel or iron-based sheet goods, used extensively for **flashing, roof gutters, pipes, and nails** to protect against rust and corrosion. A.K.A. **zinc coating**

gambrel roof   A roof with two pitches on each side.   A.K.A. **Mansard roof** See: **truss**

FURNITURE FEET

CLUB   FRENCH SCROLL   BRACKET   OGEE BRACKET   SNAKE   CLAW & BALL   DRAKE   BALL   SPADE

game room

game room   A room used primarily for recreation.

gangway   A temporary platform or boardwalk erected over an unfinished section of a building to provide access for workers and to move materials.

gantry   The heavy timber framework that supports equipment or a working platform.

gantry crane   A crane that travels along tracks to reach a more extensive area of a site than a similar-sized stationary crane.

garage   A building, either separate or attached, where motor vehicles are kept.

garage door   A large door that, raises vertically *(often motorized)*, allowing storage of motor vehicles. A.K.A. **overhead door**

garage door opener   A device, with an **electric motor, track**, and **remote control unit** to open and close a garage door.

garbage   Animal and vegetable waste. A.K.A. **trash, refuse, rubbish**

garbage disposer   A waste-disposal device installed in a kitchen sink. **garbage disposal**

garden   A plot of land used for growing vegetables, fruits, flowering plants, etc. **gardening**

garden apartment   An apartment with access to a garden.

gargoyle   A stone carving, usually of a grotesque fantasy animal. Often used to decorate the end of a rainspout or waterspout.

garland   An ornamental arrangement in the form of a band, wreath, or festoon of leaves, fruits, or flowers.

garnet paper   Sandpaper, made with a finely granulated abrasive, garnet, which is said to resist clogging and last longer than ordinary sandpaper.

gas-fired water heater   A water heater, fueled by gas *(natural, propane, etc.)*.

gas furnace   A device that produces heat, by burning gas *(natural, propane, etc.)*.

gasket   Any continuous strip of resilient material used to prevent leakage of liquids, gases, heat, cold, light, sound, etc., at a joint or around a window or door opening, as weather stripping.

gas main   The underground lines a gas company installs to supply gas to residences and businesses in the community.

gas meter   An instrument that measures the amount of gas used by a particular dwelling or building, which is used to determine the cost to the user or customer.

gas station   A structure designed to facilitate the selling of gasoline and refueling motor vehicles.

gate   A door in a fence, wall, or other barrier.

gatehouse   A building, adjoining a gate, where security personnel are stationed.

gateleg table See: **gateway table**

gatepost   The post a gate is attached to and swings from.

gateway table   A drop-lid table with a pivoting leg for support. A.K.A. **drop-lid table, gate-leg table**

gauge   A measurement relating to the thickness of sheet metal, metal tubing, and wire, usually designated by a number, the lower the number the thicker the material.   **2.** A device that measures the distance between two parallel objects, such as a depth gauge. **gage**

gauged arch   An arch of wedge-shaped bricks, shaped so that the joints radiate from a common center.

gazebo   A small, open garden shelter, often utilizing latticework.

gel coat   A gelatinlike material, such as glaze (painting) or a substance used to ease the release of a molded object from the mold in which it was made.

general conditions   A written description of the rights, responsibilities, and relationships of the parties involved in a contractual agreement.

general contractor   The primary contractor, responsible for most of the work at a construction site, including that performed by the subcontractors.

general foreman   A title bestowed on the person designated as being in charge of a construction site and all the people working on that site. Reports directly to the contractor.

generally accepted standards   A recognized standard, specification, code, guide, or procedure within the construction industry.

generator   A machine that creates electric power.   A.K.A. **AC generator**

geodesic dome   A system, developed by **Buckminister Fuller**, for creating a dome structure consisting of many triangular shaped segments.

geodesic dome

geometrical stairs   Stairs constructed around a stairwell, with a continuous handrail and balusters, but without newel posts at the angles or turning points.

Georgian architecture   A British adaptation of rigid symmetry and balanced proportions of classic, Renaissance, and Baroque details of the Palladian style.   Named after George I, George II, and George III *(1714-1820)*, that became popular, in England and colonial America, early in the 18th century and into the 19th century. *NOTE: Georgian architecture represented a final break away from the medieval architecture of England's illustrious past.*

German colonial   Predominately in the Pennsylvania area, well-built, practical,

gesso

efficient Germanic housing followed Old World traditions of combining the house with a workshop and stable/barn under one roof. A simple dwelling, three rooms around a central fireplace, built mainly of stone and/or logs, often built into the side of a small earthen mound to provide a cool storage room. A.K.A. **Swiss colonial**

gesso A mixture of plaster and glue that when dry forms an extremely hard surface. Often used in molds requiring a hard edge, as in the replication of ornamental objects and forms.

ghetto In ancient Italy, an area of the city in which Jews were confined. A similar situation occurred in Nazi-occupied Poland in the late 1930s. Today the term has taken on any economically deprived area or community. **girth** See: **girth**

gilding Affixing a very thin sheet of gold to furniture and other objects or surfaces.

gimbal A device made to suspend an object on a horizontal plane between two points, allowing it to rotate laterally. Often incorporated as part of a **gyroscope. gimbaled** A.K.A. **gimbal rings**

gingerbread Decorative woodwork, as found on a richly decorated **Victorian style** house.

girder A principal beam (wood, steel, or reinforced concrete) used over a wide span to support smaller beams or a heavy concentrated load.

girder post Any column or post that supports a girder.

girth In framing, a horizontal member between columns, studs, or posts. **2.** A heavy beam, framed into the studs, to support floor joists. A.K.A. **girt** See: **ghetto**

glare A visual annoyance of brightness sufficiently greater than the luminance to which the eyes are accustomed, that hinders or causes a temporary loss in visibility.

glass A hard, brittle, transparent material produced by melting sand (silica), which is poured into sheets (for windows and mirrors) or blown or cast into a variety of shapes.

glass block A hollow block of glass of various sizes and styles. Used decoratively rather than structurally.

glass cutter A hand tool, with a sharp, hardened steel wheel, used for scoring glass.

glass door A door made predominately or entirely of tempered glass.

glass stop See: **putty mold**

glaze A thin, glossy ceramic coating used to seal, color, and harden the surface of pottery and earthenware. **2.** A term used to describe the installation of glass in windows, doors, storefronts, curtain walls, and various other applications. **glazer, glazing**

glaze coat A thin, almost transparent, layer of colored paint that allows the color beneath to show through.

glazed tile Ceramic tile with a hard-baked, virtually impervious, surface -- the result of using a glaze.

glazing fillet See: **putty mold**

glazing mold See: **putty mold**

glazing points Pointed small, thin sheet-metal fasteners used to hold pane(s) of glass in window frame(s) in place while glazing putty dries or putty mold is applied.

glazing putty A compound *(like caulking)* applied, *at an angle*, between the glass pane and the edge of the sash, which secures the glass in place and creates a weatherproof bond. A.K.A. **glazing compound**

gliding Applying a thin surface of gold leaf or gold flakes as a surface finish.

gloss Surface luster, as defined by comparison to high gloss, semigloss, or a flat matte finish.

glue Any fluid adhesive that when cured binds various materials together.

glue block A block of wood glued to the intersecting angle of two boards (usually in furniture) to strengthen the joint or connection. The added glueing surface is what provides the added strength.

glued-laminated beam A large, strong, solid beam, made up of layers of overlapping smaller boards glued together to form one beam, of any length or thickness. A.K.A. **laminated timber, glue-lam**

glued stock Pieces of wood *(including veneers)* joined together by gluing, such as in furniture.

glue-lam See: **glued-laminated beam**

glue line The line between two surfaces that are glued together, as between layers of plywood.

gold leaf Very thin sheets of rolled gold, used for gilding. A.K.A. **gold foil**

goose neck Any curved section of pipe, flexible tubing, or anything resembling the curved neck of a goose.

Gothic architecture An early western European cathedral architectural style of the Middle Ages that emerged from the French Romanesque and Byzantine styles of the later 12th century.

Gothic revival A short-lived 18th century movement *(1830-1840)* aimed at reviving the spirit and forms of Gothic architecture. Considered brooding, romantic, and picturesque -- Gothic revival was the first **"painted lady"** of the **Victorian era**, with its vaulted ceilings, battlements, lancet arch windows, and gingerbread tracery trim. A.K.A. **neogothic**

gouache Opaque color pigments mixed with water to create **watercolors**.

gouge A chisel with a curved blade, used to remove a large amount of material, as when turning wood on a lathe. **2.** A deep penetrating scar or defect in any surface.

government house An

grab bar

obsolete term used to describe a building housing the offices of government departments or bureaus.

grab bar Handrails installed around toilets and in showers and baths, which elderly and handicapped people use to steady themselves. A.K.A. **grab rail**

gradation A gradual changing or separating of one or more attributes (**size, color, shape,** etc.).

grade A classification of materials, particularly wood, by quality. **2.** Refers, in elevation, to ground level around buildings and walls or anywhere else on a building site. **3.** The rise or fall of a roadway, usually expressed in terms of feet per 100 feet, in meters per kilometer, or as a plus *(ascending)* or minus *(descending)* percentage.

grade line A line established by measurement or computation, and usually marked with stakes at various elevations, to create a grade between two established terminal points.

grader A machine with a long angled blade, used for leveling, crowning, and spreading material.

grading plan A plan or drawing showing the desired contours and grade elevations of a particular site.

graffiti The illegal marking or decoration of walls, signs, rocks, and even municipal transportation vehicles, such as buses and commuter trains. Recognized as a developing inner-city art form.

grain Refers to the direction, arrangement, or appearance of the fibers in wood, or the strata markings in stone, slate, etc. **2.** Any small particle of material, such as grains of sand. **3.** An English unit of weight measure particularly unique to explosives, specifically gun powder: where 7,000 grains equals 1 lb.

graining A painted simulation of wood- or marble-grained surfaces, in which the paint or stain is applied with various pattern tools, combs, brushes, and rags. A.K.A. **faux bois**

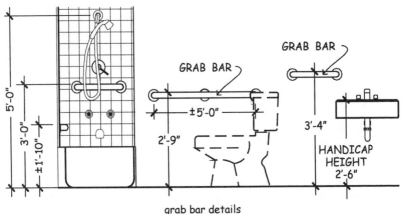

grab bar details

grandfather clock A tall freestanding clock, usually with a pendulum, made predominately of wood and highly polished brass.

grandmother clock A short grandfather clock, usually under six feet.

grandstand A structure, usually covered, that supports the seating of spectators at a ball field, racecourse, stadium, or similar public arena.

granite Extremely hard, igneous, crystalline silicate rock, used as siding, floor covering, and countertops.

granny flat A small apartment, often built over a garage, that serves as a home office, spare bedroom, or guest house.

grapery A greenhouse used exclusively for the cultivation of grapes.

graphics A general term describing the many different applications, media, and aspects of images.

graphite A form of carbon, used for many purposes, such as pencil lead and as a lubricant.

grass cloth A loosely woven fabric *(vegetable fibers)* primarily used for wall covering.

grate In a fireplace, a metal stand that holds the fuel (wood or coal) and permits air to circulate through the burning fuel. **2.** A cover with openings that allow air or water to pass-through. 3. As a bridge or walkway, a surface made of a framework of parallel or lattice metal bars that serves as a floor. **grating** A.K.A. **grille**

gravel Small, granular aggregate of various sizes, between sand and small stones.

gravel stop A metal or plastic strip used to keep loose gravel in a restricted area, as in a footpath. **gravel strip**

gray scale The many shades of grays along the path between black and white. See: **color wheel**

gray water A combination of waste and soiled water, used in an application *(as watering plants)* that does not require pure clean water. A.K.A. **foul water**

grease trap A device that allows liquid grease to cool and solidify, for easy removal.

great hall A large central room, usually two stories high, principally used for dining and entertainment. Originally the main room of a medieval castle, today it refers to a large exhibition hall.

Great Wall of China A large, 1500-mile-long wall built *(3d century BC)* by the Chinese to protect themselves from the warring Mongols. *NOTE: The Great Wall is the only man-made object astronauts have been able to identify from outer space.*

Grecian A.K.A. **Greek**

Greco-Roman architecture A melding of Classic Greek and Roman architecture characterized by traditional post-and-beam construction.

Greek revival   An architectural style *(circa 1820-1900)* that emphasized the simplicity of Roman architecture, commonly featuring **colonnade portico** supporting a **triangular pediment**, rather than its more elaborate elements.   *NOTE: Considered a natural choice of style for the civic buildings and monuments of America's young democracy, because of its association with Greek democracy.*

Greek theatre   See: **amphitheatre**

green Refers to a large grass-filled public area, such as a park. **2.** A term used to describe lumber that has not been kiln dried or mortar not yet cured.

greenhouse   A glass or glasslike structure for growing plants, fruits, and vegetables under regulated conditions.

green lumber Lumber which has not been dried or seasoned.

greenroom A theatrical term for a waiting area *(lounge)* for celebrities *(actors, singers, etc.)* waiting to appear on stage, particularly television talk shows.

grid   Equally spaced lines or elements, both horizontal and vertical, that divide a space into equal segments.

grid ceiling See: **suspended ceiling syltem**

griffin   A decorative mythological beast with an eagle's head, a lion's body, and wings.

grille A grate, usually metal, used to decoratively cover or protect an opening, as in a wall, floor, or ceiling. **grillwork**

grit   Refers to a rating (measurement) of how coarse or how abrasive a specific piece of sandpaper, emery cloth, polishing compound, or similar material is.

grommet A metal, rubber, or plastic eyelet used to reinforce a hole, as in canvas, to which a line, anchor, or fastener can be attached.

Greek Revival

groove A channel or long narrow cut in the surface or edge of a piece of material (wood, plastic, etc.). A.K.A. **channel**, **dado**

Gropius, Walter *(1883-1969)* Known as the grand old man of modern International style. *founder of German Bauhaus school of design and a professor at Harvard after WWII. Trained under Peter Behrens.*

grotesque Sculpture or paintings depicting fanciful sometimes whimsical, distortions of ghoulish human and animal figures that have no known counterparts in nature.

grotto A cavelike setting, incorporating a natural or artificial pool and/or waterfall

ground See: **ground level** 2. A wire, within an electric circuit, connected at one end to the earth and used as a common return, to prevent electrocution.

ground cover Plants that stay low and spread out over an area. **2.** Thin plastic sheeting spread over the ground, usually in a crawl space, to minimize moisture penetration.

grounded Connected to the earth.

ground fill Common dirt.

ground floor See: **first floor**

ground glass Glass whose surface has been ground with an abrasive, as in the manufacture of lenses. **2.** A term used to describe glass with a rough surface *(sandblasted or etched)*. Commonly used as a light-diffuser in lamps, or glass of similar appearance.

ground level The level of the surface of the ground *(in elevation)*, expressed by a height measurement, either above or below, to indicate the height of a structure or the depth of excavation. A.K.A. **ground line**

ground plane The horizontal plane upon which objects in a perspective drawing rest. A.K.A. **horizontal plane**

groundwater Underground water, near the surface of the earth, that feeds streams, rivers, and lakes.

grouped In close proximity to one another, as grouped columns.

grout Mortar, of various colors, made specifically to fill the voids between tiles, creating a flat, finished surface. **grouting**

growth rings Evidence of a tree's annual growth seen in the rings revealed by a cross-cut section of a harvested tree. *NOTE: The end grain of any piece of wood represents its part of the growth rings which travel the vertical length of the tree.*

guarantee A legally enforceable commitment to customer satisfaction and assurance of the quality or endurance of a product or work performed. A.K.A. **warranty**

guaranty bond See: **completion bond** A.K.A. **assurance bond**, **surety bond**, **performance bond**

guard rail

guard rail A railing used to separate and control pedestrian traffic, often used in conjunction with automatically operated doors.

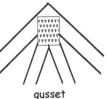

gusset

guest bedroom An extra bedroom for those who come to visit.

guesthouse A separate residence, on the same property and in close proximity to a larger house, for guests and/or a temporary residence for a parent or family loved one.

guiderail A track that acts as a guide for sliding windows and doors.

guide wire Theatrically, a steel cable that guides the vertical movement of a curtain. **2.** An arbor line that guides the movement of a counterweight.

guild A medieval term for an association of artisans, replaced, today, by contemporary craft and labor unions.

gumwood *(Wood)* A white to gray-green, high-density hardwood of the eastern and southern U.S. and used principally for low-grade **veneer**, **plywood**, and rough cabinet work. See: **red gum**

gun Refers to any of a number of tools, many pneumatic, that operate like or take on the appearance of a gun (i.e., a **staple** or **nail** gun, a **spray gun**, etc.).

gusset Refers to a vertical framing element that replicates a particular shape or profile that supports or strengthens a

framework, or to which horizontal lengths of boards are connected, to elongate. **2.** A flat bracket connecting two or more elements, as used on a truss.

gutter A channel (wood, metal, or plastic) that runs along the eves of a sloping roof to catch rainwater and direct it away from the building. **2. The point where the road meets the curb.** **guttering**

gutter spout See: **drain spout**

gymnasium A building dedicated to physical training.

gypsum A soft mineral, *hydrated calcium sulfate*, from which gypsum plaster is made.

gypsum board **Wallboard** having a noncombustible gypsum core with a paper surface. A.K.A. **plasterboard, sheetrock, gypsum lath**

- H -

hacksaw A hand saw with a fine-toothed blade used for cutting metal.

hacksaw

hairline cracking Very fine shallow cracks, usually not structurally detrimental – at least immediately.

half-bath A room containing a washbasin and toilet. Essentially, a bathroom without bathtub or shower. A.K.A. **lavatory, power room**

half-glass door

half-glass door A door with fixed glass in the upper half of the door. See: **door styles**

half-lap joint A common joint in which half the thickness of each intersecting element is removed to accommodate the other, resulting in a flush surface joint.

half round A semicircular or convex strip of molding.

half story A story within a sloping roof that prohibits the full use of that floor.

half-timbered English Tudor-inspired style of applying decorative boards to the surface of a building to replicate the structure of the building. See: **stick style architecture**

halftone Color with a tonal value between white and black. **2.** A process of printing black and white photographs that employs dots of various shades of gray.

hall A passageway or corridor between various rooms. **2.** Commonly used as part of the proper name of a public or university building, such as City Hall. **3.** A principal room, such as in a exhibition or convention hall. A.K.A. **passageway, corridor, hallway**

hallmark A mark, seal, or logo meant to designate quality.

halogen A highly efficient high-tech incandescent (lamp) lightbulb that requires special fixtures.

hamlet A small village, not large enough to be considered a town. An antiquated term, today might apply to a small commercial stop, with a gas station, market, and maybe a restaurant, along the highway.

hammer A hand tool used principally for driving nails or flattening and shaping various materials.

hammer-beam truss An early English Tudor arch truss, each end of which rested on a large wooden bracket.

hammer drill A power tool that imitates a hammer and chisel rather than rotating a cutting edge *(drill bit)*, to make a hole. A.K.A. **percussion drill**

hammered glass Embossed translucent glass that appears (on one side) to have been hammered, resembling beaten metal.

hammered finish Any finish that appears to resemble a rough-textured surface achieved from hammering on metal, particularly sheet metal.

hand Architecturally, refers to anything the human hand is expected to touch or reach, such as a handrail or handle.

hand drill A hand-driven drill.

handhold Something that the human hand can grasp on to.

handicapped accessible Buildings and facilities accessible to people in wheelchairs, by installing ramps and wider doors, especially in public restrooms. See: **ramp, grab bar**

WHEELCHAIR DIMENSIONS

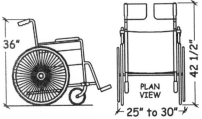

36"

42 1/2"

PLAN
VIEW

⊢ 25" to 30" ⊣

**HANDICAPPED ACCESSIBLE
REQUIREMENTS**
DOORS: MINIMUM 2'-10"
RAMPS: 1-12 MAXIMUM PITCH

handle   A general term
referring to something (**knob, pull,**
etc.) the human hand can grasp to
open a door, drawer, or any similar
item.

hand line   In rigging, a line
(rope) hand-operated and used to
lift or guide an object.

hand plane   A small
carpenter's plane that fits in the
palm of the hand. A.K.A. **jack
plane**

handrail   Any railing at hand
height meant to be a supportive
element, as a bannister.

handsaw

handsaw   Any hand-held,
manually operated saw for cutting
wood, metal, or any other material.
A.K.A. **crosscut saw**

hanger   Any wire, strap, or
rod attached to an overhead
structure, used to support a drop

ceiling, pipe, conduit, or any similar
object.   **2.** Any device used to
suspend an object from another
object.

hard copy   A computer term
used to describe a printout on
paper of what was created on a
computer. A.K.A. **printout, plot**

hardener   Any chemical
substance used to harden a
surface. **2.** One of two or more
chemical components that when
combined causes a chemical
reaction (i.e., solidification or
hardening), as happens when
cement and water are combined to
form concrete.

hardness The resistance of a
surface to damage.

hardware   Metal products,
(bolts, nails, screws, hinges locks,
etc.) used in construction and
cabinetry.

hard water   Refers to the
degree of hardness, as applied to
water, based on the amount of
mineral salts, sulfates of calcium,
magnesium, carbonates, and
bicarbonates found in the water.

hardwood   Wood (lumber)
from trees with very dense fibers,
such as oak, walnut, cherry,
mahogany, maple -- as opposed to
softwoods, like pine and fir.
Hardwoods are used primarily for
furniture and cabinets.

harem That part of a wealthy
Arab's estate where the women of
his entourage reside.

harewood *(Wood)* Common
name for **English sycamore**, a
narrow-grain hardwood ranging in
color from white to light-brown

that dries to a handsome silver gray color. Heavy, tough, and strong, used for general cabinetry and paneling. A.K.A. **sycamore**

harmonic A component of a sound containing more than one frequency.

harness An object, including the strapping, bolts, and other elements, that holds and controls another object, as in hanging and ringing a bell.

hasp A two-piece device used partly on a door or hinged cover and partly on the structure itself, enabling a door to be secured with a padlock.

hasp

hassock A large cushion or mat used as a footrest. *Same as an ottoman.*

hatch A covered opening on a horizontal plane *(floor or roof)*. A.K.A. **hatchway** 2. In drawing, the partial cover with closely drawn lines, often used for shading. In architectural drawings hatching often represents a cut section or inaccessible space. **hatching** 3. With the advent of CAD *(Computer Aided Design)*, hatch has taken on an even more encompassing meaning, which includes symbols *(brick, shingles, patterns, etc.)* of all kinds.

hatchet A hand tool which combines a hammer and a small ax.

haul The distance that material of any kind must be moved.

hazardous area An area used to store or handle highly combustible, flammable, explosive, or other potentially dangerous materials and/or chemicals.

hazardous materials Any substance, by reason of explosive, flammable, poisonous, corrosive, oxidizing, or otherwise harmful nature, is likely to cause harm or even death. A.K.A. **hazardous substances**

haze A dullness or film usually resulting from the application of a chemical that dulls or causes a chemical reaction with an existing surface.

head A general term used to describe the top or uppermost member of any object or structure.

header The upper horizontal cross member, between the jambs, which forms the top of a door or window frame. Headers are used to carry the weight of a ceiling or roof, in those parts of a wall that have been weakened by the cutting in of doors and windows. A.K.A. **lintel** 2. In plumbing, a pipe having many outlets.

header course A row of bricks near the top of a wall or building that creates a change in plane or accent. **heading course**

heading The top of a curtain extending above the curtain rod.

heading course See: **header course**

head mold See: **drip edge**

headroom The clear vertical space available for passage. **headway**

head table See: **dais**

heart Refers to the center portion of something, like a log.

hearth

hearth The floor of a fireplace as well as the area immediately in front of the firebox opening, usually **brick, tile, or stone**, meant to catch fire sparks and prevent the house or its furnishings from catching on fire.

hearthstone The materials, often of stone *(but including firebrick, concrete, etc.)*, used to form a hearth.

heat A form of energy transferred by virtue of its temperature. The higher a material's temperature, the faster the atoms are moving, hence the greater the amount of energy.

heat capacity The amount of energy necessary to raise the temperature of a given mass by $1°C$. A.K.A. **thermal capacity**

heat exchanger A device within an air-conditioning or heating system designed to transfer heat from air or water exiting the system to air or water entering the system.

heating plant A furnace or the part of a central heating system that heats air or boils water. A.K.A. **hot-air furnace**

heating unit A general term to describe some form of heating element (**baseboard heaters, radiator, space heater**, etc.).

heat loss The loss of heat due to poorly sealed or insulated window and door openings.

heat-sealed A method of joining sheet plastic or films by applying heat and pressure simultaneously.

heat sink A device with fingerlike projecting planes, that provides a large surface area from which heat will quickly dissipate.

heavy-duty A term used to indicate professional grade equipment designed to withstand intense use.

hedge A barrier formed by bushes or small trees growing close together. A.K.A. **shrubbery**

hedgerow Trees and shrubs in a row forming an organic barrier to enclose or separate a yard or field.

height The vertical distance between two points, in which one is the ground (**base**) and the other denotes how high the top of an object is from the ground.

height board See: **story pole**

heliport A helicopter **landing pad** atop a tall building. **2.** An **airport** for helicopters.

helix Any spiral, especially a small volute or twist.

Hellenistic A period in Greek art and history *(3rd century B.C.)*, under Alexander the Great. Characterized by realism and theatricalism.

hem Turning under and sewing a raw fabric edge.

hemlock *(Wood)* See: **western hemlock**

HEPA filter A High Efficiency Particulate Air filter, used as part of modern **air-cleaning (air filtration)** and **air-conditioning systems**.

hermitage An antiquated term used to describe a private retreat or secluded hideaway. **2. Hermitage,** the name of a famous Russian **museum.**

herringbone pattern A traditional diagonal **zigzag** pattern commonly used in masonry, **flooring, fabrics,** and **wallpapers.** See: **pattern types: herringbone**

hexagon A figure with six equal sides.

hickory *(Wood)* A uniquely American hardwood of the walnut family. Very strong, tough, and extremely dense. Used primarily for furniture and cabinets. *NOTE: Most baseball bats are made from hickory because of its high shock resistance and bending strength.*

hexagon

highboy A tall chest of drawers.

high-carbon steel Very strong and dense steel, because of its high carbon content.

high gloss A painted finish that drys to a shiny or highly polished surface. See: **gloss**

highlight Something that is featured, emphasized, or illuminated to stand out.

high-pressure laminates Laminated surface material, as used in countertops, that is glued and cured under pressure for a more secure bond.

high-rise A tall building with a large number of floors, usually constructed on prime, centrally located property. A.K.A. **skyscraper**

high relief See: **relief**

high school A school, in the United States, that provides education beyond elementary school, from the 8th or 9th to 12th grades. A.K.A. **middle school, secondary school**

high tech Incorporating the latest technology into the design of something.

high visibility Easily noticed or observable.

highway A long, raised paved road running through numerous cities and towns.

hinge A movable metal joint used to attach and support the swing *(open and closed)* of a door or cover.

hinge pin A metal rod, with a cap, used to hold the two sides of a hinge together. A.K.A. **pin hinge**

hinge post A post from which a gate is hung.

hinge strap An ornamental metal strap fixed to the surface of a door to give the appearance of a strap hinge.

hip The external angle at the junction of two sides of a roof.

hip-and-valley roof Intersecting gable (**hip**) roof that forms a valley at the lower edge, so that it has both hips and valleys.

hip bevel The angle between the two adjoining slopes of a roof.

hip capping A cap that runs

hip jack

above the ridge beam and along the top of a roof, which may be vented to allow air and moisture to escape.

hip jack See: **jack rafter**

hippodrome An ancient Greek arena, an elongated circle with straight runs and sharp curves, for chariot and horse racing or where a circus troupe might perform.

hip rafter See: **jack rafter** A.K.A. **angle rafter**

hip roof **hipped roof** See: **gable roof**

historical site A preserved building, structure, or property of architectural or historic significance, which is protected by law.

Hitchcock chair A black painted chair with a stencil design on the backrest. Named for its creator, an American cabinetmaker.

hog trough A stiffener created when two boards are nailed together edge to edge at 90° to one another.

hoist A machine for lifting. A.K.A. **elevator** (interior), **crane** (exterior).

hole saw A saw, made of wide spring steel, that is rounded to cut a circle (with a diameter of between one and three inches) when turned by a **drill motor**.

holiday A small area on any surface that has unintentionally not been covered or painted over, leaving it bare. A.K.A. **skip**

hollow-core

construction A method of constructing lightweight doors and folding tabletops, consisting of a wooden frame covered on both sides by plywood, Masonite, or other sheet goods material.

hollow-core door See: **hollow-core construction**

holly (Wood) A light-colored, fine-grained wood used for marquetry.

homestead A legal term used to describe a dwelling, including the land around it, that is legally protected and can not be legally taken, even to repay a bad debt. **homesteaded**

Honduras mahogany
(Wood) A **softwood** member of the mahogany family, but much lighter in color than **Cuban** or **Spanish mahogany** (which are hardwoods). Used mainly for plywood veneer. A.K.A. **baywood**

hone To file or sharpen, as in honing the edge of a chisel or knife.

honeycomb Any hexagonal structure or pattern, resembling the honeycomb chambers in which a honey bee stores honey.

hood A cover above an opening or object to shelter it.

hood mold See: **drip edge**

hook A curved or bent metal device attached to a door or wall to hang things from.

hooked rug A pile-surfaced rug made by punching threads or strips of cloth through a canvas backing.

hopper A bin or chute used to store or move loose construction materials, such as crushed stone or sand.

hopper window A window that is hinged on the bottom and swings inward. See: **window styles**

horizon The visible point where the earth meets the sky.

horizontal Parallel to the horizon.

horizontal line A line perpendicular to a vertical line.

horizontal plane Any flat surface, such as a floor.

horsepower A measure of power of a motor, equating to the number of horses it would take to accomplish a particular job.

horseshoe arch An arch resembling the shape of a horseshoe, prevalent in Moorish and Spanish architecture. Originally designed to allow horses and mules loaded with supplies to pass-through. A.K.A. **Arabic arch, Moorish arch**

hospice A care facility for terminally ill patients, where their physical and emotional needs are treated with the use of morphine and other drugs, but no effort is made to treat their medical condition.

hospital A facility consisting of a building or buildings, in which patients, regardless of sex or age, receive diagnostic and therapeutic medical and surgical services 24-hours a day, 7 days a week, for most forms of illness, injury, or disability.

hot-air furnace See: **heating plant**

hot-dip galvanizing A zinc coating to protect ferrous metals from rusting.

hotel An establishment that provides lodging and food to travelers and visitors. A.K.A. **inn**

hot-glue gun A heating element with a handle grip that melts sticks of glue that stick to virtually any surface.

hot-glue gun

hothouse A greenhouse maintained at a warm tropical temperature. See: **greenhouse**

hot water heater A device that heats water. A.K.A. **water heater**

hot wire A wire through which electricity flows.

hourglass An ancient time-keeping instrument, containing just enough **sand** to take exactly one hour to pass from its upper to lower chamber.

hourglass

house Primarily a building or dwelling for human residence. **2.** A public facility like a firehouse or a police station, which is often referred to as a house. **3.** Theatrically, the theatre itself, other than the stage, is often referred to as the house, as in turning up the house lights. **housing** A.K.A. **dwelling, residence, home**

house curtain The principal

housed

stage curtain, in a theatre, that opens and closes to indicate the beginning or end of an act, scene or show. See: **theatrical curtains**

housed Said of something that resides within. See: **housing**

household All the possessions of the individual(s) or family occupying a residence.

houselights Refers to the lights in an auditorium or theatre that provide general illumination over the audience seating area, which are on before and after performances and during intermissions, but off during the actual performance.

house wrap See: **infiltration barrier**

housing See: **house 2**. A niche, case, or cabinet, *often metal*, built to hold or enclose something. **housed**

hut

housing project A publicly supported low income residential community.

housing unit A house, apartment, or a single room intended as a separate residence.

hovel A shed, covered overhead but open at the sides. **2**. A poorly constructed and ill-kept house.

hub The center of a wheel to which spokes are attached; that part of a wheel the axile fits through. **2**. The core of a building around which elevators, staircases, public restrooms, and corridors radiate.

hue The subjective perception of color, e.g., red, yellow, green, blue, purple. White, black and gray possess no hue. *A tint is a hue with white added and a shade is a hue with black added.*

humidifier A device for adding moisture to the air in a room.

humidity Water content *(vapor)* in the air, within a given space or environment.

hut A crudely made temporary shelter, usually one room and constructed primarily of material native to the surrounding area.

hutch Shelving unit that sits on top of a desk or low chest.

hybrid Said of a plant produced by crossing two distant varieties of species.

hydrant See: **fire hydrant**

hydration Adding water.

hydraulic jack

hydraulic jack A jack that operates by means of hydraulics, (liquid) pressure acting against a piston, exerting great force.

hydraulic pump A pump that operates by means of hydraulics (liquid) pressure.

hydronic radiant floor system A system of heating a space by heating a concrete *(mass)* floor, by pumping hot water *(at controlled temperatures)* through

HUMAN DIMENSIONS

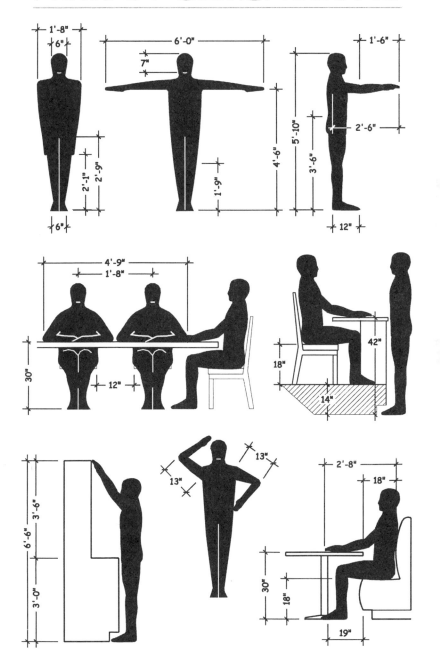

plastic tubing embedded in the floor.

- I -

I beam A structural metal beam with a cross section resembling the letter *I*.

icehouse A building equipped to make and store ice.

icon Portrait or image that represents a widely recognized person or object. **ikon**

idealism A tendency in artists to express universal or spiritual concepts.

IEEE *Abbr.* **Institute of Electrical and Electronics Engineers.**

igloo The traditional Inuit *(Eskimo)* shelter. **iglu** A.K.A. **ice block house, block ice house**

igloo

ignition The initiation of combustion, as evidenced by smoke, flame, or explosion.

illumination Lighting up or decorating with light.

illustration A conceptual drawing or picture that represents the way something should look, or an ideological representation of how things should be.

image Any representation of an object or figure.

impact wrench A pneumatically driven wrench that produces a series of impulsive torques.

impervious Impenetrability. Resistance to damage from a variety of common everyday sources.

impost The leg of an arch, beneath the spring line.

impregnated cloth Cloth saturated with a variety of materials (plaster, resin, varnish, shellac, etc.) used in many different applications.

impregnated timber See: **pressure treated lumber**

Impressionism A school of art developed in late 19th century France and exemplified in the work of Monet, Cezanne, Degas, Cassatt, Manet, Morisot, and others. NOTE: The term Impressionism was derived from a painting by Claude Monet entitled *Impression: Sunrise 1872*

improvement A change for the better in a structure's appearance, equipment, or access to public utilities, made to increase the value of the property.

incandescent lamp A lamp that emits light by heating a tungsten filament to incandescence with a continuous electric current. **incandescent bulb** A.K.A. **light bulb** *Inventor:* **Thomas Alva Edison**

light bulb

incised A pattern or figure cut into an object, as cut or shaped with a knife or chisel. **2.** Having clean and well defined lines.

incline Any sloping surface, i.e., as the side of a mountain. **2.** Architecturally, a sloping ceiling or similar element. **3.** Being neither horizontal nor vertical. **inclining** A.K.A. **inclined plane**

incombustible Not capable of starting on fire. A.K.A. **noncombustible**

incrustation Deposits of minerals and materials on the interior of pipes, vessels, or equipment from corrosive chemicals. **2.** A decorative skin or coating (**patina**) some materials naturally form when continuously exposed to the weather, as the turquoise **patina** that forms on copper.

indicator switch A device built into a lock to indicate whether or not a **restroom, dressing room**, or **hotel room** is occupied.

indigenous Said of **plants, trees, rocks, animals**, etc., that are native to a particular area.

indirect lighting Reflected light rather than direct light.

industrial area Any area zoned predominantly for manufacturing or other nonretail business.

industrial design The art of incorporating technology and modern materials to create or improve *(efficiency, safety, economy, or ease of use)* everyday consumer products.

industrial waste A waterborne chemical waste resulting from an industrial production process.

infiltration The seepage of air into or out of a room or space through cracks, particularly from around windows and doors.

infiltration barrier A sublayer of a thin sheet of material wrapped around the exterior of a house to prevent hot or cold air from escaping or invading the building, before whatever finish exterior material is applied. A.K.A. **house wrap**

infirmary See: dispensary A.K.A. **first-aid office, nurse's office**

inflammable See: flammable

infrared A light and heat source, out of the range of human sight, that is used in a number of industrial applications, including drying, baking, and transmitting electronic data.

inglenook A nook or recessed area, particularly near a fireplace, that often contains shelves and/or seating.

ingot A mass of solidified molten metal rolled and shaped into finished or semifinished product.

inhibitor A substance added to **paint** to retard drying. A.K.A. **drying inhibitor**

injection molding A process of forcing a heat-softened plastic material into the relatively cool cavity of a mold to create an object or part of a desired shape and size.

inlaid

inlaid See: inlay

inlaid work See: inlay A.K.A. marquetry

inlay A design crafted into a panel or tabletop, incorporating various hardwoods, ivory and/or other rare and beautiful materials. inlaid A.K.A. **intaria, marquetry**

inn See: hotel

inorganic material Material made or composed of minerals, plastics, etc., not animal or vegetable in origin.

insanitary Not clean, potentially injurious to health, contrary to sanitation standards.

inset A nonstructural repair of a defect. **2.** An inlay of wood veneer or a plug used to fill a defect. See **Dutchman**

inside caliper An instrument used to measure interior space, such as the **inside diameter** of a **cylinder** or the distance between objects.

inspection An examination of work completed or in progress to determine its compliance with building codes, contract requirements, or industry standards.

inspector One who inspects, such as an official or certified building inspector.

institute To establish or start up. **2.** An organization for the promotion of education, research, or any ideal or belief. **institution**

insulating fiberboard See: fiberboard insulation

insulation A nonconductive material, in many forms, used to isolate the interior of a building from the elements, by preventing the passage or leakage of heat or cold air and enabling better and more efficient control of interior temperatures and environmental conditions. **2.** Thermal insulation specifically made to prevent the breakage or clogging of pipes due to frozen water, or electrical insulation around electrical wiring to prevent fires.

insurance A legally binding agreement to, *for a price*, guarantee against specified type of loss *(property damage, general liability, special hazards, etc.).*

intake An opening through which air, water, or any other gas or fluid enters a system, chamber, pipe, or machine.

intaria A pictorial inlay. See: inlay A.K.A. **marquetry**

integrated ceiling A suspended grid ceiling that incorporates acoustical, illumination, and air handling components as an integral part of the system. A.K.A. **drop ceiling**

inter Of Latin origin, meaning space between or within.

intercom A telecommunication system restricted to a particular residence, building or specific offices within a building.

interior casing The molding used around interior door or window openings. See: **casing**

interior door Doors installed

in an interior wall of a building, rather than a exterior wall. Usually thinner than an exterior door.

interior finish   Refers to any of the finish materials *(wallpaper, paint, or trim)* or colors used on exposed interior surfaces of a building.

inter ior-grade plywood Cabinet-grade plywood, not intended for use on exterior application.

interior trim   Any molding, including casing, used on the interior of a building.

interior wall   A wall within a building, as opposed to those walls that make up the perimeter of a building.

interlocking   In modular systems, a means of locking in place one unit by virtue of its attachment to another.

international modern style   An architectural style *(circa 1920s-1960)* depicting modern clean lines with little or no ornamentation, reflecting the **"less is more"** perspective of the International Modern movement. Featured the use of steel and concrete for structural elements. Characterized by flat roofs, stucco walls, cantilevered balconies, and large expanses of flush, sliding-glass windows and doors with little or no trim. Pioneered by **Frank Lloyd Wright**, **Walter Gropius, Phillip Johnson**, and influential throughout the 1930s-1940s. A.K.A. **International style, modern**

intrados   The soffit or innermost *(inside)* curve of an arch.

invert   An exact opposite, reversed, or upside down image.

Ionic   Pertaining to and/or characteristic of Ionia, the eastern part of the ancient Greek empire.

Ionic order   One of the orders of classic Greek and Roman architecture. Of Greek origin and characterized by its light, simple lines. Not as massive as Doric and less elaborate than the Corinthian. See: **column details**

iron   An element *(iron ore)* found in the earth's crust, a principal ingredient in the production of steel and pig iron.

iron oxide   Used extensively in paints, as color pigment *(ranging from yellow through red and from purple to black)*.

ironwork   Wrought iron or cast iron, usually decorative and often elaborate.

irregular pitch   A roof whose slopes are not symmetrical or consistent.

irrigation system   Any system, with or without sprinklers, used to water vegetables and plants.

island kitchen cabinet See: **kitchen island cabinet**

isometric drawing   An axonometric projection of which three of the object's spatial axes are represented as equally inclined to the drawing surface, equal distances along the axes are drawn equally.

Italianate *(1830-1870)* Highly romanticized interpretation of the villas of Tuscany, Umbria and Lombardy. Adapted for urban row houses and typical of the brownstone-fronted row houses of New York City, with ornate doors and windows, weighty bracketed cornice, and high stoop with heavy cast-iron railings.

Italian Renaissance *(late 1880˚ - 1920)* The palazzi and country villas of Rome, Florence, and Venice translated into American palaces. A.K.A. **Italian Renaissance revival, Beaux Arts style** See: **Renaissance**

Italian villa style The style of country-house design, fashionable in England and the U.S. *(circa 1840-1880)*, characterized by (balanced) asymmetrical facades, low-pitched, heavily bracketed roofs, elaborate cupolas, narrow (often) round-arched, double-hung windows. A.K.A. **Italianate style**

- J -

jacaranda *(Wood)* See: **rosewood** A.K.A. **Brazilian rosewood**

jack A portable device that exerts a great force to raise a heavy weight, such as an automobile jack. Often used to temporarily relieve the weight on a bearing wall,

so that the bearing wall can be reconfigured or replaced. A.K.A. **hydraulic jack, jackscrew**

jacket A covering around something, to protect it from extremely cold temperatures, as around water pipes.

jackhammer A pneumatic air-hammer, similar in operation to a **hammer drill** but larger.

jack plane A medium-size, general use carpenter's hand plane.

jack rafter A short rafter with a compound cut that terminates at the **hip** or **valley** of a roof. A.K.A. **Angle rafter, hip rafter**

jack rib Any rib in a framed arch or dome that is shorter than the others.

Jacobean architecture Named after James I *(1603-1625)*, an English style of art and architecture *(circa early 17th century)* that incorporated the Elizabethan style and Italian Renaissance influences.

Jacobean chair A style of chair associated with early 17th century English architecture. See: **Jacobean architecture** A.K.A. **Yorkshire chair**

jai awning window A window having a number of top-hinged, out-swinging, pivoted sashes, side-by-side or one above the other. Most often these are squatty windows at the top of a wall that are opened to let out heat. See: **window styles**

jack

jail A building or place, usually administered by the local sheriff, where people are legally detained (short term). *Differs from a prison, which is administered and operated by the state or the federal government, and are for long-term detention.*

jalousie window A window resembling a shutter or Venetian blinds with overlapping horizontal glass louvers. See: **window styles**

jamb The vertical elements at either side of a door or window frame.

Japanese architecture

The distinct timber construction architecture of Japan in the 5th century A.D., which was strongly influenced by China. Pavilion-like structures, with tiled, hipped roofs, elaborate bracket systems, and upturned projecting eaves. A platform supporting basic **post-and-beam** construction with the bays filled with **shoji screens** -- wood-framed paper partition walls and sliding door openings. Verandas provide a transition and integration between buildings and their surroundings, that is emphasized in Japanese culture.

jardiniére *(Fr)* An ornamental tub for holding large plants.

Jefferson, Thomas Third president of the United States, a dominant influence in developing America's neoclassical *(Serlio, Palladio and Gibbs dominating)* architecture, at Monticello, his Virginia home, and in Washington, D.C.

jerkin head A clipped gable or hip roof. A.K.A. **clipped roof, sheadhead**

jerry-rigged Built in a quick and flimsy manner. A.K.A. **jerry-built**

jig A device specifically built both to hold a part and to guide a tool to make a hole or cut in that part. A.K.A. **fixture, setup**

jigsaw A power saw that vibrates *(in a reciprocating, up and down, motion)* a short, narrow metal blade. Used for a variety of cutting applications, particularly holes in the middle of something.

jimmy bar A short crowbar.

job Work on a project a worker is paid to do.

job site The place where the work is being done, as a construction site.

jigsaw

job title The position an individual was hired to fill, **carpenter foreman, mason, architect**, etc.

jog Any irregularity in a line or surface.

Johnson, Phillip American architect who coined the term International Modern, and one of its most famous practitioners.

joinery The woodworking or carpentry art of joining pieces of wood together, using a variety of methods, based on strength and longevity of that connection.

joint   The meeting of adjacent surfaces or the place where two members or components are fastened together.

joint compound   Any material used to fill the space between two adjoining surfaces, as the compound used in taping and finishing drywall joints.

jointer   A machine that turns a cutting head at high speed, which takes about a 1/16" of material off the edge of a board, to square the edges for joining.

joint fastener   See: **corrugated fastener**

joist   One of a series of parallel planks used to support a floor. Usually 2x12s on edge.

joist hanger   Metal angle pieces or strapping used to attach joist boards to a ledger, beam, or girder.

jump An abrupt change of level.

junior college An institution of higher learning, above high school, that offers a 2-year associate arts degree, and/or preparation for continuing at a 4-year university.

jute padding   A strong, durable plant fiber used in upholstered furniture to cover springs, or as backing and padding for carpeting.

- K -

kapok A filler material used to stuff pillows and upholstery.

keep A stronghold or donjon in a medieval castle.

keeper The strike plate on the jamb that holds the lock bolt.

kennel A residence, *permanent or temporary,* for dogs.

kerf   A slot or series of cuts made on the back surface of a board or sheet material, to remove material and facilitate the bending of that material or surface. **kerfing**

key A groove cut into a surface that fits a corresponding projection from another object or element, as a keyed footing. **2.** A removable metal instrument that operates a lock. **3.** The principal or most important piece, of information, or the principal stone (as a **keystone**) on which the other stones in an arch depend.

keyed Interlocking, as a tenon-and-mortised joint. A.K.A. **keyway**

keyed-alike cylinders Any number of locks, with cylinders configured to operate from the same key, as opposed to differently keyed cylinders that must be operated by a master-key.

keyhole saw   A saw that cuts a round hole large enough to insert a lock in a door.   A.K.A. **hole saw**

keypad   A digital pad, usually 10-keys, on which someone can enter numbers.

keypad lock   A lock that requires the correct set of digits to be entered on a numbered pad.

keystone   The central, often embellished, wedge-shaped stone of an arch. Until the keystone is in place, no true arch action occurs. **2.** An element resembling a keystone in function or in shape. **3.** In asphalted surfaces, a small size of filler stone.   A.K.A. **key block**   *(Fr)* **voussoir**

keyway   A slot used to interlock various elements, as in masonry walls. A.K.A. **keyed**

kicker   A temporary stiffener, used in rough framing.

kickplate   A protective metal plate, applied on the lower rail of a door to prevent marring.   A.K.A. **kick rail 2.** An area set back at the bottom of counters and built-in cabinetry to accommodate the toes of the human foot.

kilim   A flat, woven wool rug with a geometric design from the Middle East and Asia.

kiln   A large oven or furnace used to fire brick and tile or to dry *(season)* **lumber**.

kiln-dried   Using the heat of a kiln to reduce the moisture content of **lumber**.

kilo *Abbr.* **k.**   A metric unit of weight, equal to 2.2 pounds. **kilogram**

kilowatt   A measured unit of electricity, equal to 1,000 watts.

king post   The center (vertical) post in a truss.

kiosk   A small building or shelter, *perhaps a newsstand or bus stop*, that usually carries some form of information or advertising.

kitchen   The room designed and used for the preparation and cooking of food.

kitchen cabinets   A series of case pieces *(base- and wall-mounted shelving units)*, of different sizes, that makeup the counters and storage units, with doors or drawers or shelving, used to store dishes, utensils, linens, etc., used in preparing food. See: **kitchen cabinet details**

kitchenette   A small room or alcove fitted with the essential conveniences of a kitchen.

kitchen island cabinet
Freestanding, counter-height kitchen cabinets; in a large kitchen, used for additional work surface, counter, and/or storage space.

knee brace   A brace stiffener. A brace attached to another brace to add pressure or support.   **2.** A low brace, at average knee height, about 20 inches.

kneehole desk   A small, double-pedestal desk, that allows knee room for the person sitting at it.

knee rail   A rail or board that runs parallel and below the handrail, at about 20 inches from the floor.

knob   A handle, with or without a locking mechanism, used to open and close a door or drawer. A.K.A. **doorknob**

knocker   A device *(knocker, strikeplate)*, attached to a door,

KITCHEN CABINET DETAILS

STANDARD SIZES

BASE CABINETS

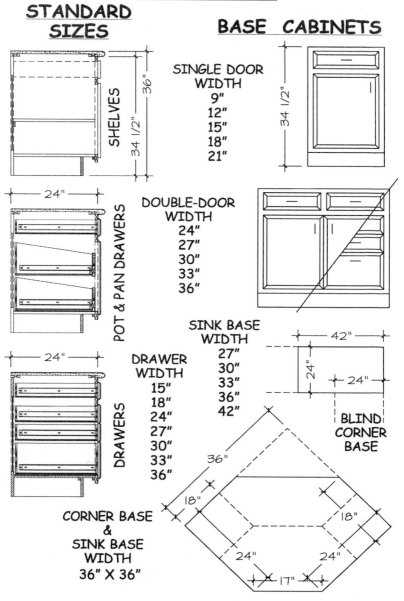

SHELVES

36"

34 1/2"

SINGLE DOOR WIDTH
9"
12"
15"
18"
21"

34 1/2"

24"

POT & PAN DRAWERS

DOUBLE-DOOR WIDTH
24"
27"
30"
33"
36"

24"

DRAWERS

DRAWER WIDTH
15"
18"
24"
27"
30"
33"
36"

SINK BASE WIDTH
27"
30"
33"
36"
42"

42"

24"

24"

BLIND CORNER BASE

36"

18"

18"

24"

24"

17"

CORNER BASE & SINK BASE WIDTH
36" X 36"

KITCHEN CABINET DETAILS

STANDARD SIZES

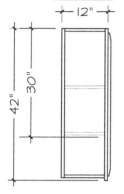

ONE-DOOR
WIDTH
9"
12"
15"
18"
21"

TWO-DOOR
WIDTH
24"
27"
30"
33"
36"

WALL CABINETS

HEIGHT
30"
42"

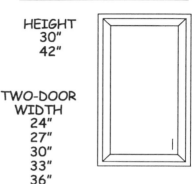

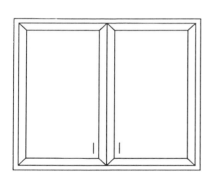

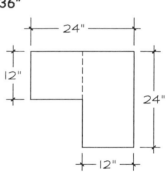

CORNER WALL
CABINET
WIDTH
24" X 24"

WALL BRIDGE
OVEN RANGE & REFRIGERATOR

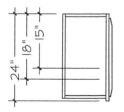

DOUBLE-DOOR
WIDTH   HEIGHT
24"   15"
30"   18"
33"   24"
36"

BLIND CORNER
WIDTH
24" X 12"

KITCHEN CABINET DETAILS

STANDARD SIZES

TALL CABINETS

HEIGHT
83"
95"

DOUBLE OVEN

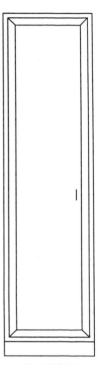

SINGLE OVEN

PANTRY CABINETS
WIDTH
18'
24"

OVEN CABINETS
WIDTH
30"

for visitors to announce themselves. *NOTE: The knocker on the front door of a house came about for two reasons: (1) as a courtesy to save their knuckles - especially ladies, and (2) to save their doors from the abuse of harder objects (metal, stones) that the visitor might use instead. In contemporary times the doorbell has generally replaced the need for* **knockers**.

knockout Predefined, partially punched-out holes in the surface of an electrical outlet, that can easily be removed, providing a semicustom installation.

knot Remnant of a branch, as it grew through that particular board. The hard, cross-grained mass of wood formed in a trunk at the place where a branch joins the trunk. **2.** In fabric, an irregularity or imperfection, common in mechanical weaving.

knotted rug An oriental rug in which the ends of threads tied (knotted) around a small-grid backing material, makes up the carpet's pile or surface.

knotty pine Pine cut so that the knots form a decorative pattern, popular as interior paneling, furniture, and cabinets.

knuckle The cylindrical parts of a hinge through which the pin passes.

korina *(Wood)* A light yellow wood, similar in character to **primavera** and used for paneling. See: **primavera**

kremlin A Russian citadel or local city hall. **2.** The seat of power for the Russian government in Moscow, which consists of a 90 acre *(36 hectares)* area surrounded by the 15th century crenelated walls, and entered into through one of five steepled gate towers.

- L -

label A tag or strip of paper attached to a container (a bottle, box, etc.) with an identifying name, descriptive mark, or reference to the contents. **2.** Architecturally, an elaborate molding hood across the top of an opening, door, arch, or window, such as a pediment. **labeled**

laboratory A workshop for chemists, or other forms of scientific work.

labyrinth A maze of winding, hard-to-follow passageways, many of which simply lead nowhere *(a dead end)*. A.K.A. **maze**

lacquer A varnish, usually enamel *(with color pigment)*, that when applied in layers, provides a hard, smooth, highly polished finish to wood and metal surfaces.

lacunar Coffers in a paneled ceiling.

ladder Portable steps or staircase. **2.** A wood or metal frame, consisting side rails *(stiles)* connected by crosspieces *(rungs)* used to climb up or down.

ladder-back chair A chair back with horizontal slats

resembling a ladder. See: **chair styles** A.K.A. **slat back chair**

ladies' room A public lavatory *(toilet)* designated specifically for female use.

lag bolt A large screw with coarse-pitched thread and a hex head, meant to be driven into wood with a wrench or ratchet. **lag screw**

lamb's tongue Refers to molding of considerable projection. **2.** The end of a handrail, which is turned out or down from the rail line to resemble a tongue. A.K.A. **tongue**

laminate A surfacing material made by bonding two or more layers of material together, such as a laminated plastic countertop or a laminated beam.

laminated beam See: **glued-laminated beam** A.K.A. **glue-lam, engineered beam, glued-laminated timber**

laminated plastic See: **plastic laminate**

laminated wood The glueing of boards together, usually to make a longer *(overlapping breaks)* or stronger element, such as a girder.

lamp A man-made light source, specifically the bulb, but including

WOMEN

ladies' room

lancet arch

the fixture in which it is installed.

lamppost A post, specifically made and wired, to support a light fixture. **2.** The post that supports a streetlight. A.K.A. **light standard**

lancet arch A Gothic arch consisting of two curved elements larger than the span of the arch, that come together at a point.

lancet window A window with a pointed arch.

land Terra firma, the surface of the earth not permanently covered by water. **2.** Real property, a legal term describing real estate (land) and any immovable improvements or fixtures attached thereto.

landfill Garbage, refuse, and trash buried within and under layers of earth.

landing A platform at the end or between a flight(s) of stairs. **stair landing**

landmark Any building, structure, fixed object, place, or marker used as a reference point. **2.** A building or structure with historic or aesthetic interest or value.

landscape architect An individual, professionally qualified, knowledgeable, duly licensed and

lag bolt

legally responsible, for the design and development of landscapes and gardens or performing landscape architectural services.

land survey A survey of real property *(land)* establishing or reestablishing and documenting its exact size, shape, and position.

land-use analysis An analysis of planned development, similar to an **environmental impact report**, but not necessarily meeting the definition as described by the National Environmental Policy Act of 1989.

lane A narrow passageway. **2.** Applied to the path(s), usually defined by painted lines on streets, roads, or highways, that vehicles travel on.

lantern A light fixture predominantly used outdoors. **2.** Architecturally, a small structure, at the crowning point of a dome, turret, or the ridge of a roof. A.K.A. **cupola**

lap Partly covering one surface with another *(overlapping)*, as in shingling. **2.** The length of the overlap.

lap joint The joining of two pieces of wood where each piece has been notched, by half its depth, to accommodate the other piece in an interlocking or overlapping manner. **2.** A joint formed by one board overlapping the butt end joint of two other boards, such as used when scabbing or laminating wood. A.K.A. **end lap joint**

larder A cool or cold room for storing provisions, especially meat and game. See: **pantry** A.K.A. **buttery**

latch A simple door- or window-fastening device, consisting of a bar pivoting at one end, which is attached to a door and free to fall into a slot or hook attached to the jamb, to deep a door closed. A.K.A. **catch, door latch**

latex A milky white emulsion (liquid) found in various trees and plants (rubber trees, milkweed, poppy, etc.), the basis of many commercial products, principally rubber. See: **foam rubber 2.** As paint See: **latex paint**

latex foam See: **foam rubber**

latex paint A latexlike synthetic polymer and water emulsion used as a base for paint.

lath Material (wood strips or expanded metal) used as a backing for plaster.

lathe A machine for shaping circular pieces of wood or metal by rotating the material at high speed, while a stationary tool is used to shape or cut away excess material.

latitude The distance, horizontally, north or south of the equator. **2.** The freedom or authority to make decisions.

lattice Diagonally crisscrossing strips of wood, used as outdoor screening. **latticework**

lattice window A window with diamondlike *(diagonal)* mullions. A.K.A. **quarrel window, quarry window**

lauan A thin plywood, usually made of **Philippine mahogany.** A.K.A. **white lauan** See: **Philippine mahogany** *NOTE: Because lauan is a product of endangered rainforests, it is recommended that alternative materials be utilized.*

laundry chute A channel or shaft for conveying soiled clothing, bed linen, etc., to a lower floor of a building. **clothes chute**

laundry room A room in a home or apartment building equipped with one or more washing machines and clothes dryers.

lattice window

laurel *(Wood)* A dark, reddish-brown hardwood with a pronounced wavy grain. Used primarily for highly polished modern furniture.

lava Any volcanic rock.

lavatory A sink for washing the hands and face. **2.** A room containing a washbasin and toilet, but not a bathtub. A.K.A. **powder room, half-bath, privy, toilet**

lawn An open space of ground, covered with manicured grass.

lawn sprinkler system A system, mostly underground, of delivering water to plants and lawns or similar applications.

layer One of many, as coats of paint or wallpaper. **2.** One material over another, that itself covers another layer of material. **3.** In **CAD**, a facility for putting objects on different layers and having the ability to turn those layers off and on.

layout Refers primarily to a full-size drawing of a scaled drawing, such as a roof truss, so that exact copies of the truss can be produced.

layout board A large piece of multipurpose, thin cardboard, *available in rolls*, used to layout a full-size diagram of the object being built for quick reference.

leaching The process of separating a liquid from a solid (as in waste liquid) by channeling it through an earthen filter (the surrounding soil). See: **leaching basin**

leaching basin A drainage pit of sand and gravel, constructed to allow water to dissipate. **2.** Part of a septic system that allows liquid to seep out into the surrounding soil. **leaching cesspool**

lead A term often used to indicate the person in charge of a crew of workers, such as the lead electrician, or the lead carpenter, as in leader. **2.** *(led)* A soft malleable metal, used between the pieces of glass in stained glass because it is very easy to cut and shape. **3.** The graphite "**lead**" found in a common pencil.

leaded glass

leaded glass Panes (lights) of glass set in lead molding. As in **stained glass**, but not generally incorporating color. A.K.A. **leaded lights, leaded window**

lead pipe Pipe fabricated basically of pig iron (lead).

leaf A hinged part, as the two halves *(leaves)* of a **Dutch door, French doors, casement windows**, or **drop-lid** tables and desks. *(pl)* **leaves** See: **door styles, window styles**

lean-to A single sloping section of a roof, the top of which is attached to a wall or building.

lease A contract transferring the right of possession, for compensation *(usually rent)*, to buildings, property, etc., for a fixed period of time.

leaseholder A tenant by lease of real estate.

LeCorbusier, **Charles Edouard Jeanneret** *(1887-1965)*, Swiss-born cubist painter, sculpture, and architect, French Modern style. The rationalism of International Modernism applied to city planning. Gave **modular** design a degree of respectability with his *(Fr. spell)* modulor theory.

lectern A stand with a slanted top to hold a book, a speech, or notes at the proper height for reading, behind which a teacher or professor gives a lecture. A.K.A. **podium**

lecture room A room, usually at a university, designed specifically for an audience,

usually students, to listen to a professor's lecture. More like a small theatre rather than a classroom. A.K.A. **lecture hall**

ledge A small shelf or projecting ridge.

ledger In stick framing, a horizontal element that carries joists. A.K.A. **ledger board, ribbon board**

leg drop A theatrical term used to describe the narrow curtains at the side of a stage. A.K.A. **legs** See: **theatrical curtain**

lens A glass or plastic surface, shaped to control transmitted light by refraction.

Leonardo da Vinci Celebrated Italian painter, sculptor, engineer, and architect *(1452-1519)*. *Interesting Fact: Leonardo learned to write backward, and wrote all his notes in that manner to protect his ideas from those who might steal them. (2) Although Leonardo left numerous architectural drawings and notes, no practical work in architecture can now be attributed to him.*

lessee The person renting property by lease.

lessor The property owner, receiving rent in lieu of possession rights.

let-in In joinery, to insert, embed, or to house, as letting in butt hinges into a door and jamb.

letter box See: **mail box** A.K.A. **letter chute, mail chute**

lettering   The art and practice of making or designing letters, numbers, symbols, etc. Particularly applicable to graphic arts and sign painting.

level

level   An instrument used by carpenters that uses water and an air bubble to determine a horizontal or a vertical line. **leveling** 2. An acoustical quantity relating to how loud, or how much bass, etc. a particular sound wave has.

leveler An adjustable device to level the footing of an appliance, equipment console, or cabinet to an existing floor. 2. Anything used to smooth or level a surface. A.K.A. **skreet** See: **skreet**

lever   A pry bar. 2. A bar used with a **fulcrum** to apply force or to move a heavy weight.

library   A room for storing and reading a collection of documents and books.

licensed architect An architect meeting the requirements *(educational and experience)* for certification by a governing authority, usually the state government.

licensed contractor A person or organization certified by governmental authority as competent to engage in construction contracting, a requirement in most areas to get insurance, bonding, etc.

licensed engineer   A licensed professional structural engineer.

lien   A legal claim against privately owned real property for payment of a debt owed for the value of services or materials rendered. A.K.A. **mechanic's lien**

lift   A small elevator on the stage or orchestra pit of a theatre. 2. A forklift or similar machinery.

lift gate   A hydraulic lifting device attached to the back of a truck for loading and unloading material.

light   A pane of glass, a window, or a compartment of a window through which daylight is admitted into the interior of a building. 2. An artificial source of illumination, as from a lamp.

light bulb   See: **incandescent lamp**

lighthouse

light fixture Any lamp that holds either an incandescent or fluorescent bulb.

lighthouse   A tower, along a shoreline, that projects a beam of light to warn ships of danger.

lighting Various forms, systems,

and/or equipment used to create or provide light and illumination.

lightning rod A metal wire or rod running from above the roof of a building to the ground *(earth)*, to divert the damage of an electrical discharge *(the result of lightning)* away from the building. *NOTE: Invented (1749) by Benjamin Franklin.*

light standard A.K.A. **lamppost, streetlight**

light well An open shaft in the center of an office or apartment building that admits daylight and allows fresh air to circulate. **2.** A shallow shaft on the exterior of a building that admits light and air, and (in the event of an emergency) provides egress from a **subterranean** *(below grade)* cellar or apartment A.K.A. **air shaft**

lime A mineral used as a hardening agent in mortar and concrete.

limestone A sedimentary rock *(calcite, dolomite, or both)* used as building stone and crushed aggregate or small stones.

line Any **string, rope, wire,** or **cable**, etc., running from one point to another. **2.** Any line drawn on a piece of paper.

line level A small level that attaches to a taut *(stretched)* string line. See: **level**

linen Cloth woven from fibers **(thread)** made from hemp *(Cannabis)* or flax -- *mostly hemp*. **2.** A strong lustrous paper made from hemp fibers.

linen closet A small closet, usually in a house, used to store linens. A.K.A. **linen room**

linenfold A carved Gothic panel representing folded or scrolled linen. A.K.A. **linen scroll, linen pattern**

linen room A room designated and arranged to store linens of all kinds, usually in commercial businesses *(hotels, restaurants, etc.)*.

linens Towels, tablecloths, bedsheets, and other articles or garments made from linen *(hemp or flax)* or resembling linen *(cotton)*.

line of sight An unobstructed view along an imaginary line, such as that between the eye of a spectator and the stage in a theatre, or as viewed through a telescope or camera lens. A.K.A. **sight line**

liner Material used to cover an interior surface, such as the inside of a jewelry box, a vapor barrier layer on a house that is covered with exterior siding, or as a backing to see-through drapery material. **lining** A.K.A. **backing**

lingerie chest A tall, narrow chest of *(usually 6 or more)* small drawers to compartmentalize a ladies' undergarments.

lining paper A layer of paper used to prepare a surface for a finished material, as is done with foil wallpaper. A.K.A. **underlayment**

linoleum A generic term used

to describe a hard, smooth, washable flooring, manufactured in 9'-, 12'-, and 15'-wide rolls, known as *"sheet goods,"* as opposed to floor tiles. *NOTE: Little or no linoleum flooring is actually produced today, it has been replaced with a product technically known as sheet vinyl.* A.K.A. **sheet vinyl**

linseed oil Common ingredient used in paints and varnishes to accelerate drying.

lintel A large, horizontal supporting beam, supported at each end, over a rough door, window, or fireplace opening, to carry the weight of the structure above the opening. A.K.A. **header**

lip An overhanging edge.

liquefaction The sudden transformation of soil from a solid state to a liquid or sandy state, usually the result of an earthquake.

liquid waste The discharge from any plumbing fixture or appliance that does not contain fecal matter.

living room A multipurpose room commonly used by all the residents. Often used to receive and entertain visitors and guests.

load Denotes the amount of weight being physically carried, *as on a truck*, or supported, *as from a cable*. **2.** Structurally, as the

lockers

weight of a bridge is carried by cables. **3.** A device that measures usage, such as the amount of electric power being used, or the number of phone calls a particular telephone company trunk line is carrying.

loading dock A platform or floor level, at the height of the bed of a truck, for easy loading and unloading of merchandise or materials. A.K.A. **loading platform**

loading platform See: **loading dock**

loam Any dark, rich fertile soil mixture, containing sand, silt, clay, and/or organic matter.

lobby An area at the interior entrance of a building, theatre, hotel, etc., often furnished and used as a waiting room.

lock A device which fastens a **door, gate, window,** etc., in a closed position.

lock box A small box or locker used to secure personal property. A.K.A. **locker**

lock corner A carpentry joint composed of interlocking fingers, pins, or cuts. See: **dovetail**

lockers One in a series of storage cubicals with locks for clothing, personal property and valuables. Used in a number of applications -- schools, gyms, bus stations, etc.

locking device Any device used as a lock. See: **lock**

lock rail A horizontal

rail, at the height of the lock, in a door.

lock set All the door hardware (locking mechanism, knobs, escutcheon plates, etc.) needed, on both sides of a door, to enable the door to be locked shut.

locksmith A person skilled in installing and fixing locks.

lockup A temporary storage building or room. **2.** Slang for jail or prison.

lock washer A washer designed to lock in place when a nut is tightened down on it.

lodge A cabin or small house in a forest area, used seasonally. **2.** A designation, *often part of a proper name*, used by resort hotels **3.** The meeting place of a fraternal organization.

loft An open or unpartitioned space in the upper part of a building or structure, such as a loft office or bedroom, a hayloft, or an organ loft.

log The trunk of a tree that has had its bark removed.

log cabin A building built of horizontal logs, notched or fitted at the ends and openings to prevent spreading. A.K.A. **log-framed house, log house** *HISTORIC NOTE: While the Swiss built the first known structures made from logs, the majority of colonial era log cabins were built by German-speaking settlers*

log cabin

between Pennsylvania and Virginia (mid-Atlantic region). With trees in plentiful supply, log cabin construction quickly spread south and west well into the 19th century.

loge The group of box seats in a theatre, either on the main floor or in the balcony.

log framing See: **log cabin**

loggia A room or gallery with an open arcade or colonnade, of the Italian Renaissance style.

lookout rafter See: **barge rafter**

lookouts Wooden brackets that support an overhanging portion of a roof. **2.** Brackets connecting rafter tails, providing a nailing surface for a soffit.

lookout tower A.K.A. **belvedere**

loom A machine to weave thread or yarn into cloth fabric.

loop Any opening resulting from a rope, wire, rod, etc., that twists back around to form a ring as it crosses itself. **2.** Any fastener with a ring-shaped section, meant to hold something, as rope **hand line**.

loose pillow-back A style of upholstered furniture with loose *(reversible)* back cushions. A.K.A. **pillow-backed**

lot A parcel of land described by survey and recorded with the local governing authority.

lotus column

lotus column A column with a lotus leaf capital motif. A.K.A. **tulip column**

loudspeaker An instrument that amplifies the human voice.

Louis XIV The Classical period in France under the rule of Louis XIV *(1643-1715)*.

Louis XV A Classical/Rococo style in France art and architecture, under the rule of Louis XV *(1725-1774)*.

Louis XVI A greater emphasis on Rococo, under the rule of Louis XVI *(1774-1792)*, terminated by the French Revolution.

lounge A room *(dining area, bar, etc.)* with an informal setting in a hotel, theatre, or other public building.

louver Horizontal slats *(overlapping blades)* that can be opened, in varying degrees, for ventilation and light, or closed for protection against the weather.

louver door A door with angled, horizontal overlapping slats or blades in the area between the rails and stiles, instead of a solid panel, allowing air to circulate while the door is closed.

louver window See: **shutters**

love seat A small sofa for two people. A.K.A. **settee**

low bid A bid based on bare-wall construction, including paint, but not including any extras or expensive upgrades. **2**. The lowest bid received from competing contractors or bidders, based on complying with all specifications and requirements.

lowboy Applied to anything made recognizably lower than usual, such as a low chest or dresser, or a truck trailer made with a low bed, to be able to transport tall items in one piece.

lozenge A diamond-shaped decorative motif.

lozenge molding Molding with a diamond-shaped motif.

lumber Dimensionally sawn **wood** (timber) for framing buildings and structures, *not usually including plywood or other manufactured sheet goods*.

luminescence The emission of light not produced incandescently.

luminous Brilliance. **2**. Giving off light.

luminous ceiling A ceiling lighting system.

luminous paint Fluorescent or phosphorescent paint that emits light for several hours after the light source has vanished.

lunch room A room set aside for employees or student to eat their lunch or take breaks. Denotes limited food service. A.K.A. **break room**

lunette An object shaped in the form of a crescent or half moon.

luster A shiny reflective finish. **2**. A surface or coating that imparts a gloss, sheen, glitter, or sparkle.

- M -

Macassar ebony *(Wood)* A *very dense* hardwood of the East Indies and China, with bold red or brown streaks in its generally black or coffee-brown color. Used for decorative paneling and applications requiring a high-impact resistant surface. A.K.A. **coromandel, striped ebony**

machinery room A room where machinery of some kind has been installed and operates. A.K.A. **mechanical equipment room**

magazine A place where explosives and projectiles are stored.

magnesium alloy Any number of alloys or additives of magnesium *(aluminum, manganese, silicon, silver, thorium, and zirconium)* used singly or in combination in the manufacture of various building products.

magnet Any piece of iron, steel, etc., with the property, either naturally or artificially induced, to attract most metal objects.

magnetic catch A door catch that uses a magnet to hold the door closed.

mahogany *(Wood)* A reddish brown, straight-grained, medium-density hardwood, found in the tropical climates of Central and South America, Africa, the West Indies, and the Philippines. Long favored for paneling, furniture, and cabinetry because of its beautiful reddish color and handsome grain. A.K.A. **Spanish mahogany** See: **Honduras mahogany, white mahogany**

mail box A postal box, in which mail to be delivered is deposited. 2. A box, or similar object, each house has in which mail to that address is delivered.

mail chute A small shaft or channel used to transport letters from an upper floor(s) to a postbox on the ground floor, where it can be easily collected. A.K.A. **letter chute**

main A major or principal pipe, duct, etc., used to distribute or collect from or to its various branches.

malachite A green-colored mineral used to artificially **age** and add a degree of authenticity to ornamental objects.

male connector The projecting side of a connecting device, made to slip into a reciprocal (female) end.

male plug The end of an electrical cord, with projecting prongs, which fits into an electric receptacle on the wall.

male thread The threads on a screw or pipe, as opposed to the female threads of a nut or flange.

mall An area or structure designed for pedestrian traffic,

malleability

originally meant outdoors. **2.** A large, enclosed commercial marketplace where people walk through a plaza lined with various stores, restaurants, theaters, etc.

malleability A property of metal that allows it to be hammered, pressed, forged, rolled, etc., into various shapes without breaking.

mallet A soft-headed hammer used (1) to force something into place without damaging the surface, (2) to absorb the shock of striking a hard material, such as chiseling a stone sculpture.

malt house See: **brewery**

mandoral Decorative element in the general shape of an almond.

manger A trough in a stable for feeding cattle.

manhole A small, covered opening in a street to access the sewer and underground electric cables.

man-hour The amount of work one worker can accomplish in one hour.

manifold A distribution hub. Used to run several lines from a central supply.

manor house The lord of a manor's house. **2.** The most important house in a country or village neighborhood.

mansard roof

Mansard roof A roof of French design, with two slopes on all four sides, the lower slope being much steeper. *Architect: Francois Mansart (circa 1660)*

mansion A large, imposing, and usually very costly house. **2.** A manor house.

mantel A general term used to describe all the elements of a fireplace surround. A.K.A. **mantelpiece 2.** Refers to the horizontal projection shelf atop a fireplace. A.K.A. **mantelshelf**

mantelpiece The surround, *including the shelf and its supports*, around a fireplace. A.K.A. **mantel**

mantelshelf A horizontal shelf above the opening of a fireplace. A.K.A. **mantelboard**

manufactured building A structure substantially or wholly built in a factory and shipped, in pieces, to the site for assembly. A.K.A. **prefabricated building, prefab building**

manufactured housing See: **prefabricated housing** A.K.A. **prefab housing**

map A graphic depiction, *to scale*, of the earth's surface.

maple *(Wood)* A handsome, strong, straight-grained, high-density hardwood, native to North

America and Europe. Used for furniture, flooring, paneling, wood turnings, etc.; the curly or bird's-eye varieties are used for veneers. Light to dark brown in color with a uniform texture. Similar in character to **beech** and **birch**, and used in similar applications.

maple

marble Highly impervious metamorphic rock *(calcite or dolomite)*, cut and smoothed to a polished finish. Used primarily for countertops, wall and floor coverings, and fireplace hearths and surrounds.

marbled Having the appearance of veined marble, achieved with paint to look like marble. **marbling, marbleized, marbleizing**

margin An area left blank around a picture or text specifically to highlight it. **2.** A border around a hearth.

margin strip In wood flooring, a border strip.

marine glue Glue that is insoluble in water.

marine paint Paint formulated to withstand exposure to sunlight and water.

marker Anything used to pinpoint a specific point, as on a map or as a road marker. **2.** Large, felt-tipped, colored pens, used for a variety of artistic effects.

market Any open area or building where merchandise, particularly fresh local produce, is displayed or kept for sale. A.K.A. **marketplace**

marketplace See: **market**

marking gauge An instrument used by carpenters to scribe a parallel line along an edge. **butt gauge**

marquee A structure over the entrance of a theatre used to advertise the show and players. **marquise**

marquetry See: **inlay**

masking Temporarily protecting surfaces adjacent to that or those being painted from accidental paint splatters, by covering with masking tape, or tape plus plastic or paper. **2.** A theatrical term meaning to screen off part of the stage from the audience's view. **3.** Rendering one sound inaudible or unintelligible by introducing an even louder sound.

masking tape An adhesive paper tape, made for easy removal.

masonry The art of building with brick or stone and mortar.

masonry anchor A fastener, embedded in concrete, with the holding power to secure or attach something to it.

masonry block A.K.A. **concrete block**

masonry drill A drill bit made to go through concrete.

masonry veneer A finished layer of brick, stone, etc., that is not structural in nature. A.K.A. **stone face, stone veneer**

mast That part of a derrick or

master bedroom

crane *(the arm)* that carries the load. **2.** A tower that carries one or more load lines.

master bedroom The largest and most elaborately finished bedroom of a house.

master plan The drawings, physical model(s), or written documentation describing anticipated or approved future construction.

mastic A strong, pasty adhesive available in many forms *(tape, sheets, paste)*.

mat A small or thin mattress. 2. See: **matte finish 3**. Very heavy blanket of steel mesh, woven wire rope, or chain, used to confine fragments of rock during blasting.

match Uniformity and equality of objects of like form, shape, and color. As wood planks are matched for tabletops and flooring, giving a uniform, overall consistency.

matte finish A dull surface finish, with little or no gloss or sheen. **matt, mat, matted**

matting Plant material woven into a carpet, typically found in tropical climates and used to provide an informal setting.

mattress That part of a bed that directly supports the body. A fabric bag surrounding an inner spring core and padding. Part of the modern standard bed. See: **bed** A.K.A. **mattress and box spring**.

maul A heavy wooden mallet.

mausoleum A large and elaborate tomb for one or more people.

maze See: labyrinth

MDF *Abbr.* medium density fiberboard. See: **medium density fiberboard**

measured drawing A scaled drawing, meaning distances between lines on the drawing can be measured.

mechanic's lien See: lien

medallion A decorative circular or oval plaque on which is represented an object (figure, flower, etc.) in relief. **2.** A prominent or central sculptured tablet, panel, or similar decorative object.

medicine cabinet A small bathroom storage cabinet for medical supplies, toilet articles, etc., either embedded into the wall or attached to it.

medieval A term used to describe the period in Europe known as the Middle Ages *(5th to 15th century)*. **2.** Architecturally, relating particularly to the art and architecture of the Byzantine, pre-Romanesque, Romanesque, and Gothic styles. **3.** Denotes ancient or outdated, at best, often dangerous and threatening.

medium A universal environment, such as white latex paint *(the base)*, used with a combination of colors to produce a spectrum of colored paints. **2.** A vehicle or field of endeavor for artistic expression, such as working in glass, watercolor, stone, canvas, paper, film, etc.

medium density fiberboard

medium density fiberboard *Abbr.* MDF
Structural sheeting material, similar to plywood but not made from layers of thin **ply**.

meeting bar
See: **meeting rail**

meeting rail
An element in a double-hung window sash where the two sashes meet when the window is closed. A.K.A. **meeting bar**

megalithic
Literally, a huge stone. **2.** A term applied to prehistoric ancient monuments distinguished by their unusually large size.

member
Structurally, any of the elements or component part of a building or structure.

membrane
Denotes a one-piece rubberized, weather-resistant covering or liner.

memorial arch
An arch of monumental size commemorating an event or individual. *Examples:* **Brandenburg Gate** *(Germany)* and **Arc de Triomphe de l'Etoile** *(France)* See: **monument**. A.K.A. **triumphal arch**

memorial park
A designation given to cemeteries of national significance, such as the Arlington National Cemetery. ***Interesting Facts:*** Arlington lies on property, *actually the rose garden and house,* once owned by Gen.

men's room

Robert E. Lee before he became a Confederate general.

men's room
A public restroom for males.

mesa
A small plateau or flat plain in a area of relatively low rolling hills.

mesa dwelling
A house built on the summit of a mesa, common in Arizona and New Mexico.

mesh
A skintight structural grid whose form is shaped by the object it covers. **2.** Structurally, expanded metal (light-woven steel, or welded steel) used as a security barrier or to reinforce concrete. **3.** A network of metal wires.

mess hall
A room or building where a group of people *(particularly military)* regularly eat their meals.

metal ceiling
See: **tin ceiling** A.K.A. **metal coffering**

metal-clad door
A fire door, made of a standard wood-framed door covered with metal. There is no wood in modern fire-rated metal doors.

metal grating
A surface or covering made of metal components.

metallic paint
A paint or lacquer containing fine metal flakes to reflect light.

metropolis
A capital or major city.

Arc de Triomphe

mews

mews A terrace, alley, or court in which stables are, or once were located.

mezzanine A partial second floor of a large building with an open area that looks down on the first floor. **entresol** 2. Theatrically, the first few rows of the lowest balcony.

Michelangelo, **Buonarotti** *(1475-1564)*, Renowned Italian Renaissance poet, painter, sculptor, and architect. Father of Mannerist style of architecture, influenced nearly all subsequent classical styles.

microphone An instrument, *connected to other equipment*, that when spoken into amplifies, records, or broadcasts the voice.

Mies van der Rohe, Ludwig *(1886-1969)* German modern architect, and leading proponent of the Ultra-Expressionist style. Director of the Bauhaus (1930) and pillar of International Modernism.

mildew A fungus that grows and feeds on paint, natural fabric, etc., exposed to moisture, causing discoloration and decomposition of the surface.

mill A workshop with large machinery to cut, shape, and fabricate various objects and structures. See: **millwork**

milled Parts produced in a mill.

millennium The name used to mark our entry into the 21st century. *NOTE: Turn-of-the-century marks our entry into the 20th century.*

millwork The fabrication of doors, door frames, window sashes, railings, bannisters, cabinets, moldings, etc., all better accomplished in a **mill**, rather than on the job site. See: **mill**

minaret The tower of a mosque, with a balcony from which the call to prayer is given.

mineral spirts A solvent and thinner for paint and varnishes.

mineshaft architecture A popular architectural style that features long clean lines with a single-plane, slanted *(shedlike)* roof.

miniature A scaled down version of a normally larger piece. 2. Unusually small furniture, picture, or other object.

mint A building where money is coined.

mirror A nearly perfect reflecting surface.

mismatched Said of adjacent boards or veneers in which there is an absence of symmetry.

mission architecture Reminiscent of the early 18th century adobe buildings and churches with red tile roofs that Spanish missionaries built along the California coast. See: **Spanish colonial** A.K.A. **Monterey style**

miter An angled cut, used to connect two pieces of material, as in a picture frame.

miter box An electric saw that can quickly be set for a

miter cut

variety of angled cuts. **2.** A device for guiding a handsaw at a specific angle through wood.

miter cut Any oblique cut across two pieces of board or molding, so that when joined they form an angle.

mitered joint Any angled joint.

miter gauge An instrument for determining an angle.

power miter box

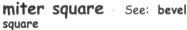

miter square See: **bevel square**

mixture A blend of ingredients, such as of concrete or mortar.

mobile home A portable home on a wheeled carriage, and usually pulled or made part of a truck. *NOTE: Many of the "mobile homes" built today are actually not designed to be mobile, but are delivered almost fully constructed on wheeled trailers.*

mock-up A full-size or scale model of an object, in the design stage, for further study or judging.

model A physical representation in scale, for study or illustration.

modeling Forming or shaping a clay, plaster, or plastic object.

modification An authorized change. **2.** A written or graphic amendment to an existing contract document, signed by both parties.

modillion One of a series of projecting corbels or brackets supporting a cornice or roof.

modular construction A system of construction using mass-produced, prefabricated parts of equal or similar size with various functions, affording custom configuration. Follows **LeCorbusier's theory of the Modulor.**

module One of many dimensionally similar but often unique pieces that can be configured in a variety of different ways. **2.** A unit of measurement.

moisture barrier A vapor barrier.

moisture content The amount of water, by weight, in a particular material.

mold A device used to shape a substance *(plastics, plaster, clay)* into 3-dimensional objects. Usually, a 2-piece mold with the interior shaped as a negative of the positive form to be duplicated.

molding The decorative wood trim, interiors (rooms), and exterior (buildings), particularly around doors and windows. Traditionally used as trim to give a finished look to doors, windows, ceilings, floors, and walls. Also used to cover a surface where two elements or surfaces meet. **moulding** *(Br) NOTE: Generally divided into three categories; **rectilinear**, **composite**, and **curved.** **moulding** See: **molding details**

MOLDING

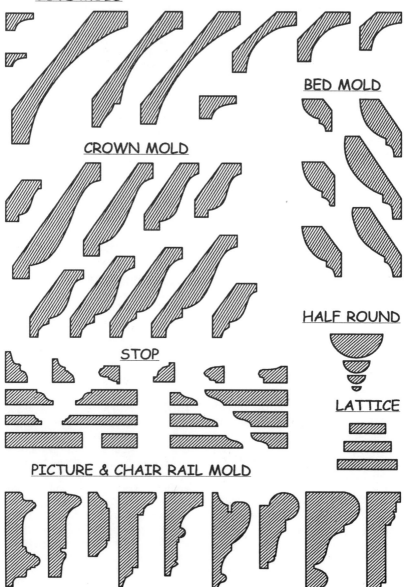

COVE MOLD

BED MOLD

CROWN MOLD

HALF ROUND

STOP

LATTICE

PICTURE & CHAIR RAIL MOLD

MOLDING

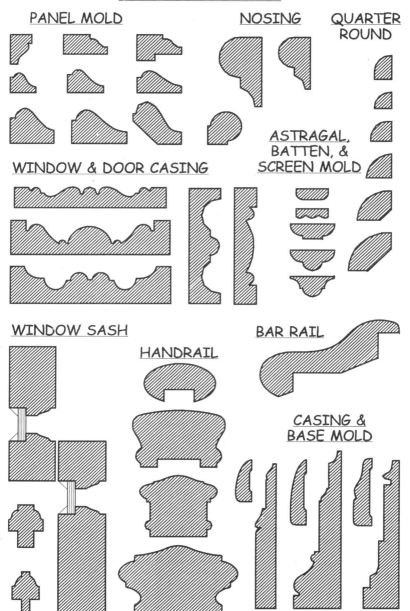

PANEL MOLD

NOSING

QUARTER ROUND

WINDOW & DOOR CASING

ASTRAGAL, BATTEN, & SCREEN MOLD

WINDOW SASH

HANDRAIL

BAR RAIL

CASING & BASE MOLD

MOLDING DETAILS

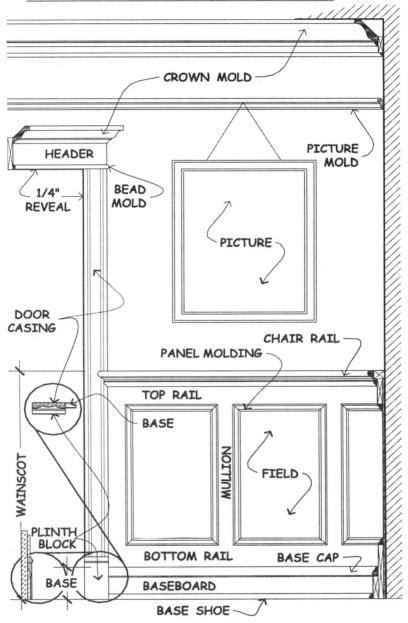

CROWN MOLD

HEADER

PICTURE MOLD

1/4" REVEAL

BEAD MOLD

PICTURE

DOOR CASING

CHAIR RAIL

PANEL MOLDING

TOP RAIL

BASE

WAINSCOT

MULLION

FIELD

PLINTH BLOCK

BOTTOM RAIL

BASE CAP

BASE

BASEBOARD

BASE SHOE

molded plastic   Plastic objects that are formed or shaped in a mold, as a skylight of transparent or translucent plastic.

monastery   A building or group of buildings occupied by members of a religious order.

monkey wrench   A wrench having one jaw fixed and one adjustable jaw.

monochromatic   Use of various tints and shades of a single color.   **monochrome**   A.K.A. **monotone**

monolith   A solid structural mass, like a concrete wall, an obelisk, the shaft of a column, etc., consisting of a single stone.

monolithic   Shaped from a single block of material. 2. Said of concrete that is cast in a single piece.

montage   See: **collage**

Monterey style   See: Spanish colonial A.K.A. **mission style**

monument   A statue, structure, building, or similar object erected in memory of the dead or to mark a historic event.

moon gate   In Chinese architecture, a circular opening in a wall large enough to walk through.

mop-board See: **baseboard**

mopping   Applying a hot tarlike substance, to form a waterproof membrane, on a roof or deck.

morgue   A place, usually at a hospital or coroner's office, where bodies are stored before an autopsy or release to a private mortuary for burial or cremation.

mortar   A general term to describe an adhesive material used to attach tile to a wall or floor or to bond bricks together to build a wall.

mortgage   A loan for the purchase or improvement of real property, in which the property itself is used as security for the loan.

mortgagee   The mortgage lender.

mortgage lien   A lien against property used as security for repayment of a loan.

mortise   A hole, cavity, or slot of specific size and position to accept the tenoned end of another structural element or object, such as a lock mechanism.   See: **mortise-and-tenon joint**

mortise-and-tenon joint   The joining of two structural elements, formed by fitting a tenon *(projection)* at the end of one element into a mortise *(cavity)* in the other, as a male / female connector.   **mortised joint**

mortised latch   See: **mortised lock**

mortised lock   A lock designed to be installed in a mortise rather than applied to a door's surface.

mortuary   A commercial business that makes funeral arrangements and services.

mosaic

mosaic An image or design formed by inlaying small pieces of stone, tile, glass, or enamel into mortar to form a surface.

mosque A Muslim house of worship.

motel A roadside business that provides sleeping accommodations for transient motorists.

motif Refers to a principal style or orientation followed in the design of a room, building, etc.

motive Artistically, the subject of or the peculiar character of a work of art, in either detail or in its entirety.

motor A device that converts electric power into mechanical power by means of a rotating shaft, such as a drill motor.

moulding British spelling of molding. See: **molding**

mound A pile of any material.

mounts Ornamental metal, such as handles, drawer pulls, escutcheon, etc., used on cabinets.

moving The process of removing a building from one site and placing it on another site.

muck Moist organic soil of very soft consistency.

mudroom A small entryway where muddy footwear, coats, and hats may be removed and stored until needed again.

mudsill An early American foundation timber placed directly on level ground. A.K.A. **groundsill**

muffler Something used to muffle sound.

mulch Material (leaves, hay, straw, or the like), spread on the surface around newly planted shrubs or trees to protect their roots from extremely hot or cold weather.

mullion A large vertical divider of structural significance, as between two windows. See: **molding details, door styles**

multifolding door Refers primarily to folding wall panels *(hung on a ceiling track)* that section off a large, multipurpose meeting room into smaller rooms. When open, the panels stack against each other and are housed in a relatively small space. A.K.A. **accordion doors**

municipal building A building that houses the offices and personnel needed to conduct the business affairs of the collective community.

muntin A secondary framing element used to hold panes of glass in a window or door. A.K.A. **glazing bar, sash bar** See: **window styles**

mural An image *(painting)* applied to a wall.

Murphy bed A bed made to fold vertically *(into a cabinet, closet, or cavity in a wall)*, allowing the space in the room to be used when the bed isn't needed.

museum A building(s) to house and display a collection of art, decorative, or historic objects, and/or interesting items to the general public.

music hall A large room or auditorium designed for an audience to be entertained by musicians and musicals of all kinds.

music room A room, *usually in a private home*, designated for practicing or performing music.

Muslim architecture The architecture of the Middle East, including Syria, Egypt, Mesopotamia, Iran, North Africa, Spain, Central Persia and India, *(circa 7th to the 16th century A.D.).* Incorporated many variations of basic architectural elements such as interlaced, ribbed bulbous, conical, and melon-shaped arches, vaults, and domes, with geometric, floral, and calligraphic decorations executed in stone, brick, stucco, wood, and glazed tile.

muslin A strong, coarse cotton cloth used for a variety of purposes, such as for cushion casings.

myrtle *(Wood)* A yellow-blond wood with fine markings, used in cabinetry, inlays, and veneer.

- N -

nail A thin, straight piece of metal, pointed at one end and having a head at the other, driven in with a hammer or pneumatic gun to hold two or more pieces of wood together. *NOTE: Nails are usually driven into what is considered softwoods, such as pine, fir, popular, etc., the kind of wood used to stick frame a building. Nails are, generally, not driven into hardwoods.*

NAIL & MATERIAL SIZES
Nails are identified by **penny weight**, which refers to their length.

16(d) penny nails *(3½" long)* are used for 2x *(1½" thick material)* construction *(i.e., 2x4s, 2x6s, and 2x12s, etc.).*

8(d) penny nails *(2½" long)* are used for attaching 1x *(3/4")* material *(i.e., 1x3, 1x6, 1x12, etc.).*

4(d) penny nails *(1½" long)* are used to attach ¼" sheet material.

6(d) finish nails *(2" long)* are most often used for attaching molding.

KINDS OF NAILS

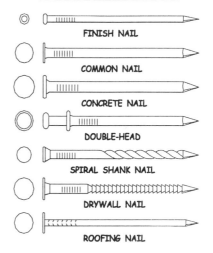

FINISH NAIL

COMMON NAIL

CONCRETE NAIL

DOUBLE-HEAD

SPIRAL SHANK NAIL

DRYWALL NAIL

ROOFING NAIL

nail box A box sectioned off to hold a variety of sizes and kinds of nails.

nail gun A pneumatic tool that implants a nail into wood, used

nail gun

instead of a hammer.   A.K.A. **nailer**

nailhead   The end of a nail that is driven by a hammer into wood. **2.** A decorative ornament resembling the head of a nail.

nailing The process of affixing one object or material to another by driving nails through or into both objects.

nailing strip A strip of wood to hold the nails used to fasten one object to another.

nail punch See: **nail set**

nail set A tapered metal tool used to drive the head of a nail slightly below the surface of the wood. A.K.A. **set punch**

nanmu *(Wood)* An aromatic, Far East cedar commonly used in China for building and decoration (softwood). Turns a deep rich brown with age.   A.K.A. **Persian cedar**

natural gas   A colorless, odorless, combustible hydrocarbon gas commonly used for cooking and heating.

naturalism   The artistic replication of natural objects.

near colors Colors that have an imposing tendency, which tend to make the things around it appear smaller, particularly dark colors *(red)*.

neck   A narrow connecting, elongation, or projection, or any object that resembles the neck of a bottle or a human neck.

needle A slender piece of steel with a sharp point at one end and a hole, which thread passes through, at the other, used for sewing by hand. *NOTE: Sewing machine needles have a hole, for thread, near the pointed end of the needle.* **2.** The sharp slender tube at the end of a hypodermic syringe. **3.** Any object resembling the various parts of a needle. **4.** A short timber, or the like, which passes through a hole in a wall.

needle-nose pliers
A pinching tool with pointed jaws; also contains a wire cutter.

needle-nose pliers

needle spire   A tall thin column, such as the **Seattle needle**.

needlework Any work done with a needle.

negligence Failure to exercise a reasonable and prudent degree of care or judgment, as would normally be exercised, even expected, by others under similar circumstances.

neighborhood   An area consisting of several or many blocks of houses, possibly with a local shopping center.   A.K.A. **community, village**

neoclassical   *(1900-1940)* Reminiscent of the last phase of European classicism *(late 18th and early 19th centuries)*, based on a rational approach to design and a more realistic interpretation of Greco-Roman architecture. Characterized by simple shapes and monumental size, with two-story pedimented porticos and colossal columns.

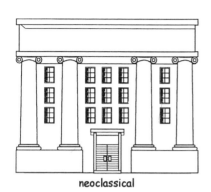

neoclassical

neo-Gothic   See: **Gothic revival**

neon   An inert gas that produces a reddish orange glow when used in an electric discharge lamp.

neon lamp   A cold-cathode lamp that produces light by passing an electric current through neon gas.

nested tables   A group of three small tables made progressively smaller so they fit beneath each other.   A.K.A. **nest of tables**

net   A loosely woven fabric made of string, cord, etc., used to catch or snare, particularly fish, but including most small animals.

nested tables

2. Any of a variety of meshed fabric used to hold or protect something, as a hair net. **3.** That which remains, as profit, after all expenses and deductions are paid.

network   A support system made up of organizations and individuals.   **2.** A series of broadcasting stations that transmit or operate as one.

neutral colors   Colors of several hues that are of low chromatic value or highly tinted or shaded *(dark or light)*. Usually produced by mixing a secondary color with the opposite primary color on the **color wheel**. **2.** Having little or no distinctive color of its own, unobtrusive, e.g., **lt. beige**.

newel   See: **newel post**

newel cap   The trim *(molding, turning, or carving)* at the top of a newel post.

newel post   A large post at the foot or head of a staircase that supports the handrail, and into which the handrail terminates. **2.** The central post or column around which the steps of a circular staircase wind, and which provides support for the individual steps.   *NOTE: newel posts are often named by their location, e.g., starting newel, landing newel, and an intermediate or angle post.*

New England Colonial

The art and architectural style of colonial America *(17ᵗʰ & 18ᵗʰ centuries),* heavily influenced and reflective of America's British heritage. Basic, boxlike, heavy construction; typically, one multipurpose room or two-story *(one room deep)* buildings with little or no decorative trim and simple batten doors. Characteristics include steeply pitched gabled roofs without overhangs, massive central fireplace with stacked chimneys,

niche

weatherboard siding, and small **casement windows.** A.K.A. **saltbox style, English Colonial**

niche A recessed space in a wall made to hold a statue or ornament.

noise Any annoying, unwanted sound.

noise abatement
Regulating noise to an acceptable level.

nonbearing wall An interior partition wall, not intended to support a ceiling or upper floors.

noncombustible Any materials that will withstand high temperatures without igniting or burning.

nonconforming Any building or structure that does not comply with applicable code, rules, or regulations.

nook An alcove or intimate space, such as a breakfast nook, where family members eat together.

normal consistency The expected physical condition of mixed concrete or mortar at the time of application.

Norman *(Normandy)* The English name for Romanesque architecture, exemplified by Westminster Abby *(1065)*.

nosing Rounded molding added to the edge of any horizontal surface, such as a table or step.

notching Rough joining of timbers by cutting a notch in one or both pieces. A.K.A. **lap joint, rabbet joint.**

nozzle A device at the end of a hose or pipe that controls the flow of fluids.

nuance A slight variation in tone, color, meaning, etc.; small difference.

nuisance A pest. 2. A condition detrimental to public health or dangerous to human life. A.K.A. **public nuisance**

nursery A room for small children. 2. A place where plants, shrubs, and small trees are grown.

nursery school A school for children aged 3 to 5 years.

nurse's office See: **dispensary** A.K.A. **first-aid office, infirmary**

nursing home A facility offering inpatient care and lodging for the physically ill or elderly, on a 24-hour basis.

nut A short metal block having a threaded center hole to receive a bolt.

- O -

oak *(Wood)* Perhaps the most-used high-density hardwood for stained or varnished furniture, cabinetry, and structural and decorative interior trim. Native to temperate climates, oaks are divided into over fifty species *(all with similar characteristics)*. Broad-ranging colors from light brown to red with a robust grain. English and French oak is said to have finer graining than American varieties.

oak

obelisk A monolithic, tapered, shaftlike monument with a **pyramidal** tip, such as the Washington Monument. Prominent in Egyptian art, as a cult symbol to the sun god.

obscure glass Sheet glass with one face roughened.

observatory A rotatable dome structure designed around large telescopes, to observe the stars. 2. Usually, a top-floor room of a house, which affords a wide view, in which a devotee of astronomical observations has set up and regularly uses a telescope.

occasional furniture Small unique tables, tea carts, etc., used as accent pieces. A.K.A. **occasional table**

observatory

octagon An eight-sided object or figure.

oculus A round window 2. The opening at the top center of a dome. A.K.A. **eye**

odeum A small ancient Greek or Roman theatre, usually with a roof. **odeon**

off center An axis not along the geometric centerline or center point.

office A room or series of rooms where management, technical, and clerical work is done, opposed to a workshop.

office building A building used to house the offices of management, technical, and clerical staff of one or many companies.

offset A change in direction, such as in a wall or pipe. 2. A parallel distance from one object to another. See: **reveal** A.K.A. **set-in**

off white A common paint color that is a slight shade or hue of white. White, but not pure white.

ogee Molding with an S-shaped curve, consisting, *in profile*, of two opposing cyma curves. A.K.A. **O.G.** See: **reverse ogee**

O.G. See: **ogee**

O.G. door A standard door, so called because it is made with stock ogee molding.

oil painting Any painting done in oil-based paint, usually linseed oil.

old colonial architecture See: **New England Colonial**

olive *(Wood)* A light yellow hardwood with a greenish yellow grain. Takes a high polish, commonly used in veneers and inlays.

on center A measurement from the center of one stud, *or similar object*, to the center of the next. *NOTE: In modern stick framing, studs are usually spaced on 16" centers, enabling 4'x8' sheets of plywood or drywall to be nailed at 16" intervals.* A.K.A. **center-to-center**

on grade Directly on the ground or ground level.

onyx

onyx Quartz, with bands of color, used as polished slab floor and wall coverings.

opacity The quality of being opaque, as the capacity of a paint to cover the surface to which it is applied.

opal glass A light-diffusing glass of milk-white appearance.

opaque Impervious to the transmission of visible light; not transparent.

open bidding Competitive bidding open to all interested qualified contractors.

open newel staircase A staircase with an open well at its core and newel posts at each landing or right angled turns to hold and stabilize the handrail.

open-plan office A large, open office space, divided by freestanding partitions.

opera house A theatre designed primarily for performing operas.

optical balance Symmetry created when the two halves of a composition are similar in appearance but not identical in detail.

optical fiber cable See: **fiber optics**

option An agreement between a property owner and prospective buyer or lessee that, for a specified sum of money, grants the buyer, for a specified period of time, the right to exercise the purchase or lease of the property.

orangery A conservatory for growing oranges. **orangerie**

orbital sander An electric-powered hand tool that utilizes an elliptical pattern to rotate sandpaper or abrasive cloth in order to sand a surface.

orchestra pit The area immediately in front of a stage, which is at or below the audience level, and from which musicians or a full orchestra perform. A.K.A. **parquet circle**

order Directions or instructions of things to do or for things to be supplied. 2. See: **column details**, A.K.A. **architectural order, classical order**

organ A musical instrument, operated by keyboard, from which sound is produced by the vibration of the air in pipes of wood and/or metal.

organ chamber A room or space where the organ is placed. A.K.A. **organ loft**

organic Said of vegetable or animal-based materials or compounds.

organic architecture A philosophy of architectural design in which structure and appearance harmonize with its natural environment.

oriel window A bay window that appears to be supported by brackets or corbels.

oriental rug A handwoven rug native to the Middle and Far East.

orientation The placement of a structure on a site, with regard to its surrounding views and its relationship to exposure to sun, wind, etc.

oriented strand board

oriented strand board
Structural sheeting material, similar to plywood but made from chips of wood and other material glued together under pressure.

ornament An architectural detail used for decorative or stylistic purposes.

ornate Highly ornamented.

oscillating sander An
electric vibrating sander, used primarily for finished sanding. A.K.A. **vibrating sander**

ottoman A generic term for Turkish *(Ottoman Empire)* art and architecture from the late 14th century. 2. An upholstered footrest.

ou tbuilding Building(s) on the same piece of property but separate from the main house or building.

outhouse A detached outdoor toilet, without plumbing.

outlet An access point to something, as an electric outlet in a wall is an access point for electric appliances to obtain electric power.

outlet box A small metal or plastic box, *installed within the wall cavity*, that holds one or more electrical receptacles and the attached wiring in place.

outlet vent A vent leading directly out of a building.

out-of-center See: **off center**

out-of-plumb Not truly vertical.

outrigger A horizontal steel beam with an attached leg used to stabilize a large crane, cherry picker, or other equipment. 2. A structural member supporting a roof or floor from a point beyond the exterior walls. 3. A beam that projects beyond the walls of a building, that supports a pulley or hoist, as found on a barn to move hay to the hayloft.

outshot See: **outshut**

outshut A small extension or wing built off the main structure. A.K.A. **outshot, wing**

oval Anything shaped like an egg or ellipse.

overall The total linear dimension of a building including any projection, such as a porch or deck. A.K.A. **overall dimension**

overdrape See: **valance**

overflow The amount that flows over the edge of a container that has been filled beyond the container's capacity. 2. A pipe or drain that is expected to take up an overflow of some kind of liquid.

overhang The distance one element *(e.g., a **roof**)* projects beyond the vertical wall plane.

overhead door A swing-up or roll-up type door, such as a garage door or a metal security door.

overlapping See: **lap**

overload A load *(weight or use)* exceeding that which a structure or system was designed to carry.

overmantel Refers to paneling, mirror, etc., placed above a fireplace mantel.

160 **ovolo**

ovolo A convex molding element resembling a quarter circle.

owner The person or company holding legal title to property. **2.** An architect's or contractor's client.

oxidation A chemical reaction to the air (oxygen) of some compounds, such as a paint that dries to a hard dry film when exposed to the air and sun.

overmantel

oxyacetylene welding A welding process utilizing heat from the combustion of acetylene and oxygen to produce a flame.

ozone A slightly blue form of oxygen (O_2) that makes up a protective layer around the earth, that fends off the sun's harmful rays.

- P -

pace A slightly raised section of the floor, broad step, or raised space, such as a dais. Most often used to refer to a landing.

packing Refers primarily to material used to cushion merchandise from damage during transit. **2.** Small stones embedded in drying mortar to fill gaps and prevent movement of larger stones while mortar cures.

pad That portion of land prepared for the construction of a building or structure. **2.** A soft material used as an underlayment for carpeting, that prolongs the life of the carpet. **padding 3.** A number of pages bound together at one edge, for writing and drawing. A.K.A. **tablet 4.** To lengthen a speech or essay with unnecessary or irrelevant material. **5.** To fraudulently claim reimbursable expenses.

padding A general carpentry term used to denote the building up of a surface, usually to match the height of an adjoining surface. **2.** See: **pad** (carpet), **furniture pad**

pagoda A tower of Chinese or Asian origin with several stories. Usually part of a Buddhist temple.

pail A small bucket for carrying liquids and compounds.

paint A liquid solution of color pigment, which when applied to any surface dries to a durable protective and decorative coating.

paintbrush A tool made of bristles or hair, bound to a handle, that a painter uses to apply paint.

painting The physical act of applying paint, applicable to both portrait artists and house painters alike.

painting room A room, studio, or workshop designated for use by painters, for the purpose of painting.

paint remover A commercially produced chemical designed to cause dry paint or varnish to soften or loosen its adhesive properties, for easy removal.

paint roller   A cylindrical tube covered with various materials that rotates around a metal rod / handle, used to apply paint to large flat surfaces, such as walls and ceilings.

paint spray booth
See: **spray booth**

paint sprayer   See: **spray gun**

paint thinner   A volatile liquid used to dilute and lower the viscosity of paints, adhesives, etc. A.K.A. **thinner, solvent**

palazzo

palazzo   An Italian term generally applied to any impressive public building or private residence.

pale   The lack of intensity or brilliance in color or light.   **2.** Diminished in importance when compared to something else.   **3.** The flat strip (slats) pickets of a fence.   **4.** An area enclosed by such stakes.

palette   The board an artist mixes colors on. **2.** A broad range of colors.

palette knife A thin flexible blade, with a wooden handle, used by painters to mix colors or apply paint to a canvas.

palisade   A series of stout poles, with pointed tops, driven into the ground and used as a fence or fortification.   A.K.A. **stockade**

palette

palisander *(Wood)*   A brown hardwood with a violet cast, native to Brazil and the East Indies, and used principally for modern furniture.

Palladian architecture
The neoclassical architecture of Italy as interpreted by prolific Venetian architect Andrea Palladio *(1518-1580)*, known internationally as Palladianism.   Particularly popular in 18th century England where it was known as classical revivalism. *NOTE: It is believed that Palladio was named after Pallas, the goddess of wisdom, by his employer, Gian Giorgio Trissino, a scholar and poet who trained Palladio as an architect.*

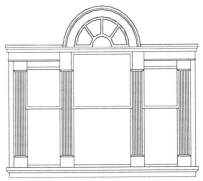
Palladian window

Palladian window A window style (**Italian neoclassical**) associated with Palladian architecture, having a central arched sash flanked on both sides by smaller windows. A.K.A. **Venetian window, serlian window**

pallet A low platform on which merchandise or materials are stacked to facilitate handling or loading by forklift.

palm The inner flat surface of the hand, between the fingers and wrist. 2. That part of a glove that covers the palm of the hand. 3. Any of several varieties of tropical trees having tall branchless trunks and a bunch of large leaves at the very top. *NOTE: Grows 60 to 80 feet high.* 4. Any broad flat blade at the end of an arm or handle, such as a oar. 5. To hide something in the palm or about the hand, as in a **sleight-of-hand** disappearing coin or card trick.

palmette Decoration based on the palm leaf.

pane A flat sheet of glass glazed into a window or door. A.K.A. **window pane, light, window light** *NOTE: Double-hung sash windows are often described by the number of panes of glass each sash contains, such as 6 over 6, 9 over 6, 6 over 1, etc.*

panel A flat piece of material, usually rectangular, used to form walls, doors, and cabinets, such as an end panel, back panel, etc. 2. Any raised or sunken section of a door, wall, ceiling, or mantle with a framelike border. 3. A flat surface for instruments and controls. 4. A thin board, plywood sheet, or similar material with all its edges inserted in a groove of a surrounding frame of thicker material. 5. A group of people empowered to look into and decide an issue. 6. A section of floor, wall, ceiling, or roof, usually prefabricated, that is one of several panels needed for assembly and erection of a building. A.K.A. **paneling**

panel door A door having stiles, rails, and possibly a mullion, forming one or more frames around (thinner) recessed panels.

paneled door See: **door styles** *NOTE: paneled doors are often described by the number of panels the door has, such as a 4- or 6-panel door.*

paneling A large, relatively thin board or sheet of lumber, plywood, or other material used as a wall covering. 2. A decorative wall or ceiling treatment with raised framelike borders and recessed surfaces.

panel insert A panel made to be inserted into a channel or frame, such as the face of a kitchen appliance, so that it matches the kitchen cabinetry.

panel mold Molding, traditionally used to cover the exposed or stepped edge of paneling. A.K.A. **panel molding**

panel saw A saw with closely set teeth for cutting a clean edge on sheet material. 2. A saw, set up to operate vertically, to cut plywood and other sheet material.

panel strip See: **batten**

panic hardware A device installed on exterior doors of public buildings that enables occupants, *by pushing a bar*, to quickly open the door and exit the building in an emergency.

panorama An unlimited view in all directions. **2.** A picture or series of pictures of a landscape, historical event, or discovery seen on a continuous surface.

pantheon A Roman temple dedicated to the gods. Specifically the Santa Maria Rotunda, built in 27 B.C., rebuilt in the 2nd century, and used as a Christian church since A.D. 607 **2.** A religiously ornamented church, like Westminster Abby, where famous people are buried.

pantograph An antique drafting instrument for copying drawings, plans, etc., either on the same scale or on an enlarged or a reduced scale. *NOTE: Writers used pantograph technology (circa 17th and 18th centuries) to make a duplicate copy of what they had written.*

pantry A cabinet or room for storing beverage and food supplies. A.K.A. **buttery, larder**

paper cutter A device with a long blade and table for cutting large sheets of paper.

paper felt See: **felt paper, construction paper**

papier-maché A material used for artistic expression, made principally of damp shredded paper and a flour paste, which can easily be molded into a desired shape or form.

papyrus A plant traditionally associated with the art and architecture of Egypt. *NOTE: The word **paper** is derived from papyrus, as the Egyptians made a paperlike writing material from papyrus around 3500 BC, later replaced by **parchment** (lambskin).*

parabolic reflector A reflector, often used in a light fixture, that directs the light in a particular direction.

parallel The juxtaposition of two lines or objects that are side-by-side to one another, such as railroad tracks.

parallelogram

parallelogram A slanted rectangle.

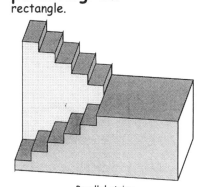

Parallel stairs

parallel stair A staircase consisting of flights that are parallel to each other and separated only by one or more intermediate landings.

parapet wall A low wall or railing, such as at the edge of a terrace or a sudden drop in grade

parascenium

(ground level), over which a view of the landscape can be seen. **2.** A dividing element, used both on the interior and exterior of a building.

parascenium An ancient theatrical term referring to projecting structures or wings flanking the stage, which included the actor's apartment.

parcel A legally recorded division of land subject to single ownership. **2.** Part of a larger area.

park A publicly owned area or parcel of land dedicated to recreation and the preservation of woodlands, pastures, and other open areas.

parking garage A structure with two or more tiers or levels designed exclusively to park or store automobiles and light trucks. *NOTE: Not for automobile repairs or service work.* A.K.A. **parking structure**

parking lot An open space for short-term parking and storing motor vehicles. A.K.A. **parking area**

parking space A marked-off space designated for one vehicle.

parking structure See: **parking garage**

parlor A room primarily for entertaining and conversing with guests. A.K.A. **sitting room** See: **living room**

parquet Strips or blocks of wood laid out in a geometric pattern. Used primarily in flooring and tabletops. A.K.A. **parquetry** **2.** Theatrically, the lower floor of

a theatre normally reserved for the orchestra, but used instead for seating.

parquet circle See: **orchestra pit**

parquetry Ornamental plaster objects applied to a flat surface, in relief. A.K.A. **parge work**

Parsons table A plain square or rectangular table with square straight legs, named after the **Parsons School of Design** where it was developed.

Parthenon In ancient Greece, a group of temples and religious statues within an area known as the *acropolis* meaning "uppermost city," considered the highest and most defensible part of the city.

partial payment Less than a full payment or a series of payments based on progress.

particleboard A durable building board (4' x 8' or 10' sheets) made of wood fiber chips glued together under heavy pressure and heat to various thicknesses. Used primarily for sheathing and construction grade decking. A.K.A. **chipboard**

parting bead A long narrow strip between the upper and lower sashes in a double-hung window. A.K.A. **parting stop, parting strip**

partition A interior dividing wall that separates one space from another.

parts per million *Abbr.* **ppm** A measurement describing the amount of a particular substance in water or air.

party wall A wall built on

the property line between two parcels of land owned by two different parties. Building this kind of wall requires an agreement between the two parties.

pass To go over something once, such as one layer of paint on a wall, scanning a page for content, or as an airplane passing over an airport.

passageway A corridor connecting one area or room of a building with another. A.K.A. **corridor, hallway**

passenger lift See: elevator

passive solar energy system Refers to solar collectors on the roof of a building that turn sunlight into electric power.

pass-through An opening in a wall for passing things from one room to another, usually between a kitchen and a dining room.

pastels Pale, soft, light shades of colors. 2. Pigment, in a chalklike form and available in a variety of colors, used by artists to create drawings.

patch In carpentry and joinery, a piece of wood or veneer glued into a recess to replace defective portions or to fill a void. A.K.A. **dutchman, plug** 2. A hole in a wall repaired with plaster or plastic compound.

patchwork A combination of many different things, often with no real connection to one another.

patchwork quilt A blanket,

bedspread, or comforter that is made from small pieces of fabric sewn together to form a unique design.

path See: footpath

patina A thin incrustation that forms on exposed wood and metal surfaces, which over time changes the color and character of the object, as exists with old wood or the greenish brown crust or film that forms on bronze and copper.

patio A paved courtyard, terrace, or enclosed area open to the outdoors, adjacent to a residence.

pattern A reoccurring design, such as in wallpaper and flooring. 2. A category of, or typical of. 3. A full-size model made in some easily worked material (such as paper) which serves as a layout or guide, with respect to form and dimensions.

patterned brickwork The various patterns, consisting of two or more colors, used to add interest to plain masonry walls. **dichromatic** brickwork describes a pattern using two colors of brick, while **polychromatic** brickwork describes patterns containing more than two colors.

pattern repeat In fabric and wallpaper, the actual distance between the start of a pattern object to the start of the next repetition of the same object.

pavement The durable surface material used in roads, sidewalks, or other outdoor areas.

paver Stone, brick, or tile used to pave a walkway or driveway. A.K.A. **paving stone**

PATTERN TYPES

MASONRY

AMERICAN BOND

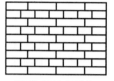

ENGLISH BOND

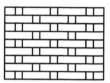

HONEYCOMB BOND

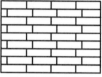

RACKING BOND

FLEMISH BOND

HEADER BOND

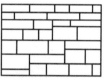

BROKEN RANGE

RUNNING / STRETCHER BOND

STACK BOND

PAVING

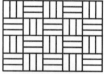

BASKET WEAVE

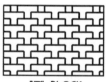

"T" BLOCK

HERRINGBONE

FABRIC

FLAME STITCH

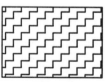

ZIG ZAG

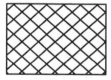

DIAMOND

MISC.

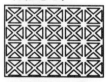

UNION JACK

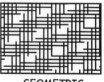

GEOMETRIC

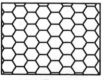

HONEYCOMB

paving The actual physical act of laying pavement or paving stones.

pavilion A detached or semi-detached structure used for entertainment or special occasions. **2.** A prominent portion of a facade, usually a central projection identified by height or form. **3.** A temporary structure or tent erected in a garden.

pavilion roof A roof hipped equally on all sides, so as to have a pyramidal form. See: **roof styles**

peak The highest part of something, such as the top of mountain.

peaked roof A roof, of two or more slopes, that rises to a ridge or peak.

peanut gallery The topmost balcony in a theatre.

pearlite A lightweight aggregate used to create a stuccolike finish. **2.** Used as thermal insulation and as an aggregate in concrete.

pearwood *(Wood)* A pinkish brown, finely grained hardwood frequently used in fine cabinetry and inlayed tops.

peat See: **peat moss**

peat moss A fibrous organic material in various stages of decomposition, generally dark brown to black in color. A.K.A. **mulch**

pedestal A decorative *(with molding)* supporting base or block for a statue or column. *NOTE: Without the decorative molding it would more correctly be called a plinth.*

pedestal sink A washbasin supported from the floor by a column-like base. A.K.A. **pedestal washbasin**

pedestal sink

pedestal table A tabletop supported by one or two pedestals, rather than the standard four legs.

pedestal table

pedestal washbasin See: **pedestal sink**

pediment A triangular or curved ornament, representing a Greek gable end roof, used over the entrances of buildings and windows of prestigious rooms. A.K.A. **fronton** See: **segmented pediment, broken pediment, scroll pediment,**

triangular pediment door

Pembroke table A small table with hinged leaves on all four sides of the top and a small drawer, Designed by **Thomas Sheraton**.

penalty clause A clause in a contract that spells out the

pencil

consequences (financial penalty) of the parties for failing to comply in a timely manner to the terms and requirements of the contract.

pencil An instrument used for writing and drawing that uses lead *(graphite)* to make a mark.

pencil rod Any rod having a diameter approximating that of a pencil.

pendant A suspended or hanging ornament.

pendentive arch A triangular transition piece that serves to connect and support a rotunda or vaulted dome over a square room. A.K.A. **compound arch**

pendentive arch

penetrating finish Any paint, varnish, etc., that penetrates below the surface of the material to which it is applied.

peninsula- base kitchen cabinet An isolated, counter height cabinet in the middle of a kitchen. **2.** A kitchen cabinet that extends into the room. A.K.A. **island cabinets**

penitentiary A facility built to house convicted criminals. Originally, a place where penance was performed.

pentagon An object with five equal sides. **2.** A 5-sided building, *once the world's largest office building*, and headquarters of the U.S. military.

The Pentagon Washington D.C.

penthouse An apartment or office on the top floor of a building.

percussion drill See: **hammer drill**

perforated metal Refers to sheet metal with a design, produced by a series of small holes (usually a small nail). Once used to decorate a kitchen cabinet, providing a safe place for baked goods to cool off.

performance standard Refers to the level of performance specific material or equipment is expected to meet.

pergola A covered walk on which garden plants are grown.

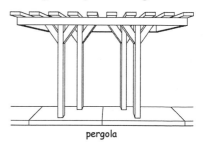

pergola

perimeter The outer boundary of an area or figure, such as a fence marking the extent of a piece of property.

perimeter-attached floor Flooring material that is glued only at the seams and along the perimeter.

period A theatrical term denoting a particular era, such as the Roaring '20s or the Victorian era.

periphery wall An exterior wall.

peristyle A continuous row of columns surrounding a building or court. **peristylium**

permafrost Permanently frozen subsoil in arctic or subarctic regions.

permit A document issued by a local municipality authorizing the applicant to do specific work.

perpendicular A line or object at right angle to another line or plane. 2. Refers to the vertical lines of English Gothic architecture (14th to 16th centuries), particularly in its intricate tracery, often rising into a curve or arch.

perron An exterior flight of stairs leading to an exterior landing and entrance.

personal injury A legal term referring to the bodily injury of a person, or to their reputation.

personal property Any property other than **real property** (land and the buildings and/or structures found on it).

perspective The position from which an object is viewed. 2. Point of view.

perspective drawing A 2-dimensional drawing depicting a 3-dimensional view of a room, building, or structure.

petit-point An embroidery term used to describe areas with a large number of stitches per square inch.

pew Wooden bench seating, as typically found in a church.

pewter An inexpensive substitute for silver, made from an alloy of tin and lead, with a dull gray appearance, used for tableware and ornamental objects.

phantom line
Architecturally, a broken line on a drawing indicating something above or below the plane of the drawing.

Philippine mahogany
(Wood) Refers to a variety of trees found in the rainforests of the world, particularly in the Philippines. Not a true mahogany, but resembles mahogany in grain. Used for interior carpentry, plywood, and general construction. See: **lauan**

Phillips-head A screw with a cross-slotted head, enabling a better grip with a screwdriver.

Phillips-head screwdriver A screwdriver with a Phillips-head bit or end to turn a Phillips-head screw.

phosphor A substance capable of radiating light (**luminescence**) for some time after exposure and absorption of ultraviolet light. **phosphorescence**

phosphorescent paint
Paint made with phosphor and used for its luminescent properties.

physical stability The ability of material to maintain its physical shape and size when exposed to conditions normally encountered in its service environment.

piano hinge See: **continuous hinge**

piano nobile Refers to the

piazza

first floor of a house and its elaborate large rooms with high ceilings, meant to impress and entertain influential guests. Particularly associated with Renaissance architecture.

piazza Italian word describing a public open space or square surrounded by buildings.

pick A hand tool, with a curved, pointed, double-sided steel head, used to break up compacted soil and rock.

picket fence A fence formed from a series of vertical stakes, often sharpened at the top and joined together by horizontal rails supported by posts at uniform intervals.

pickle finish A finish in which the base color, often green, comes through a whitewash glaze. **pickled finished** A.K.A. **washed finish**

picture light A small light fixture attached to a picture frame.

picture molding Any of many styles of moldings, at a level near the ceiling, where picture hooks are attached to avoid damage to the surface of the wall. A.K.A. **picture rail**

picture window A large fixed window, usually between two narrower operable windows, that is located to take advantage of an attractive view of the outdoors.

piece-dyeing See: **dip-dyeing**

piecrust table A small table with a scalloped or carved edge.

pier A heavy, usually unexposed vertical column *(a structural support)* buried deep into the ground as part of the foundation. 2. A column or pilaster lacking any finished or decorative details. A.K.A. **piling**

pigeonhole See: **egg crate**

pigment The finely ground organic or inorganic insoluble powder of various colors, used to produce paint when mixed with oil or water. As opposed to spectral colors as seen through an optical prism.

pigtail A connecting device, shaped like a "Y" that enables two electrical appliances to be plugged into one outlet.

pilaster A flat-faced column projecting from a wall, that is finished and detailed *(capital, base, etc.)*, as a traditional column. See: **engaged column** A.K.A. **engaged, pillar**

pilastrade A line of pilasters.

pile Reinforced concrete, steel, or wood column, embedded into the ground to carry a vertical load or to provide lateral support.

pile driver A machine with a tall shaft and a heavy weight, used to drive, with repeated blows, a steel pier or piling into the ground.

pilings A.K.A. **pier** 2. See: **carpet pile**

pillar Functionally, a supportive structural element, similar to a **column**, or **post**, but not circular in shape. See: **pilaster** A.K.A. **engaged pier, engaged column**

pillow back   Refers to upholstered furniture that has or appears to have loose back pillows. See: **attached pillow back, loose pillow back**

pilot hole A hole driven to (1) guide a screw along a path, and (2) to remove material to prevent **splitting** or **cracking** the increased pressure of a screw could cause.

pilot punch   A slight indentation, usually in metal, made with a hammer and pointed steel punch, to guide a high-speed drill bit and prevent it from straying.

pin Refers to a hardwood dowel used to lock together a mortis-and-tendon joint.

pinch bar   See: **crowbar** A.K.A. **wrecking bar, pry bar**

pin drill   A small finger-operated drill, used to bore a starter hole.

pine *(Wood)* A general term used to describe the wood of the pine tree. While all pine is considered **softwood**, there are two distinct types of pine, (1) **soft pine** (A.K.A. **sugar pine**) which is straight-grained and easy to mill, and (2) **hard pine** (A.K.A. **yellow pine**) used for general construction. See: **sugar pine, yellow pine**

pine cone

pine tar   A viscous black substance distilled from **pine** tree **sap** and used in paint, roofing materials, and disinfectants.

pin hinge See: **hinge pin**

pinhole A hole made by a pin or through which a pin passes. **2.** A descriptive term used to describe a very small hole or blemish.

pinnacle The apex of an arch or circle. **2.** A slender, pointed object at the top of a building, structure, or mountain peak. **3.** A turret, or part of a building elevated above the main building.

pipe A leakproof hollow tubular conduit for transporting liquids or gases.

pipe cutter   A tool with a sharp wheel used for cutting pipe or tubing by rotating and tightening around the pipe.

pipe elbow See: **elbow**

pipe hanger   A device used to support a pipe or group of pipes from a ceiling or other structural element.

pipe insulation   Thermal insulation manufactured to slip around pipes to prevent the contents *(usually water)* from freezing.

pipe thread   he screw threads *(either interior or exterior)* at the ends of pipes and fittings to facilitate connection from one to another.

pipe wrench   A hand tool with adjustable toothed jaws, used to rotate a pipe and tighten a connection.

piping An upholstery term that describes the covered cord used at cushion edges or at seams, giving a finished appearance. A.K.A. **welt, welting**

pit

pit An excavation resulting in a hole in the ground. **2.** A drop in the surface plane of a floor, such as occurs where an orchestra pit meets the stage.

pitch A term used to describe the slope of a roof, stairs, or grade expressed as a ratio of vertical rise to horizontal run, such as an 8-12 or 12-12 pitch. See: **roofs & pitches** **2.** An acoustical attribute describing a high or low frequency of sound. **3.** A dark, viscous distillate of tar used in paving. A.K.A. **coal tar pitch**

pitched roof A roof having one or more surfaces with a pitch, usually greater than 10 degrees. **2.** A roof having two slopes that meet at a central ridge. See: **roofs & pitches**

pitting The development of many small cavities on any surface.

pivoted window A window whose sash opens and closes by pivoting on pins vertically aligned at the top and bottom of the sash.

pivot point See: **fulcrum point** **2.** The axle or pin around which a window or door rotates.

placard A sign or notice displayed in a public place. A name plate or decorative panel. A.K.A. **plaque**

placement The placing or positioning of an object, such as a picture or piece of furniture. **placing**

plan A 2-dimensional drawing of a horizontal plane, as viewed from above, of the design, location, and dimensions of the project or parts thereof.

plancier The exposed underside of a projecting box, **cornice**, or **soffit**.

plane The line of any surface, as the surface of water. A.K.A. **surface plane** **2.** A carpenter's hand tool, with a slightly exposed inclined blade, used for removing, shaping, and smoothing wood surfaces. A.K.A. **wood plane**

plane

planer A machine, either stationary or portable, with a cylindrical cutting head to shave a surface or edge of a wooden plank until smooth. A.K.A. **planing machine**

planing The process of smoothing a wooden surface by evenly shaving off a small amount of material.

planing machine See: **planer**

plank Denotes a substantial machined wooden board, such as a 2x10 or 2x12 (See: **dimensional lumber**), that when set between two points will support the weight of an individual walking across it. **2.** Any of the articles or principles in a political party's platform.

planking The laying of **planks**, as in **flooring** or **decking**.

planning The process of analyzing and developing (**look and function**) the utilization of space to meet the clients needs. A vital part of any project that includes every aspect, both interior and exterior, insuring the completed building or facility operates at maximum efficiency.

plant Vegetation 2. A facility built to house a manufacturing operation.

planter A container *(ceramic pots, wooden boxes, or plastic container)*, in which a plant or tree is planted.

planting To plant organic vegetation, either from **seed** or **cutting**.

planting box See: **planter**

plant mix Any mixture of organic material, usually including various nutrients, used for planting trees and plants. A.K.A. **potting soil**

plant on A separately prepared object fastened to any surface.

plaque Any flat tablet used as decoration. 2. An inscribed tablet given to honor or in recognition of an accomplishment or service. A.K.A. **placard**

plaster A pastelike material applied to wall surfaces and ceilings that dries to a hard smooth surface. A material used in casting a variety of decorative objects. A.K.A. **plaster of Paris**

plasterboard See: **drywall**

plastic A natural or artificial polymer (predominately petroleum) that can be molded, shaped, extruded, cut, or worked into a variety of objects; available in numerous shapes and forms (sheets, rods, etc.), in various thicknesses and sizes.

plastic laminate A thin composite material, consisting of a stiff backing covered by a pictured or textured layer under a clear, hard-plastic, protective membrane, used extensively on countertops, furniture, and cabinets. A.K.A. **laminated plastic** NOTE: Also widely known as **Formica**, a trademarked brand name.

plate bolt A bolt used to secure the plate rail of a wall to the foundation. A.K.A. **expansion bolt, anchor bolt**

plate glass A large sheet of *(strong)* tempered glass, used for display windows, sliding glass doors, etc.

plate rail A narrow shelf, usually with corbels, along the upper part of the walls of a room, which is grooved to hold plates or other decorative items.

plates A stick-framing term used to describe the horizontal timbers, usually 2x4s, to which the studs are attached, top and bottom. A.K.A. **wall plates**

platform A raised floor of any size, such as a stair landing.

platform framing See: **framing**

plating A process for applying a thin coating of one metal to another, such as plating tin with brass. 2. The doubling of panes of stained glass to modify its appearance.

play A separation between moving parts to reduce friction.

plaza A Spanish word referring to a public square or open area in a town or city.

plenum The space either partly

Plexiglas

or fully filled with some kind of material, as opposed to a vacuum, such as an air-conditioning duct or the space between a suspended ceiling and the structure supporting it, that contains wiring, air ducts, lighting fixtures, etc.

Plexiglas An *(oil-based)* plastic material available in sheets of various thicknesses. *NOTE: Plexiglas, although a brand name, is a popularly used term to describe a variety of sheet plastic products, as Frigidaire (also a trademarked name) was used in the 1940s to describe the refrigerator, or Kleenex to describe facial tissue.*

pliers A pincerlike hand tool, usually with serrated jaws, used for gripping, holding, bending, and cutting.

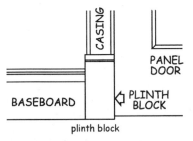

plinth block

plinth block A square or rectangular base, with little molding, that **columns**, **pilasters**, or **door casings** rest on and into which the baseboard **dies** (terminates). A.K.A. **skirting block** 2. A solid monument base, supporting a statue or memorial. 3. The base or base courses of an external wall or building collectively, so treated as to give the appearance of a platform.

plot A parcel of land consisting of one or more lots or portions thereof, which is described by survey and legally recorded. 2. A small area of ground. 3. The **printout** of a computer-generated drawing. See: **plotter** A.K.A. **printout**

plotter A large-format printer that produces a hard copy (plot) of a drawing, drawn on a computer. *NOTE: Some plotters are capable of producing drawings up to 52" wide by several hundred feet long, depending on the length of the roll of paper.*

plough To cut a groove or channel. **plow**

plug A short wooden dowel used to fill a recessed screw hole. 2. Any solid material used to fill a hole or opening. 3. Fibrous or resinous material used to fill a void and otherwise patch a surface. 4. In plumbing, a stopper for a drain opening or a fitting for closing the end of a pipe 5. A device on the end of an electrical cord that inserts into a wall outlet.

plumb Exactly vertical.

plumb bob A weighted, pointed piece of metal suspended from the end of a line to determine true vertical.

plumber An individual certified and licensed to install and repair plumbing.

plumbing A system of pipes, fixtures, and other apparatus that supplies water and removes liquid and waterborne wastes from a building.

plumbing contractor A

licensed individual or company specializing in the installation of pipes and plumbing fixtures. One of the many subcontractors (tradespeople) found on a construction site.

plumbing fixture
A receptacle (sink, toilet, tub, etc.) that receives and discharges water, liquid, or waterborne wastes into the drainage system to which it is connected.

plumb line
A cord or line attached to a metal bob or weight.

ply
Thin sheets of peeled log veneer that makeup the various layers of laminated plywood. See: plywood

plywood
A material consisting of pressure glued layers of ply. Available in a variety of thicknesses (1/8" increments), wood finishes and grades, in either 4'x8' or 4'x10' sheets. Used in cabinetry, structurally and as sheeting material. NOTE: Alternating layers of ply are stacked cross-grain to one another to prevent twisting or cupping.

PLYWOOD GRADING
The top and bottom layers and the type of glue are the primary determining factors in the 2 or 3-letter (either A, B, C, D, or X) plywood grading system. As a general rule, all plywood is made with a lesser grade of ply on the bottom than on top.

A = Finish grade, meaning it is a hardwood surface and can be stained, rather than painted.

C = Construction grade (paint grade), made from softwoods and used structurally. Expected to be covered over or painted. No voids

D = As "C," but with voids.

X = Used to denote that an exterior grade of glue was used and the plywood meets the basic standards for exterior use.

Cabinet grade is plywood with a hardwood (Birch, Oak, etc.) face and a smooth-finish softwood back without voids. Identified as AC grade.

Construction grade Any plywood other than Cabinet grade. Identified as CD, or CDX.

pneumatic drill
A drill powered by compressed air.

pocket
Any recess or cavity made to receive another object.

pocket door
A chamber, in a wall, that receives a sliding door when in the open position. NOTE: Often used in applications where swinging doors would be inconvenient, and especially useful for people in wheelchairs, as it enables a slightly wider opening.

podium
An elevated platform, such as a speaker's stand or an orchestra conductor's stand. 2. A balcony in an ancient Roman theatre for the emperor and others of high rank. 3. A low foundation wall, or raised platform upon which a building is built.

point
The exact location where something begins or ends, as the ends of a line.

pointed arch
A general term referring to any arch that comes to a point. A.K.A. equilateral arch

pointing
In masonry, the final treatment of joints by the troweling of mortar or a puttylike filler into the joints. 2. The

pole

removal of mortar from between the joints of masonry units and the replacing of it with new mortar. A.K.A. **repointing**

pole A long, slender, sometimes tapered log or round piece of wood.

police station A facility built specifically to meet the special needs and requirements of the police in a particular area.

polished finish To give, by rubbing and buffing, a sheen or gloss to the finished surface. A.K.A. **buffing**

polyester resin One of a group of synthetic resins that hardens when cured.

polyurethane finish An exceptionally hard and wear-resistant clear gloss or matte finish.

poplar *(Wood)* A durable, white to yellow, medium-dense softwood with a uniform grain. Easy to work, excellent surface for painting, and used in numerous applications, including flooring, shelving, and furniture parts. Similar in character to **cottonwood** A.K.A. **yellow poplar**

porcelain A hard, glossy, transparent, fine-grained, nonporous, baked-on finish coat, used primarily for dishes and plumbing fixtures. A.K.A. **china, ceramics**

porcelain enamel Vitreous (glassy), baked enamel finish.

porcelain tile A smooth, dense, impervious ceramic tile or paver.

porcelain tub A ceramic, usually over cast iron, tube having a slight shoulder on one side to accept a tub enclosure.

porch An open or semi-enclosed covered entrance to a building, with a separate roof, usually large enough for seating and walk space. May be screened or glass-enclosed. A.K.A. **portico, veranda, sun porch**

porch rail A handrail, usually extending between the posts that support an overhanging roof.

porte cochere An attached, covered **portico** projecting over a driveway to shelter passengers arriving in automobiles, carriages, other vehicles.

portfolio A representative collection of an artist's work that demonstrates their ability and artistic style.

porthole A round, sealable window on a ship.

portico An elaborate covered entrance to a building, usually with columns, often **colossal columns** *(two story)*, supporting a separate roof. A.K.A. **porch, veranda**

portland cement A cementitious binder for most structural concrete, made of lime, fly ash, air entraining agents, or other materials. Used primarily as mortar and as a main binding ingredient in concrete. Available in various mixes depending on the application.

portrait A picture, usually of a person(s), by either a painter or a photographer.

post Any vertical upright element, either supportive (supporting a roof) or not, that affords a firm point for lateral attachment (fence or rail). 2. To publicize or advertise by posting notices, etc. 3. A place (military base, guard station, country) where soldiers are stationed. 4. A position or job, particularly one which is made by appointment. 5. Mail. 6. A point in time after an event.

post-and-beam framing A type of construction in which the primary structural elements of a building are horizontal elements *(beams, lintel)* which rests atop a vertical **post**. A.K.A. **post-and-lintel**

post bracket A projecting bracket at the top of a post.

poster An advertisement or drawing.

poster board A thick, stiff paper used for signs and presentations.

post hole A hole dug in the ground to hold a post, such as a fence post.

Postimpressionism Describes a generation of artists *(late 1880s -1910)* in painting, that followed the influences of the Impressionists, but whose subject matter is seen through more realistic eyes, often in a less than picture-perfect setting. The artists most associated with Postimpressionism are Cezanne, Gauguin, Redon, Bonnard, Seurat, Toulouse-Lautrec, and van Gogh.

postmodernism A 1970s arts movement rejecting the stark austerity of the **international modern style**. Postmodernism reintroduced a decorative ornamental motif with garish colors and the illogical juxtaposition of objects, instead of a symmetrical relationship.

post office In the U.S.A., an office or building of the U.S. Postal Service, where letters and parcels are received, sorted, and distributed to various destinations for delivery. Post offices provide a number of services, including selling stamps and postal money orders.

pottery

pottery Clayware either fired or not.

pounce bag A bag filled with colored powder, used primarily by sign painters to transfer the position of a line, object, or letters through a series of small holes in a full-size pattern to the surface below.

powder room A public toilet for women. See: **lavatory** A.K.A. **Ladies room** 2. A small first-floor toilet in a house.

power Refers principally to electricity, which powers electric tools and appliances.

power drill A drill powered by electricity. See: **drill motor**

power house A building that houses a generator, which produces and/or distributes electricity.

power of attorney

power of attorney A legal document authorizing another to act as one's agent.

prairie architecture A more modern, simplified Frank Lloyd Wright rendition of the classic craftsman-style house, popular from 1900-1920. Emphasized horizontal lines with low-pitched overhung roofs, shading casement windows that look out onto long balconies or terraces. Also characterized by its detailed built-in furniture and fixtures that are treated as importantly as any architectural element. A.K.A. **prairie school** NOTE: Prairie style architecture has been making a comeback in popularity in recent years.

precast Said of concrete members produced off site.

preclassic A term used to describe the art, culture, and architecture of the people preceding the Greek, Roman, and Egyptian civilizations.

prefab Anything made in part or whole off site. **prefabricated**

prefab building A building (not including mobile homes or trailers) that is fabricated in a factory, rather than on site, but actually assembled on site. See: **manufactured building** A.K.A. **prefabricated building**

prefab construction A method of construction that relies on the use of standardized manufactured components assembled rather than fabricated on site.

prefab housing See:

prefabricated housing A.K.A. **manufactured housing**

prefabricated building See: **manufactured building**

prefabricated housing Housing, except for the foundation, that, through the use of computers, are custom designed and manufactured in a factory and shipped, in finished parts, to the construction site for assembly. NOTE: Prefab houses are usually less expensive because manufacturers are able to purchase materials in larger quantities, and because component parts are put together in an assembly line process, which is far more economical than standard building methods. Many prefab home builders are using state of the art technology or construction methods, which are accomplished more economically in a factory than on the job site. A.K.A. **manufactured housing**

printer A device attached to a computer that prints out a hard copy of text or drawings.

preliminary drawings Drawings prepared during the early stages of the design process to enable decisions to be made on future development.

preservation See: **restoration**

preservative A commercial chemical product used to treat wood so that it becomes waterproof and/or immune against attack by insects, etc.

presidio A Spanish word meaning a frontier outpost or fort.

pressed glass

pressed glass   Glass ornamented or shaped, in relief, by pressing into a mold.

pressure   Force that is exerted, for example, on the walls of a pipe or container, from the constraint of liquids or gases.

pressure treated lumber   Timber into which flame retardants, chemical preservatives, insect poison, and/or fungicides have been forced under pressure. A.K.A. **impregnated timber**

primary colors   The three primary colors are red, yellow, and blue, from which all other (secondary and tertiary) colors are made. Primary colors cannot be produced by combining any other colors. See: **color wheel**

primary light source The principal, or most dominant source of light when several sources of light are present, such as the sun during daylight hours or a specific lamp, in a room, at night.

primavera *(Wood)* A smooth blond hardwood with handsome graining, native to Mexico. Used primarily for paneling and highly polished contemporary furniture. Similar in characteristics to **korina**. A.K.A. **white mahogany**

primer A layer of paint, a first or base coat meant to seal and fill the wood, plaster, etc., to inhibit rust, and to improve the adhesion of subsequent layers of paint to the surface. A.K.A. **primer coat** 2. An explosives device into which a detonator or detonating cord is inserted or attached.

primer coat A base coat of paint, made specifically to address the needs of various materials, as opposed to a finished coat of paint containing color.

primitive   A term used to describe the art of early native, often extinct, cultures.

principal   A legal term referring to the person on whose behalf, or in whose name, an agent is operating. 2. In stick framing, the most important structural element, such as a truss, that supports the roof. 3. The amount still owed on a loan to which interest is applied.

printout A copy of a computer-generated drawing or report, printed on paper. A.K.A. **hard copy, plot**

prism An extruded multisided glass object that refracts and disperses light into a spectrum of color. **prismatic glass**

prism

prison   See: **penitentiary**

private residence   A dwelling occupied only by a single individual or the members of a single-family unit. A.K.A. **home, dwelling**

privy A lavatory or bathroom.

producer   Someone who manufacturers, processes, or assembles a commercial product. 2. Theatrically, a title applied to the person(s) leading or responsible for overseeing all aspects of a production.

produce stand

produce stand A small stand a farmer sets up to sell produce. A.K.A. **farmers market**

production designer A film and television industry title given to the art director in charge of the artistic look of a production.

profile A side view of the shape of something, such as a section through a piece of molding, or as through the numerous underlying strata of earth. **2.** An engineering term used to describe the shape of an object at various points along an elevated plane, such as in the construction of airplanes and ships, which at various points take on different shapes and measurements.

produce stand

project The planning and construction of a particular building, structure, remodel, or creation of any setting, from conception to completion.

project budget The sum of money established by the owner as available to cover all the costs (land, professional services, materials, labor, etc.) associated with all aspects of the project.

projecting window See: **bay window**

projection Any element, part, member, or component that juts out from a building or structure.

projection booth Theatrically, a booth or projection equipment room at the rear of a theatre or auditorium from which, through small openings, motion pictures or still film slides are projected.

project site The property on which the project (building, structure, etc.) is to be constructed.

promenade A place suitable for walking for pleasure, as a mall.

prop A post or brace. **2.** Theatrically, any object (guns, magic tricks, explosions, etc.) used to add interest, reality, and/or authenticity to a performance. A.K.A. **property**

propeller fan A fan that looks and operates like the propeller of an airplane (non-jet), used primarily to circulate and exhaust air.

property The ownership of any real or personal assets. **2.** See: **prop**

property line The recorded boundary of a plot of land.

property room Theatrically, a room where furnishings and props are stored when not being used. **2.** In a police station, a room where property (recovered property, prisoners personal property, evidence, etc., are kept for safekeeping.

proportion The artistic and harmonious relationship between things or the various parts of the whole, in terms of their size, quantity, or importance.

proposal An offer to provide certain materials and labor to perform a specific job at a specified price.

proscenium A theatrical term describing the whole stage.

prosce nium arch An arch over a stage.

protection See: alarm system A.K.A. **security**

prototype An early sample of a particular product.

protractor An instrument for measuring an angle, in degrees.

protractor

Prussian blue *(Color)* A deep blue pigment. Denotes royalty. A.K.A. **Chinese blue**

pry bar See: **crowbar** A.K.A. **wrecking bar, pinch bar**

public access Open to the general public.

public address system A system designed to audibly project, as to magnify, the human voice or replication thereof, so that people in the back of an audience can hear as well as those within normal speaking and listening range. A.K.A. **sound-amplification system**

public area Any area that is always free and open to the general public.

public corridor A common or publicly used passageway or corridor connecting sites, buildings, suites, etc., to staircases, exits, parking, etc. **2.** Refers to the common areas the occupants and visitors of a particular floor of a building use.

public garage Denotes an enclosed facility, often a multistoried building, for the temporary parking or storage *(only)* of motor vehicles, and made available to the general public for a specified price per hour, day, or longer.

public housing Low-cost housing owned, sponsored, or administered by a municipal or other government agency.

public nuisance An individual or condition that has caused a disturbance or disruption in the normal calm of a street, neighborhood, community, etc. A.K.A. **nuisance**

public space All interior or exterior space designated for use by the general public.

public utility Refers to companies, either publicly or privately owned, that are contracted to provide, at least, basic water, gas, electricity, telephone, sewers, and other services to a particular community or area.

pueblo Refers to both the ancient communal dwellings of the Pueblo Indians and the Spanish colonial heritage of the American Southwest, characterized by adobe flat roof dwellings. Other than the basic look of the structures, the two styles are vastly different, with the large, Spanish, walled-in haciendas contrasting dramatically with the

pueblo revival

small communal dwellings cut into or built onto and excavated hollows in the face of cliffs or on mesas, with ladder access. Obviously, both groups were extremely concerned about security.

pueblo revival   Refers to the art and architecture of the early Southwest, with flat roofs, rounded adobe walls, and stepped or terraced upper stories.

pull   A handle for opening a door, window, drawer, etc.

pulley   A wheel with a grooved rim to carry and guide a rope or other line attached to a sheave (or block) prohibiting the line from getting tangled. A.K.A. **block-and-fall**

pulley block   A frame or case containing one or more pulley sheaves, such as found in a **block-and-fall**.

pulpit   An elevated speaker's stand. *NOTE: Teddy Roosevelt spoke of the presidency as a "bully pulpit" because everyone listens to what the president has to say.*

pumice   Lava having a highly porous, loose, spongy, or cellular structure, used for polishing because of its slightly abrasive properties.

pumice stone   A solid block of pumice, used to polish or rub painted or varnished surfaces.

pump   A device (using pressure, suction, or both) to move fluids from one location or level to another.

pump room   A room in

which a pump is installed and operated.

punch   A small, pointed metal tool used to mark a starter hole.

punch list   A list of items or work still remaining to be finished or completed. A.K.A. **to-do list, inspection list**

punch press   A large machine that punches sheet metal into various shaped parts.

purchaser   The buyer or agent for the buyer, of property and materials.

pure design   An artistic theory that says our ideals of beauty, in art and design, are ruled by a universal set of fundamentals and principles.

purge   To eliminate, as bleeding the pressure out of an air line or blowing out a gas line.

purlin   A piece of timber laid horizontally to support or brace principal rafters. **2.**   Often attached to rafters as nailing for the roof covering. **purline** See: **rafter details**

push-button   A device to trigger or start an electrical device in motion.

push plate   A plate applied to the lock stile of a door to protect it against soiling and wear. **finger plate, hand plate**

putty   A general term applied to a heavy, pastelike composite material, such as that used to fill holes and cracks in wood prior to painting.

putty knife

putty knife A knife with a broad flexible blade used for laying on putty.

putty mold Wood molding used instead of glazing compound. A.K.A. **glazing mold, glazing fillet, glass stop**

pylons A monumental mass or tower flanking an entrance or gateway. Usually at a ceremonial entrance to a city, temple, or the entranceway to a bridge.

pyramid A massive memorial structure of stone or brick, with a square base and four sloping, triangular sides meeting at the apex, used by ancient Egyptians and Central American Indians to bury royalty.

pyramid hipped roof A pyramid-shaped roof with four equal sides.

- Q -

quad Refers primarily to an open courtyard at the University of Oxford. 2. See: **quadrangle**

quadrangle A large open triangular or rectangular area surrounded by buildings, typically found on university campuses.

quality assurance The process of randomly analyzing, inspecting, and testing parts to ensure they meet required standards and quality, so that in the final assembly of a product, everything will fit together and work as expected. A.K.A. **quality control**

quarrel One of the many diamond-shaped windowpanes in a **lattice, quarrel,** or **quarry window**. A.K.A. **quarry**

quarrel window See: **lattice window** A.K.A. **quarry window**

quarry Refers to a stone quarry, which is an open excavation where stone for buildings is extracted. 2. See: **quarrel**

quarry window See: **lattice window** A.K.A. **quarrel window**

quarter A term used to describe the thickness of roughly milled lumber, usually hardwoods. Each quarter is a quarter inch, e.g., 4-quarter or 5-quarter stock.

quartering Dividing anything into four equal, or nearly equal, pieces.

quarter round Refers to a (convex) quarter circle of molding.

quarters Generally a military term referring to housing.

quartz A brilliant crystalline mineral, silica dioxide, most abundant in a colorless transparent form, but also found in various colored, semiprecious stones. Very hard, will scratch glass.

quartz-halogen lamp A lamp with a tungsten filament encased in a quartz envelope that is capable of working at higher temperatures, thereby emitting more light than a glass bulb.

quaternary A term used to describe a hue, the result of mixing tertiary colors with adjoining primary or secondary colors.

Queen Anne An art and architectural style popular in England and named after Queen Anne, *early 18th century*, revived *in the U.S. (1870-1910)*. Another of the Victorian "ladies," but not as frilly as most. Characterized by multiple steep roofs, porches with decorative gables, and windows of various styles including bay windows, and the use of a variety of colors, textures, and materials. Many featured large verandas, turrets, and sleeping porches.

Queen Anne sash
The incorporation of small squares of stained glass along the outer edge of the upper sash of a double-hung window.

Queen Anne sash

quilting A method of sewing together many pieces of small fabric to make one large piece of material.

quoins Large blocks of stone, wood, or brick arranged to accentuate the corner of a building. Normally laid in alternating large and small blocks. May also serve as a structural element. A.K.A. **coins, coin stones**

quoins

-R-

rabbet A longitudinal channel, groove, or recess cut out of the edge or face of a surface. Often created to receive another element, such as a backing or interlocking *(joinery)* end panel of a cabinet. A.K.A. **rebate**

rabbet joint See: **rabbet**

raceway A facility built especially for racing, includes people, cars, motorcycles, bicycles, etc.

rabbet joint

radial-arm saw A circular saw which is suspended from above and travels along a cantilevered arm, used to cut boards or planks to length; however, the blade can be set at any angle or tilted for compound miter cuts. A.K.A. **cut-off saw**

radiance The rate of radiant heat emitted from each heating unit.

radiant floor heating system See: **hydronic radiant floor system**

radiant heat Heating transmitted by radiation from a central source, such as a heater, rather than from conduction or convection.

radiator Anything that radiates. **2.** A system of coils or pipes through which hot water or steam circulates, so as to radiate heat within a room or series of rooms.

RAFTER DETAILS

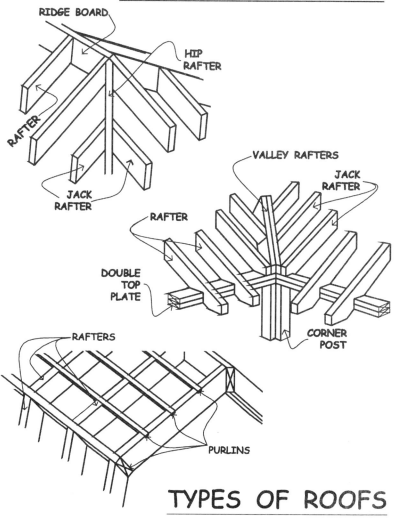

RIDGE BOARD

HIP RAFTER

RAFTER

JACK RAFTER

VALLEY RAFTERS

JACK RAFTER

RAFTER

DOUBLE TOP PLATE

CORNER POST

RAFTERS

PURLINS

TYPES OF ROOFS

GABLE

GABLE & VALLEY

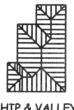

HIP & VALLEY

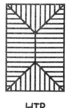

HIP

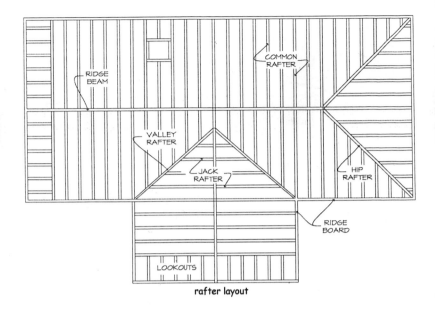

rafter layout

rafter One of a series of inclined structural lumber that runs from the ridge beam down to the wall upon which it rests, and to which a roof covering is affixed. A.K.A. **common rafter** See: rafter details

    TYPES OF RAFTERS
     common rafter
     hip rafter
     valley rafter
     jack or cripple rafter
     principal rafter
     false rafter
     show rafter

rafter ends See: rafter tails

rafter tails That portion of the rafter that overhangs the wall on which it rests. A.K.A. **rafter ends**

rag-rolled finish A painting technique achieved by rolling a piece of twisted rag over a coat of wet paint or glaze, so as to remove or build up portions of

RAFTER TAILS

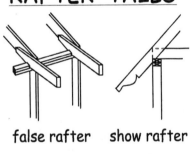

false rafter   show rafter

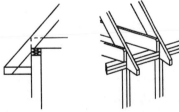

box cornice   rafter tail

it, and also showing the color of the base coat. A.K.A. **ragging** See: **bagging**

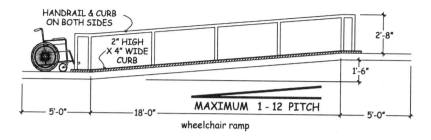

HANDRAIL & CURB
ON BOTH SIDES

2" HIGH
X 4" WIDE
CURB

2'-8"

1'-6"

MAXIMUM 1 - 12 PITCH

5'-0"   18'-0"   5'-0"

wheelchair ramp

rail   A horizontal or angled element, such as a handrail, or the horizontal parts of a panel door or window sash.   **2.** Any openwork construction or railing used to designate a path, provide a barrier or anything similar. **railing**

railroad The system of tracks that a train runs on.   **2.** An expression used in upholstery to indicate that the material is to run horizontally rather than vertically.

railroad station A depot where trains regularly stop and passengers and freight are loaded, unloaded, or wait while in transit.

rain spout   The tube or pipe that allows rainwater collected by the roof gutters to move to ground level and away from the building.

raised floor   An area where the floor level   rises (intentionally) above the floor level of the house or building.

raised panel   A panel with the center portion on the same plane or thicker than its border or frame.   A.K.A. **fielded panel** *NOTE: When exposed on both sides (as on both sides of a door), it is called a double raised panel.*

rake   Refers to the slope or inclination from a horizontal plane, such as a ramp, auditorium floor, staircase, pediment gable, etc.

rake mold   A board or molding along the sloping edge of the roof. A.K.A. **rake board, raking mold, barge mold, barge board**

ram   A heavy weight used to drive pilings into the ground. **2.** *A* computer term meaning **random access memory**, which is the memory in the computer that programs operate in, as opposed to **rom**. See: **rom**

ramp   A sloped surface connecting two or more planes at different levels.

Ramset A tool used to drive *(with an explosion)* a concrete nail through a plate rail and into a concrete footing. *NOTE: this tool is literally a gun and requires certification to operate.* Ramset is a trademarked brand-name.

ranch A relatively large parcel of land, generally dedicated to raising livestock, but not always and not exclusively.

ranch house   The main residence on a farm or ranch. **2.** A sprawling, low-pitched, one-story house with an open interior plan, large picture windows, sliding glass doors, and few if any steps; for informal casual living and entertaining in an indoor/outdoor atmosphere.

random course A masonry term used to describe a pattern of various-sized block or stone, so that there are no continuous horizontal lines.

random widths Shingles, boards, etc., of nonuniform widths.

range An appliance that provides heat, at several outlets, for cooking. A.K.A. **stove top 2.** Open land.

range hood A device installed over a cooking surface that draws in air to capture and expel smoke, hot air, and odors.

rasp A coarse file with varying degrees of protruding pointed teeth.

rattan Furniture that is made from bamboo.

raw edge An unfinished or cut edge. See: **factory edge**

rayon Continuous-filament yarn synthetically produced by pressing and solidifying cellulose filament strand.

razor blade The kind of disposable blade commonly use by painters and artists.

razor blade

readily accessible Direct access without obstruction.

reading room Often a room in a library, furnished with comfortable chairs and/or desks A.K.A. **library**

ready-mixed concrete Concrete, mixed to specifications and delivered to the site, ready to pour into concrete forms.

real estate Real property in the form of land, including any and all buildings erected on it. A.K.A. **real property**

realism An artistic representation of forms and objects as they actually are, to photographic accuracy.

real property Land, everything growing on it, and all improvements made to it. Usually includes rights to everything beneath the surface, and some rights to the airspace above it. A.K.A. **real estate**

reamer A tool with a tapered spiral or fluted cutting edges along its shaft. Used, usually, on pipe material to enlarge an opening or remove the burrs left from cutting.

rebar Reinforcing steel bars or rods, that are shaped and wired together to form a skeleton within a concrete wall or structure, to better resist stress and force. See: **reinforced concrete** A.K.A. **reinforcing rod**

rebate A.K.A. **rabbet 2.** A monitory give back, given as an incentive to purchase something.

receptacle A device installed in an outlet box to receive a plug from an electrical equipment or appliances. See: **duplex-receptacle**

reception room A room dedicated to receiving clients or

patients, with comfortable seating where people can temporarily wait.

recess Any shallow depression in a surface.

recessed fixture A light fixture installed into the ceiling, so that only the lower edge of the fixture is exposed.

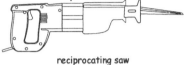

reciprocating saw

reciprocating saw A power tool that quickly moves a saw blade back and forth, used to rough cut virtually anything. A.K.A. **Sawzall** *(a trademarked name)*

rectangle A figure consisting of two sets of parallel, equal sides.

rectangle

recycling bin A container to collect recyclable material.

recycling symbol The international symbol for recycling.

red cedar *(Wood)* See: **western red cedar**

recycling

red gum *(Wood)* A handsome, reddish brown, fine-grained hardwood, used primarily for veneered doors, paneling, and furniture. Selected specimens may even be found to imitate the striking figure of **Circassian walnut**. (See: **Appendix: Woods**) In addition to various stained finishes, used to imitate a variety of other woods, including walnut, mahogany, and maple. A natural finish and wax produces a handsome satiny effect that wears remarkably well. *NOTE: Sap gum is the sapwood of the same tree, and is much lighter in color.*

red oak *(Wood)* A coarse-grained oak (hardwood) of eastern North America, of light brown or red color. Used predominately for furniture, built-in cabinets, and wainscoting. See: **oak**

red oxide A natural or synthetic red pigment used in paints.

reducing coupling A transition connector between two different sizes of pipe.

redwood *(Wood)* A strong, durable, straight-grained softwood from the Pacific Coast of the U.S. Light red to deep reddish brown in color and used extensively for exposed exterior applications because it is resistant to decay and insects. *WARNING: REDWOOD TREES ARE AN ENDANGERED SPECIES.*

redwood bark Shredded bark of the redwood tree; often used as loose fill around plants or as a decorative ground covering.

reed A strawlike material prepared for thatching a roof.

refectory A communal dining hall at a college or church.

refectory table A long narrow dining table, used for communal dining.

reference line Any line that serves as a reference or base to measure from. **2.** A line used to

reference mark

indicate the direction and limitations of any dimensioned space.

reference mark A usually small, precisely placed, permanent **ground marker** enabling the reestablishment of a surveying point (**station**), to which it is related by an accurately measured distance and azimuth (**bearing**).

reference point Any point on a drawing from where something is referenced as to distance or size.

refinements Intentional deviations from mechanical exactness in architectural design; to subtly add artistic variety and interest.

reflected ceiling plan A plan view *(from above)* drawing of a building depicting information relating to the ceiling structure, rather than the floor, such as for the tile and fixture layout for a dropped ceiling.

reflection Light bouncing off a reflective surface.

reflective glass Window glass with an outside, transparent metallic coating to reflect, rather than absorb, the light and radiant heat that strikes it.

reflector A polished metal or glass surface positioned to reflect the light from a particular source.

reflector lamp An incandescent bulb containing a reflective material, thus increasing *(almost doubling)* the amount of light omitted by the lamp, without increasing energy input.

refrigerator A large kitchen appliance used to keep food cold and fresh. **2.** A temperature-controlled cold room or series of rooms used to temporarily store large quantities of fresh food.

refuse See: **garbage** A.K.A. **rubbish, trash**

Regency style A style of architecture reminiscent of America's colonial period, *circa 1870s*, copied from Europe; **Georgian** and **Federal**, in particular. Characterized by a balanced facade with large double-hung windows, Palladian windows, gambrel roofs, and an emphasized front **portico** entrance, including decorative door crowns, pediments, fanlights, and/or sidelights.

register A grille with a damper to regulate the quantity of air passing through it. A.K.A. **registered vent**

regulation Refers primarily to rules established by the administrative agency pursuant to authority delegated to it by legislation that permits or forbids conduct.

rehabilitation The repair, alteration, or modification of a building to a useful state. A.K.A. **retrofit**

reimbursable expenses Money advanced, on behalf of the owner, to purchase parts or materials.

reinforced concrete A concrete wall or structure within which is embedded a skeleton of steel rods *(rebar)*, meant specifically to tie together and strengthen the overall structure. A.K.A. **ferro-concrete**

reinforcing rod
Any of a variety of steel rods used in reinforced concrete. A.K.A. **rebar**

related trades
In building construction, the various subcontractors with specialized skills or specialized equipment, such as framers, plumbers, drywallers, plasterers, painters, electricians, heating and air-conditioning specialists, pavers, etc., required to complete the project.

release agent
In molds or concrete forms, any coating or material used to prevent a molded or formed object from bonding to the mold or form.

relief
Carving, chasing, or embossing raised, *for prominence,* above a background plane. See: **bas-relief** A.K.A. **undercut, high relief** 2. Used generally to describe an elevation or projection from a surface or plane. **3.** In topographic mapping, the representation of the variation in height of the earth's surface, often mapped relative to a mean-sea level.

relief map
A map depicting the contours of the earth's surface by means of contour lines, shading, tinting, or a 3D relief model. A.K.A. **hypsometric map**

reliquary
A small elaborately decorated receptacle designed to hold a sacred relic.

relieve
Refers to temporarily or permanently redirecting structural support, for repair or renovation.

relieving arch
A soldier course arch *(decorative rather than structural)* that appears embedded in the building because it does not protrude beyond the plane or surface of the wall.

remodel
A renovation.

rendering

Renaissance

remodeling A.K.A. **alteration, renovation**

Renaissance A rebirth. Refers to the Italian Renaissance in art and architecture from 1420 to the mid-16th century, which rejuvenated the motifs and principles of ancient Greek and Roman classic architecture and integrated it with the Italian architecture of that period.

rendering A usually colored perspective or elevation drawing illustrating the various colors, materials, etc., of a proposed project or portion thereof, giving all those involved in the project a common image of its planned outcome.

rent Financial compensation by a renter to a landlord for one month's use of a dwelling or commercial space. Differs from a lease in that the renter is obligated only for a short period of time. See: **lease**

reproduction The recreation, *not necessarily an exact copy*, of an original design.

reservoir A receptacle or enclosed space for the collection or retention of fresh clean water.

residence Any dwelling. Someone's home or the family dwelling, not necessarily owned by the occupant.

residual sound See: **reverberation**

resilient flooring Refers to manufactured flooring material *(linoleum sheets and tiles)* that is impervious to minor liquid spills, stains, permanent marks, and is long lasting.

resin A general term used to describe various nonvolatile, semisolid synthetic or organic material, used for a variety of applications, but generally a material that when mixed with another compound hardens into a solid object.

resistance The power of any substance or building material to resist force, often the forces of nature.

resistor A device used to control the flow of current within an electrical circuit.

resonance Vibrating or oscillating sound waves.

restaurant A building or part thereof that houses a business that prepares and/or serves meals.

restaurant booth
Separated dining tables with upholstered bench seating, typically used in restaurants.

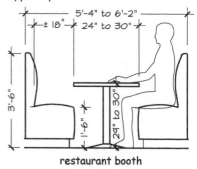

restaurant booth

restoration Recreating the original splendor, form, and details of an object or building.

restriction

restriction On land, an encumbrance limiting its use, imposed by the local authorities for community or mutual protection.

resurfacing The replacing or reconditioning of the finish of an existing surface.

retaining wall A wall built to restrain the lateral movement of earthen fill. Used in instances when there is a sudden drop in the contour of the land, as in step grading.

retardation Reduction in the rate of hardening, or prolonging the setting time to produce a harder final set strength.

retention The rate at which a material retains a chemical, as cloth accepting a coloring dye. **2.** The contractual withholding of final payment for a stipulated period of time after acceptance of the completed work.

reticulated molding Molding with a design of a geometric network of interlaced repeating lines. Popular in the Byzantine and Romanesque styles.

retrofit A commercial space or facility that is renovated and used for something other than for what the building or structure was originally designed. See: **rehabilitation 2.** An option added after a product was originally manufactured, such as installing a radio in an automobile.

return The continuation of a molding or cornice in a different direction, usually at right angles, such as around a corner. Often a small piece of molding that finishes off a molding detail by returning it into the wall.

reveal A standard offset, usually a 1/4" from the surface of a jamb, where door and window casing is placed. A.K.A. **offset, set-in**

reverberation The persistence of sound in an enclosed space (room or auditorium) after the source of the sound has stopped. A.K.A. **residual sound**

reverse Refers to using the scheme of a dwelling in reverse profile, for variety. **2.** Using the side of fabric or material not intended as the finished face. **3.** The side of the coin with the least important design.

reverse ogee A cutting bit with a profile opposite that of a standard ogee profile. Used for applications such as a drop-lid table, where the leaf (that portion of the table which moves) hinges on the legged portion of the table. See: **ogee** A.K.A. **reverse O.G.**

revolving door An exterior door consisting of four leaves (at 90° to each other) which pivot about a center post, usually within a cylindrically shaped vestibule. Used predominately in cold weather areas to prevent the direct passage of air through the vestibule and eliminate drafts of cold air from the outside. A.K.A. **turnstile door**

rheostat An electric device that controls the flow of electric current. A.K.A. **dimmer switch**

rib

rib A curved structural member, the equivalent of a stud but with a shape, not straight, that forms the shape of the object it is a part of, such as the exoskeleton ribs of a ship or plane. **2.** A raised ridge or fold that is formed in sheet metal to provide stiffness.

ribband back Chair backs designed to look like interlaced flowing ribbons. Characteristic of Chippendale style. **riband back**

ribbed panel A panel either decorative or structural that consists of a series of beadlike ribs.

ribbon A decorative ribbon belt that runs around a house or room. **2.** A long thin strip(s) of wood, as used in marquetry. **3.** In stained glass, a bar of lead to hold the edge of the glass. A.K.A. **came**

rich mix A concrete or mortar mixture containing a high ratio of binder to aggregate, thus providing better spread and workability. A.K.A. **fat mix**

ridge The horizontal line at the top of a mountain or roof.

ridge beam A longitudinal beam that supports the upper ends of the rafters, forming the apex of a roof. A.K.A. **ridgepole, ridgeboard, ridge piece, ridge plate**

ridgecap Any material used to cover the ridge of a roof. A.K.A. **ridge capping, ridge cover** *NOTE: Modern insulation techniques suggest the use of a vented ridgecap to allow moisture to escape from an otherwise sealed structure.*

riding house A building designed specifically for riding horses indoors.

rigger The person(s) that plans and sets up the required rigging. **2.** A thin, long-haired brush used in precision painting.

rigging A system of ropes and pulleys used to move or set heavy objects, including theatrical scenery.

rigging line A rope or cable that controls the contraction or relaxation of the **block-and-fall** system used in stage rigging.

right angle A 90° angle.

right-of-way Any strip or area of land, which includes the surface, underground, and overhead space, granted by deed or easement for the construction and maintenance of roadways and public utilities (power and telephone lines, and gas, oil, water, and sewer pipelines, etc.

rigidity The property of inflexibility of a material or the ability to resist changes in the object's shape.

rim The border or outer edge of anything circular or continuously curved. **2.** Descriptive of any finish hardware designed to be applied to the face of a door or window, rather than mortised in.

rim joist Refers primarily to the doubled joist that runs around and structurally supports the joists of a section of floor.

rinceau *(Fr)* Ornamentation that incorporates, either carved or painted, intertwined foliage as a design element.

rinceau

ring Refers primarily to a boxing or wrestling ring. Often referred to as the *squared* ring.

rink Refers primarily to an ice-skating rink, but also a roller-skating rink.

rip Cutting board or plywood into long strips. **ripping**

ripsaw See: **table saw**

rise A term used to describe the vertical distance from one level to another, such as the height of a flight of stairs from landing to landing or from one step to the next. See: **staircase details** 2. The slope of a roof, expressed in terms of its vertical height. See: **roof pitch** 3. In an arch, the vertical distance from the spring line to the highest point (**apex**) of the arch. 4. The vertical distance of travel of an elevator. See: **travel**

rise and run A numeric description of the vertical rise of an inclined surface or stairs compared to its horizontal run. See: **roof pitch**

riser Any *(vertically)* raised surface, such as a raised step, platform, or floor. 2. A general term used to describe a supply pipe or duct, used to distribute electric power, air, water, gas; or a vent pipe, vertically, one full story or more.

rivet Any of a number of metal fasteners used to connect two metal plates together, by passing a rivet *(a short pin with a head on one end)* through a hole in both plates. Once in place the rivet is either mechanically altered or is hammered down to form a second head, so it can't be removed.

riveting The process of uniting various parts with rivet fasteners.

rock Solid natural mineral material, found as small stones or as large masses, which are excavated from a stone quarry.

Rococo A style of art and architecture of early 18th century France *(the final phase of the Baroque period)*, characterized by lightly colored, elaborate, and profuse ornamentation accomplished with delicacy and refinement. *NOTE: The name originates from the prominent use of rocaille and coquille (meaning rock and shell in French) motifs in its decoration.*

rod A solid, long, round **dowel** of metal, wood, or plastic.

roll Any material distributed in rolls of long narrow sheets, such as wallpaper, felt (tar) paper, even metal sheeting.

rolled Any material formed into a cylinder by running it through a series of rollers to bend it.

roll-up door A manual or motor-driven door made of narrow horizontal slats that travel *(as a unit)* along a track or that curls around itself to open and close.

rom

196

rom A computer term meaning **read only memory**, representing hard disk space where programs are stored. Computer programs operate in **ram**. See: **ram**

Roman architecture
The architecture of ancient Romans.

Romanesque The style of art and architecture that emerged in western Europe early in the 11th century, incorporating Roman and Byzantine elements. Characterized by massive intricate walls and structures with round arches and vaults.

Romanesque revival
(1870 - 1890) A more stylistic version of Romanesque but certainly as a robust, with massive masonry foundations of stone under a brick upper facade. Rich textures include deeply recessed windows, splayed stoop, and densely carved decorations.

Roman shade A flat fabric shade that folds into horizontal pleats when raised.

roof The protective covering on top a building, including all the materials used in its construction (such as supporting rafters, plywood sheeting, and tile covering), necessary to carry it.

roof covering The material used on the surface of a roof that is exposed to the weather. The most popular roof covering today is asphalt shingles, because of their fire-retardant properties and ease of installation. A.K.A. roofing material

TRADITIONAL ROOFING MATERIALS
Natural
 bark, sod, thatch, wood boards, wood shingles, slate
Metal
 copper, zinc, lead, tin-plates, galvanized aluminum
Manufactured Materials
 ceramic tile, tar and gravel, asphalt shingles

roof garden A small garden on the flat roof of a building.

roof hatch A hinged panel cover that provides a weather-tight means of access to a roof.

roofing Any material *(shingles, slate, sheet metal, or tile)* used as a roof covering.

roofing material See: **roof covering**

roofing nail A short galvanized nail with a barbed or rink shank and a large flat head, made and used specifically to attach roofing felt and shingles to a plywood roof-deck or roof boards.

roofing tile A tile, of any material (asphalt, concrete, or clay), manufactured specifically to protect a roof from the weather, especially rain.

roof light See: **skylight**

roof line The contour or shape of a roof.

roof pitch The slope of a roof, expressed in terms of its vertical rise and horizontal run. See: **roofs & pitches**

roof structure See: **roof** 2. A structure that sits on a roof, such as an antenna, cooling tower, or sign supports.

rooftop   The very top of a house or building.

room   An area within a dwelling or building that is separated from other parts of the house or building by walls.

root   That portion of a plant that grows underground. 2. Often used to describe the origin of something, like a word.

rope   A strong thick line, comprised of a number of twisted or braided strands of fiber (such as hemp). When made of twisted wire it is called **cable**.

rope molding   Wooden or plaster molding made to resemble the look of a piece of thick rope.

rosette   A circular or oval decorative wood plaque, usually in a floral motif, traditionally used as a decorative element around doors, windows, and staircases.

rosette

rose window   A circular window with muntins radiating from its center. Often filled with stained or beveled glass.

rosewood   *(Wood)* A high-density hardwood with fine reddish brown to violet color and black streaks. Native to West Africa, East India, and Brazil. Used for highly polished modern furniture, paneling, cabinetry, and musical instruments.   A.K.A. **Brazilian rosewood, bubinga, jacaranda**

rostrum   A slightly elevated platform for addressing an audience.

rot   A wasting away, crumbling, or chemical decomposition of wood by fungi and other microorganisms that reduce strength, density, and hardness. **rotted, rotten, rotting** A.K.A. **decay**

rotary drill   A hydraulic, pneumatic, or motor-driven, heavy-duty tool with a rotating cutting bit, to chisel openings or holes in rock or earth.

rotunda   A large circular hall or auditorium topped by a round dome or cupola.   Usually the centerpiece of a large building or complex.

rough coat   Refers to a base coat of plaster, as opposed to a smooth finished coat.

rough cut   Wood pieces cut slightly longer or wider than actually needed.

rough-in   In framing or cabinetry, early placement and accommodations made for window and door openings, fireplaces, counters, plumbing, electrical fixtures, etc. **roughing-in** A.K.A. **rough-out**

rough lumber   Lumber that is only planed straight on one edge and one surface.   A.K.A. **undressed lumber**

rough opening   An opening framed into a wall of a building, such as for a door or window, that is bigger than required by the window or door by the width of the jambs, including the header and sill jambs.

ROOF STYLES

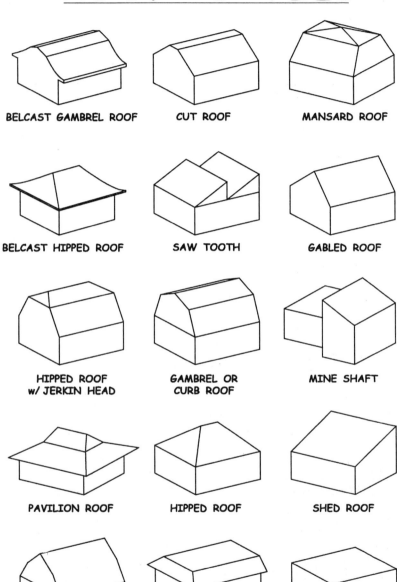

BELCAST GAMBREL ROOF

CUT ROOF

MANSARD ROOF

BELCAST HIPPED ROOF

SAW TOOTH

GABLED ROOF

HIPPED ROOF
w/ JERKIN HEAD

GAMBREL OR
CURB ROOF

MINE SHAFT

PAVILION ROOF

HIPPED ROOF

SHED ROOF

PENDENTIVE ROOF

SKIRT ROOF

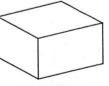

FLAT ROOF

ROOFS & PITCHES

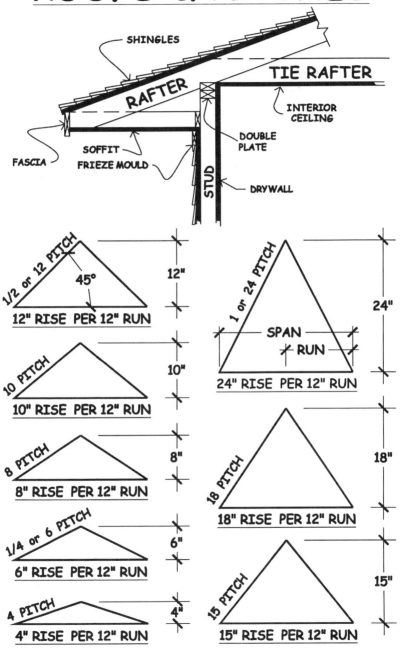

SHINGLES

TIE RAFTER

RAFTER

INTERIOR CEILING

DOUBLE PLATE

SOFFIT
FRIEZE MOULD

FASCIA

STUD

DRYWALL

1/2 or 12 PITCH — 45°
12"
12" RISE PER 12" RUN

10 PITCH
10"
10" RISE PER 12" RUN

8 PITCH
8"
8" RISE PER 12" RUN

1/4 or 6 PITCH
6"
6" RISE PER 12" RUN

4 PITCH
4"
4" RISE PER 12" RUN

1 or 24 PITCH
24"
SPAN
RUN
24" RISE PER 12" RUN

18 PITCH
18"
18" RISE PER 12" RUN

15 PITCH
15"
15" RISE PER 12" RUN

ROOF TRUSS DETAILS
PREFABRICATED

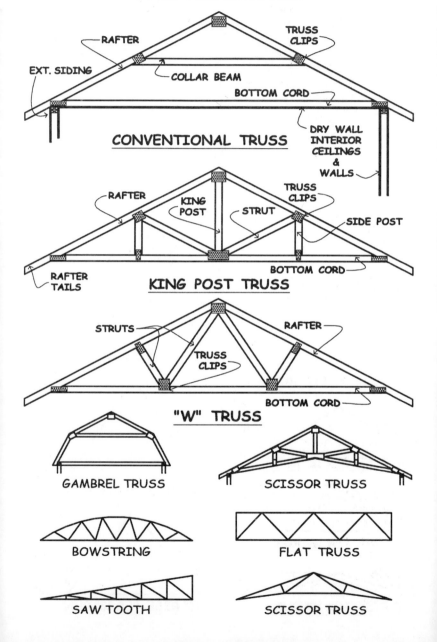

CONVENTIONAL TRUSS

- RAFTER
- TRUSS CLIPS
- EXT. SIDING
- COLLAR BEAM
- BOTTOM CORD
- DRY WALL INTERIOR CEILINGS & WALLS

KING POST TRUSS

- RAFTER
- KING POST
- STRUT
- TRUSS CLIPS
- SIDE POST
- RAFTER TAILS
- BOTTOM CORD

"W" TRUSS

- STRUTS
- RAFTER
- TRUSS CLIPS
- BOTTOM CORD

GAMBREL TRUSS

SCISSOR TRUSS

BOWSTRING

FLAT TRUSS

SAW TOOTH

SCISSOR TRUSS

rough-out See: rough-in

rough-sawn lumber
Lumber that has not been planed.
A.K.A. **undressed lumber**

round house A building specifically made to turn train engines around, to head the opposite way.

round over bit Refers to a quarter-round router bit used to round the edge of, for example, a tabletop.

rout To **cut, groove,** channel, or **furrow** into wood with a router.

router A power tool with a high-speed, revolving, vertical spindle that holds various shaped bits to cut and shape wood and other metals.

router

row house One of a number of similarly constructed houses in a row, with little or no open space between them. Usually, a housing development, built side-by-side in an unbroken line of houses along a common street. A.K.A. **row dwelling**

rubber A highly resilient elastic material made from the sap of the rubber tree, as well as other trees and plants, that can be formed into a waterproof membrane. 2. Any of a variety of synthetically produced materials with similar properties.

rubbish See: **garbage** A.K.A. **refuse, trash**

rubble A pile of unusable material, often the result of demolition.

rubble masonry A wall or structure, without mortar, made of local stone.

rule An instrument with straight edges and marked off in inches or centimeters for measuring distances on a drawing. **ruler**

run Denotes a distance in a horizontal straight line to be covered or followed. 2. In staircase layouts, the width of a single tread. 3. The horizontal distance covered by a flight of steps. 4. The length of channel or track that a window sash or elevator travels. 5. A small stream of paint flowing vertically on a painted surface. A.K.A. **tear** 6. A long straight section of pipe, cable, or wire.

rung The step of a ladder, or anything of similar appearance.

runner A wheel or flange that runs along a track or within a channel.

run-off Refers primarily to rain exceeding the amount absorbed in the ground. 2. Waste products, as those created in various manufacturing processes. 3. A final race to decide a winner.

runway Theatrically, a long narrow stage that projects from the main stage, permitting the actors to perform in close proximity to the audience. 2. A path within which something travels, such as a race track or a sliding window. A.K.A. **channel, track**

rust

rust   A light reddish brown substance that forms on steel or iron, the result of oxidation, that eats away at the metal on which it is allowed to form.

rustic   Descriptive of simple, rough, somewhat unsophisticated and unrefined handmade country elegance.

rustication   The beveling of exposed edges in a block or stone masonry to extenuate the joints.

- S -

s4s   *Abbr.* for **surfaced four sides**   See: **dressed lumber** A.K.A. **surfaced lumber**

Saarinen, Eero   *(1910-1961)* Innovative Finnish-American architect of a branch of International Modern style, known as an expressionistic modernism for his design of TWA's futuristic terminal at New York's JFK Airport.

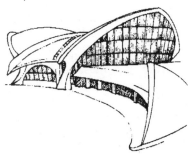

TWA terminal at JFK, New York

saber saw   A power saw with an oscillating blade extending through

the base *(table)* of the saw. A.K.A. **jigsaw**

saddle   Any object resemblin (hollow-backed structure) or functions as a saddle.

saddleback roof   See: **gable roof**

saddle flange   A type of plumbing flange, either specially manufactured or custom made, connecting a boiler or tank to a pipe. Called a saddle because of the shape of the flange needed to fit the curved surface of the boiler or tank.

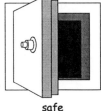

safe

safe   A small, strong, metal box or cabinet, usually with a combination lock, used to store valuables.

safe-deposit vault   A walk-in safe, usually in a bank, where valuables are stored.

safety belt   A device, usually worn around the waist and required when operating certain equipment, that prevents a worker from falling.

safety cage   A rig, attached to a power-driven winch, designed to hold workers safely, as they work on the exteriors of skyscrapers. **2.** Any metal cage or platform used to transport or temporarily support people safely.

safety glasses   A plastic covering to protect the eyes, usually made to fit over existing glasses.

safety glasses

sagging An irreversible downward bending in any material for any reason, such as excessive weight.

sail cloth A strong heavy cloth or light canvas, as was once used on ships with sails, and traditionally made of hemp linen.

sally port A below-grade entrance. 2. An underground passage or concealed gate.

saltbox style A style of house popular in the colonial America era, characterized by a nonsymmetrical roof, with the entrance on the side rather than the end of the building. Often two stories with a short roof in front and a long sloping roof in back *(known as a catslide)*, to a single story in the rear. *NOTE: The shape of the house resembles the kind of container that was commonly used to store salt, hence the name saltbox.* See: **New England Colonial** A.K.A. **English colonial**

saltbox

sample A small specimen of material use to check compatibility with other materials and colors or to verify the material's specifications to whatever standards are required.

sampler Needlework, usually an early sample of a child's ability to embroider, circa early 19th century America.

sanctuary A place considered sacred.

sand Granular material, predominantly found on beaches, available in various grades. Used for a variety of purposes, such as a base for a concrete or for paved sidewalks and paths.

sandbag Burlap or plastic bags filled with sand, used primarily to restrain the flow of water in flood conditions, or to support an existing barrier. 2. Theatrically, a counterbalanced weight enabling the easy movement of hanging scenery or equipment.

sandblasting A device that uses sand, propelled by compressed air, to remove dirt, rust, paint, etc., from virtually any surface, leaving a decorative rough surface. Also used to create a rough translucent texture on glass, which clouds the glass (providing privacy) and defuses light (often used in lamps).

sander A power tool or machine designed specifically for sanding various surfaces. There are a number of different shapes and sizes of sanders *(hand tools to large machines)*, but there are only three basic types -- disk sanders, belt sanders, and vibrating sanders.

sanding block Refers basically to a piece (block) of wood, used to keep the sandpaper flat to avoid creating unwanted valleys. *NOTE: To avoid splinters, always use a full sheet of sandpaper folded in quarters, which provides more protection for the fingers.*

sanding sealer An initial coating made specifically to seal and fill the wood pores, without hiding the grain. The object is sanded before applying the sealer and between subsequent coats.

sandpaper Heavy paper coated with an abrasive material such as silica *(sand)*, garnet, silicon carbide, or aluminum oxide, and used to smooth and polish a surface or object. Sandpaper is graded by grit size, where the lower number (60-grit) is very coarse, while 220-grit is very fine. *NOTE For best results, sanding is done to a universal consistency in each of the three or four grit levels. Most sanding projects start with 80-grit paper, this takes off most of the major scratches, 120-grit is a good medium transition grit, and 220-grit produces a nice smooth finish. Always sand with the grain to avoid scratches.*

sandstone *(Masonry stone)* Sedimentary rock that appears to be grains of sand naturally cemented together.

sandwich construction Any assembly of materials that appears as a sandwich, such as ridge insulation sandwiched between and glued to plywood sheeting. **2.** A process for constructing composite material made of several layers of various materials chosen for specific properties and bonded together.

sanitary engineering A branch of engineering concerned with the public health.

sap The fluid that circulates in trees and oozes out of unsealed lumber.

sarcophagus A coffin for ancient Egyptian royalty.

sash The frame of a window that holds the glass. A.K.A. **sash frame**

sash bar The rail in the center of a double-hung window or sliding window that the two sashes meet. A.K.A. **meeting rail 2**. The muntins that surround each pane of glass. A.K.A. **muntin**

sash pocket A hollow channel behind each side jamb of a window that holds a counterbalancing weight for easy sash movement. *NOTE: Modern windows are no longer made with counterweights.*

sash window Any frame made to hold window glass, whether fixed or sliding sash (vertically) hung or (horizontally) swinging. A.K.A. **sash, sash frame**

satellite dish A device to receive telecommunications and pictures transmitted by a satellite.

satellite dish

satin finish A smooth semigloss paint finish.

satinwood *(Wood)* A light blond hardwood with a satiny finish and a handsome grain, cut from various species of trees that grow in India, Florida, and the West Indies. Rare and expensive, largely used for furniture and inlaid table tops. Similar to aceitillo. See: **Appendix: Woods**

satisfaction A contractual condition deemed met upon final payment or the cancellation of any encumbrance on real property secured by it.

saturated Having absorbed all that can be taken in. A.K.A. **soaked** 2. Said of the purity and intensity of color, without white. **saturation**

saw A hand tool or machine used for cutting various materials.

sawhorse A four-legged support, usually used in pairs, to hold wood while sawing. A.K.A. *(Antiquated)* **sawbuck**

sawtooth roof A roof system with a profile similar to the teeth in a saw. See: **roof styles**

sawtooth wall A sheer wall that is shaped to support a sawtooth roof.

scab A wood or metal piece used to fasten together the butt ends of two boards with nails, screws, or bolts. A.K.A. **fishplate**

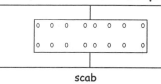

scab

scaffold An elevated platform or series of platforms temporarily erected on the exterior of a building or structure to support workers and materials.

scale In a measured drawing, the proportional ratio between the drawing and the actual size of the project or object being

satisfaction 205

constructed. *For example:* At 1/4" scale *(1/4" = 1'-0")*, the actual building will be 48 times as large as the drawing, because every 1/4" distance on the drawing represents a full 12" in real world terms. See: **architect's scale**

Typical scales used by architects:
1/4" = 10'-0", 3/4" = 1'-0", 1 1/2" = 1'-0", 3" = 1'-0", and full scale, meaning 12" = 12".

scale drawing A drawing, reduced in size, proportionally, to the actual structure or object being designed and constructed. A.K.A. **measured drawing, working drawings**

scaling The act of measuring a drawing with a ruler to determine the actual size of any one of its various elements. 2. To climb a wall or mountain.

scallop One of a continuous series of half circles, traditionally used as a decorative element on the outer edge of a strip of wood, molding, etc.

scallop shell A furniture motif. See: **shell**

scantling Sizing dimensional lumber and timber *(large pieces)* by its thickness and width, such as a 2x4, 6x12, etc.

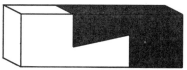

scarf joint

scarf joint A joint used in

scarf lap

connecting large pieces of timber with several angles, so that the pieces interlock.

scarf lap A severe angle cut in molding to blur the visual appearance of a joint or seam in a long straight run.

scene dock Theatrical term for the place where scenery (sets) or components thereof are stored when not being used.

schedule An allotted segment of time within which specific work is to start and is expected to be finished. *NOTE: The contractor normally breaks the project down into its various elements -- framing, plumbing, electrical, drywalling, etc., and schedules subcontractors to come in at the appropriate time to accomplish their specialized work.* A.K.A. **project flowchart** 2. A detailed listing of a specific components, items, or parts needed to complete the project, as a door schedule.

schematic design phase

The first phase of the design process, resulting from an initial consultation with the client, to determine the client's overall requirements and establish a relationship of various components of the project, through the use of basic illustrations, scaled drawings, and/or a model of the project. Approval to continue or revise are usually based on the results of this phase of the project, along with a projection of construction costs.

school A facility designed to house and operate as an educational institution, dedicated to a specific level of education, elementary, high school, etc., or dedicated to the study of a specific subject, such as the school of architecture at a particular university. Schools may consist of a single-room structure with one instructor teaching numerous subjects and grades, or may be a series of buildings; under either private or public auspices.

schoolhouse Refers, generally, to a single-classroom building.

school of architecture

A school within or branch of a university that is dedicated to the teaching of architecture.

scissor brace **scissor bracing** See: **X-brace**

scissor truss A type of truss that has a cross- or **X-brace** as part of its configuration.

sconce An ornamental wall bracket made to hold a light or candle.

score To make a slight straight impression or cut on the surface of a material, to weaken the strength of the material at that point, so the material will bend or break there when proper pressure is applied. 2. To scratch the surface. **scoring**

scotia A concave molding that produces a shadow. Scotia means *dark one* in classical mythology.

scraper Generally refers to a hand tool with a sharp edge, used to remove paint or other material from a flat surface.

scratch A thin, fine groove in

any finished surface, usually the result of an accident.

scratch coat A term used primarily in plastering to describe the initial rough coat of plaster, which is scratched to provide a bond for the second (brown) coat. A.K.A. **base coat**

screechier A nail coated with glue, for added holding power.

screen A nonstructural decorative partition, *(solid or see-through, fixed or movable),* used to separate or conceal. Often made in three sections and hinged together to fold. A.K.A. **folding screen** 2. A finely woven wire cloth, mounted in a suitable frame or holder, and usually found on the exterior side of windows and doors to keep flying insects out while the door or window is open. **3.** A wire screen of various sizes used to separate material *(such as pebbles)* by size. **4.** A frame covered with any material that serves to protect from the sun, fire, wind, rain, or cold.

screen door A lightweight exterior door, usually of wood or aluminum, that holds a finely woven mesh screen, which permits ventilation but excludes insects.

screening The separating of various sizes of sand or aggregate by passing it through a series of various-sized meshed screens. **2.** Theatrically, a private showing of a yet-to-be-released film.

screw A metal fastener with slightly angled threads for going through and grasping the material or the nut into which it is installed.

SCREW TYPES

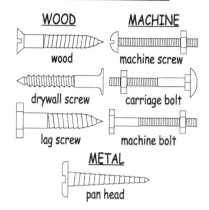

WOOD

wood

drywall screw

lag screw

MACHINE

machine screw

carriage bolt

machine bolt

METAL

pan head

screwdriver A power or manual hand tool used to drive or remove screws. *NOTE: The most popular screwdriver today is a battery-powered screw gun, with easy to replace bits conforming to whatever kind of screw (slotted, Phillips, etc.) being used.*

screw eye A heavy-gauge self-taping wood screw with a long shaft bent into a loop (eye), often used to anchor a rope that holds something in place. A.K.A. **eye hook**

scribe A pointed instrument used to mark cutting lines on wood, metal, bricks, etc.

scrim A plastering term used to describe a coarse, meshlike material (wire mesh, fiberglass, or heavy cloth) used to bridge, reinforce, or serve as a base for plaster. **2.** A decorative term to describe a light, open-weave fabric, often used for curtains because they allow the air to flow through while maintaining a degree of privacy.

scroll A traditional decorative motif, resembling ancient scrolls.

scroll pediment A broken pediment with a reverse curve, instead of a straight rooflike structure. See: **pediment**

scroll pediment

scroll saw A powered or handsaw with a very narrow blade, used to cut intricate details and curves.

scrollwork The creation of any ornamental object that is scroll-like in character.

scrub sink A large sink, installed adjacent to a hospital operating room, designed specifically for doctors, nurses, and technical personnel to use to scrub their hands and lower arms prior to a surgical procedure. The water temperature and volume controls on these sinks have traditionally been control nobs with a long handle that could be adjusted or turned off by the person's elbow, but more-modern scrub sinks have controls operated by the person's knees.

scullery A room attached to a kitchen where dishes, pots, and pans are washed.

sculpture A 3-dimensional, carved, molded, or assembled object of art.

scuttle A covered ceiling access hatch or opening.

seal An embossing device or stamp placed on construction drawings by architects, structural engineers, and other design professionals, as evidence of license or registration with the state where the construction is to take place, ensuring that all regulations and codes have been met or exceeded. 2. The material used to make an air- and water-tight connection. **sealant**

sealer A liquid coat that seals wood, plaster, etc., and prevents the surface from absorbing paint or varnish. 2. Any material used to seal the surface of another material.

seam A joint between two sheets of materials, such as plywood or metal.

seam weld Two sheets of steel joined together with a continuous weld along the seam. 2. See: **piping**

seasoned Wood dried by air or in a kiln. A.K.A. **seasoned lumber, seasoned timber** 2. The curing or hardening of concrete.

seat Any kind of furniture made to sit on. 2. Theatre seating, bench seating, or individual stacking chairs that connect together, in rows, to accommodate a group of people. **seating** A.K.A. **gang seating**

seating capacity The total number of seats, for public safety reasons, authorized for

CONFERENCE & DINING TABLE SEATING CAPACITY

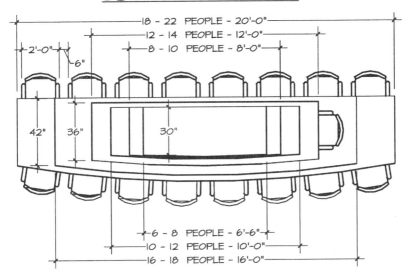

18 – 22 PEOPLE – 20'-0"
12 – 14 PEOPLE – 12'-0"
8 – 10 PEOPLE – 8'-0"
2'-0"
6"
42"   36"   30"

6 – 8 PEOPLE – 6'-6"
10 – 12 PEOPLE – 10'-0"
16 – 18 PEOPLE – 16'-0"

auditoriums, restaurants, or any other place where people gather.

sea wall A retaining wall built to protect property from the waves of the sea.

second Manufactured goods with a slight flaw, and not sold as meeting top (first) quality standards.

secondary colors Colors produced by mixing equal amounts of two primary colors, i.e., orange, purple, and green.

secretarial chair A swivel chair, on wheels, without arms, that a secretary would use at a desk.

secretarial chair

secretary A high, narrow, drop-lid desk, with storage below and usually a glass enclosed bookcase above. A.K.A. **drop-lid desk**

section A portion of an object, usually separated by a partition or space, such as a section of seating in a theatre or a section of paneling. 2. Architecturally, a drawing or model that shows the internal structure or mechanism of something through an imaginary plane or cut view.

security alarm system See: **burglar alarm system**

security glass Thick, strong glass *(often Plexiglas)* used to protect cashiers from armed robbers, or as a view port in security door or areas. A.K.A. **bullet-proof glass, bullet-resisting glass**

security screen A system of establishing the security of a particular area. 2. Heavy metal screen, *usually*

sediment

expanded sheet metal or wire mesh, used as a barrier to prevent unauthorized access or to restrain someone in a jail cell.

sediment   Organic material, often microscopic, that settles to the bottom of water or any other liquid.

sedimentary rock   Rock formed from layers of materials deposited as sediments, such as limestone or sandstone. A.K.A. **stratified rock**

seepage   Water that has slowly been absorbed into the soil or other porous material.

segmented arch   Any rounded arch that is less than a true semicircle. **2.** An arch (less than semicircular) embellished, on its face, with tapered segments of an **arch**. *NOTE: Segmented refers to that part or segment of a circle used as the radius of an arch.* See: **arches**

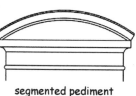
segmented pediment

segmented pediment   A style of pediment. See: **pediment**

semicircle   Half of a circle divided by its diameter. **semicircular**

semicircular arch   An arch with a round top. See: **arches**

semigloss   A medium glossy finish, between flat (matte) and high gloss.

senate chambers   A large room designed to accommodate a branch of the legislature known as the senate.

sensor   A device designed to detect movement, sound, smoke, or fire, that triggers or engages another device.   For instance a motion detector light switch that turns on a light, for a specific length of time, when motion *(someone walking)* is detected. A.K.A. **detector, sensing device**

septic system   A large tank to receive *(through pipes)* and harmlessly store solid sewage or other organic wastes from a dwelling or drainage system, while allowing liquids to seep or leach out into the surrounding subsoil. Utilized when no city-provided sewage system is available. A.K.A. **cesspool**

septic tank   A self-contained sewer system, *buried into the ground*, used in rural areas where city sewer lines are not available.

serlian window   See: **Palladian window** A.K.A. **Venetian window**

serpentine curve   A design element in furniture, utilizing an undulating curve that forms the fronts of drawers or doors on chests, desks, etc., a demonstration of cabinetry skills.

service   The equipment necessary to deliver electricity, telephone, cable, water, gas, etc., to a building or residence.

serviceability   All the components necessary to provide and maintain equipment at an expected level of service.

service box   Any box through which a mechanical device or electrical equipment are designed to be serviced. **2.** A *(usually metal and wall-mounted)* box that houses the switches and connections needed to connect a building's electrical system to the power source provided by the local power company.

set   A condition of rigidity or hardness, either achieved or approaching, in cement, mortar, plaster, resin, adhesive, or any other material that has cured; usually measured in terms of resistance to penetration or deformation. **2.** Theatrically, the setting *(room or series of rooms reflecting a particular period or theme)* within which actors perform. **3.** A term often used to describe a finish coat of plaster. **4.** To drive a nail below the surface of the wood (using a nail set). **5.** Something built and installed in its designated place.

setback   The minimum distance, *required by code or ordinance*, between a reference line (usually a property line or sidewalk) and a building.   **2.** An offset in the plane of a wall **3.** A distance behind something else. **4.** An offset A.K.A. **reveal**

set designer The equivalent of an architectural draftsman specializing in the design of theatrical sets. See: **set**

set-in A.K.A. **offset**

set punch See: **nail set**

setscrew   A machine screw used to affix a collar, knob, or other detachable part to

something else, such as a shaft. A.K.A. **grub screw**

settee See: **love seat**

setting-up   The thickening that occurs when paint stands in an open can. **2.** The increasing viscosity of a paint film as it dries.

settle   A term to describe the shifting of weight or the force of gravity, weather, or rotting timbers as it affects the structure of a building.   **settling**

setup   A device built to hold a piece of material in place and guide a particular tool to cut or groove a specific part. A.K.A. **jig, fixture, appliance** **2.** A term used to describe an executable file that automatically installs a program on a computer.

sewage   Liquefied waste material containing chemical, animal, or vegetable matter.

sewage treatment plant
A facility designed to reduce the organic and bacterial content of sewage waste so as to render it less offensive or hazardous to public health.

sewer   A system of collecting and transporting sewage and other liquid waste for proper treatment and disposal.

sewer pipe   A large pipe or conduit, buried below the streets, part of the city sewer system, used to collect and transport sewage.

shack See: **shanty**

shade A slightly darkened area shielded from direct sunlight. **2.** A window-covering consisting of

shading and blending

material hung from a ratcheted spring roller, that can be easily raised and lowered to block the direct rays of the sun or to provide privacy. **3.** A color or pigment that contains some percentage of black.

shading and blending
Altering the color of paint by adding equal parts of black in several stages to achieve a subtle blending or to create a gradation.

shadows See: **shade**

shaft
The extended (dowel like) portion of any object between two specific items, such as that part of a column or pilaster between the base and the capital, or that part of a hand screwdriver between the handle and the screw-turning head. **2.** The main body of a column.

shake
Any edge-grained shingle or clapboard.

Shaker furniture
A simple style of furniture originally produced (late 18th century) by a religious sect known as Shakers, living predominately in the New York area. Its characteristic simple, functional design quickly spread throughout New England.

shale
A thinly laminated argillaceous sedimentary rock, used on roofs; used decoratively rather than structurally because of weakness along its various layered planes.

sham door See: **dummy door**
A.K.A. **blind door**

shanty
A small structure of rough character, often with an earthen roof. A.K.A. **shack, hut**

shaper
A large, powerful woodworking machine with a vertically revolving cutter head, used for cutting a contoured edge on material. Predominately used to make all kinds of molding.

shear strength
The maximum stress on the lateral movement any material is capable of sustaining.

sheathing
A covering *(boards, plywood, wallboard, drywall, etc.)* placed over exterior stud walls or rafters of a building, that ties the building together, adds stability by preventing lateral movement, and provides a base (nailing) for the exterior roofing material and wall cladding. A.K.A. **sheeting** *(when 4'x8' sheet material is used.)* **sheathing board, board sheathing**

sheathing board See: **sheathing**

shed
A roughly constructed shelter, storage room, or workshop, either separate or attached to an existing building.

shed dormer
A style of dormer with a shedlike (flat inclined) roof. See **dormer**

shed roof
A roof shape having only one sloping plane. Predominant in **mineshaft architecture.** *NOTE: Similar to a lean-to roof except that a shed roof does not need to be supported by another structure.*

sheet
Refers to a flat material produced and purchased in sheet form, as plywood, glass, or wide rolls of continuous material of various thicknesses.

sheet glass   Ordinary window glass. A.K.A. **single-pane glass**

sheet metal   A category of metal products sold in a flat sheetlike form.

sheet-metal screw   A short, coarse-threaded, self-tapping screw used to fasten sheet metal parts together or to attach something to a sheet metal surface, without having to predrill holes or use nuts.

sheetrock   See: **drywall**

sheet steel   Refers to one of the various forms steel is available in -- a sheet form, used for a variety of applications.

sheet vinyl Known generically as **linoleum**. See: **linoleum**

shelf A flat, horizontal surface, as found in a bookcase or mounted on a wall, used to support or store various objects. **2.** A projecting, flat, near-horizontal surface, such as a rock ledge.

shelf bracket   A device used to support a shelf when attached to the plane of a wall.

shelf life The period of time an adhesive, chemical solvent, paint, sealants, or any other product can be stored and remain suitable for use.

shell   A thin, exoskeleton *(hollow)* structure, similar in look or construction to a sea shell. **2.** Any uncompleted framework. **3.** A sea shell motif traditionally found on furniture. A.K.A. **scallop shell**

shellac   A thin, usually clear varnish containing shellac resin and alcohol, used to seal the surface of wood furnishings.

shelving   A series of shelves, often adjustable, as found in bookcases, linen closets, kitchen cabinets, etc.

shield   Anything made to protect something from something else, such as a metallic layer within shielded electrical cable that protects against electrostatic interference.

shim   A thin, flat, pie-shaped piece of wood or metal, or small stone, usually tapered, inserted under or behind an object to adjust its height or to provide a stable, flat surface for it to rest against. **shimming**

shingle   A roofing material (wood, asphaltic material, slate, tile, concrete, etc.) cut to stock lengths, widths, and thicknesses and applied in an overlapping fashion to look like actual wood shingles. *NOTE: While the look of wood shingles is desirable, genuine wood shingles are considered an extreme fire hazard in most areas, and are not allowed to be used.*

shingle style   A popular American style *(1880-1915)* of architecture that featured shingled siding on exterior walls, as well as the roof, of a house, with shingles in various patterns. Particularly favored for rambling seaside estates and resorts on the New England coast, featuring free-flowing floor plans with large rooms and porches arranged around a **great hall** dominated by a large staircase.

shiplap

shiplap Horizontal wood siding or sheathing whose upper and lower edges are rabbeted to accommodate the next board, so that each board overlaps the one below. A.K.A. **shiplap boards, shiplap siding**

shirring Gathering fabric along a string or curtain rod.

shoe Any element or object made to receive or hold the lower end of a vertical element. A.K.A. **soleplate** 2. A base shoe molding. See: **shoe mold** 3. See: **shoe rail**

shoe mold Refers to the lowest piece of molding, which would receive most of the scuff marks from people's shoes. **shoe molding**

shoe rail The lowest part of a railing, which holds the balusters, and is susceptible to receiving scuff marks from people's shoes.

shoji screen A lightweight, Japanese wood-framed paper screen, used as interior and exterior walls, sliding doors, or decoratively in traditional Japanese architecture. Often made with intricate *geometric patterns* formed with delicately cut lacquered muntins, backed by translucent white rice paper.

shooting gallery A long room with targets at one end, used to practice the skills of shooting a gun or rifle.

shop A store or workshop, usually a commercial building. **2.** Any space where something is produced, such as a mill.

shop drawings Drawings, diagrams, illustrations, etc., which illustrate how specific portions of the work is to be fabricated and/or installed. A.K.A. **working drawings**

shop front See: **storefront**

shopping center Refers primarily to a neighborhood planned development containing a concentration of large and small stores, often including a supermarket, with ample parking.

shopping mall Refers primarily to large, regional shopping centers containing one or more department stores and a number of specialty shops.

shore See: **brace**

shore up To close up, hold, or support by means of shoring. **shoring up**

short circuit An abnormal connection in an electric circuit.

shoulder A projection element or break in the profile of molding, where the width or thickness suddenly changes. A.K.A. **ear, elbow** 2. The surface alongside a paved road where a vehicle can make an emergency stop. **3.** A supportive element that another member rests on or in, such as the base of a tenon.

shower Plumbing, created within an enclosed area configured to spray water on the body from above. A.K.A. **shower bath**

showerhead The nozzle the water comes out of in a shower, often with spray adjustment control.

shower pan A tiled-over

metal pan with high sides that forms the base of a shower and to which the drainpipe is attached.

showroom Refers, generally, to a wholesale display room, operated by a manufacturer or a local distributor, to assist local dealers and the dealer's clients, not the general public. See: **wholesale showroom** A.K.A. **to the trade**

show window A display window in a shop, arranged with some of the merchandise sold inside. A.K.A. **display window, storefront window**

shrine A splendidly adorned receptacle for sacred relics.

shrinkage A reduction in size of any material, usually produced by drying, a change in temperature, or by the constant exposure to the elements.

shutter blind An exterior adjustable louver used as a window blind.

shutters A movable window covering with louvers instead of glass panels. Used either on the exterior of buildings to protect windows from storm damage or decoratively on the interior side. A.K.A. **louver window, jalousie window**

sideboard A serving table in a dining room.

side cut See: **cheek cut**

sidelights Refers generally to a pair of framed, fixed-glass windows along both sides of a door

or window opening. A.K.A. **wing-light, flanking window, margin light**

sidewalk A paved pedestrian footpath at the side of a street or roadway.

siding Any exterior finished covering on a framed building. A.K.A. **cladding**

sight line See: **line of sight**

sign A surface of any size used to inform, warn, or advertise. A.K.A. **signboard**

silhouette In drawing, a profile or outline of any object, usually in a single color, often black. **2.** Theatrically, a silhouette accomplished by placing a person or object between a light and a semi translucent screen.

silhouette

silicone resin A silicone substance, found in a number of products because of its heat and chemical resistance and waterproofing properties, that is used by the various construction trades.

sill Horizontal timbers, attached to a concrete foundation, that support a wood-framed structure. A.K.A. **sill plate 2.** The horizontal finish piece *(that the casing dies into)* forming the bottom of a door (A.K.A. **threshold, door sill**) or window (A.K.A. **windowsill**), which is slightly sloped to allow water to fall away.

sill cock

sill cock See: spigot

sill course In stone masonry, a course of brick, block, or stone set at windowsill height that is commonly different in form, thickness, size, or color from those found in the rest of the wall.

sill plate See: sill

sink A plumbing fixture, consisting of a basin, a water supply, and a drain. A.K.A. **washbasin, lavatory**

sisal An organic fiber from the sisal plant used in a number of applications, such as carpet padding, or in upholstered furniture and bedding where it is used to cover springs.

sistered In framing, a second stud or rafter, perhaps stronger, attached to an existing stud or rafter. A.K.A. **sister stud, sister rafter**

sister rafter See: sistered

sister stud See: sistered

site The land on which a building, project, park, etc., is planned and built.

site drainage A network of underground pipes intended to drain rainwater away from buildings.

site plan A scaled drawing of the property (land), including a plan of the proposed building or project, and the placement and orientation of its various components. Usually includes topographic contour lines of the property.

sitting room A room arranged for social gatherings. A.K.A. **living room, parlor**

size The physical dimensions of any object.

sizing A gelatinous solution used to stiffen fabric, like starch. 2. A paper underlayment used beneath foil wallpaper. A.K.A. **heading tape**

skeleton A frame without a covering.

skeleton construction A type of high-rise construction that transmits the load and stress of the building onto the foundation through a steel framework of beams and columns, while the exterior walls (usually a glass **curtain wall**) is supported by only a light framework.

skew Any member cut with a sloping surface.

skewed Having a twisted shape.

skillsaw The popular name for a worm-drive, powered hand saw, commonly used in the construction industry, and first manufactured by the S-B Power Tool Company.

skim coat A thin coat of plaster, usually a finish coat.

skin Refers to a thin, dense, outer covering, that gives shape to a wire- or stick-frame structure or object.

skirt In cabinetry, a wooden strip that lies just below a shelf, window, sill, or tabletop. A.K.A. **apron, frieze** 2. A fabric strip fitted around the lower edge of an upholstered sofa or chair.

skirt board

skirt board See: baseboard
A.K.A. **skirting board, mop-board**

skreed To level a concrete slab, using a straight-edge (2x4) dragged over the top of the parallel forms to set the height of the wet cement. **skreeding** A.K.A. **skreet**

skreet **skeeting** See: skreed

skylight A water-tight (fixed or open) window in a roof, usually of frosted or clear **Plexiglas**, used primarily to admit light into the space below.

skyline

skyline A view or silhouette of the a city's major buildings, often identifying a particular city by its unique buildings and features.

skyscraper A very tall building, usually the city's largest, with many stories. *NOTE: Originally built in the U.S., circa early 1880s, and made possible by the invention of the elevator.* See: **elevator**

skyscraper

slab Any thick, flat slice or plate of material *(stone, wood, concrete, etc.)*. **2.** Any mass of concrete poured to form a flat surface, such as a floor or sidewalk.

slab door A flat, smooth-surfaced door. A.K.A. **flush door**

slab floor A reinforced concrete floor. A.K.A. **concrete floor**

slack Loosely fitting. **2.** A rigging term used to describe a no-strain condition on a line. **3.** A fine grade of coal.

slant A slight change of direction or angle, such as the tilt of the blade of a table saw. **2.** A sewer pipe that connects a building (at one level) to a common sewer line at a lower level.

slat One of several thin, narrow strips of wood, plastic, or metal, such as individual **slats** of a **venetian blind**.

slat-back chair See: **ladder-back chair**

slate A smooth, hard, brittle metamorphic rock that splits easily along parallel layers and is used extensively as a flooring and roofing material.

slaughterhouse A facility where animals are butchered for food.

sleeper As furniture, a sofa with a built-in collapsible folding bed. **2.** In stick framing, any long, horizontal beam used to distribute a load from posts or framing. **3.** A railroad car built to accommodate overnight travelers. **4.** A construction term used to describe the pressure-treated 2x4s or 2x6s laid flat on a concrete slab floor to which a wood floor is nailed.

sleeve That part of a garment that covers an arm or any part of an arm, anything that functions in a similar capacity. **2.** A tube or tubelike part that fits over or around another part, or within which it travels.

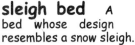
sleigh bed

sleigh bed A bed whose design resembles a snow sleigh.

slew An open channel, using gravity to transport material from one place to another, as used on concrete mixing trucks to deliver the concrete. A.K.A. **shoot, slue, flow trough**

slicker A hooded raincoat and pants, warn by emergency road crews and utility workers during inclement weather. Often yellow for safety, because they can be better seen. A.K.A. **darby**

sliding door Any door mounted on a track to slide horizontally, such as a glass patio door, a pocket door, or a heavy sliding fire door in a manufacturing plant or warehouse.

sliding window A window sash (wood or metal) that slides horizontally. A.K.A. **sliding sash**

slip A narrow passage between buildings. **2.** A parking spot for a boat.

slipcover A fabric covering custom-fitted to a sofa or chair, with separate cushion covers. A solution short of completely reupholstering.

slip-joint pliers Pliers with an adjustable pivot point, enabling the jaws to open wider and grasp larger objects. A.K.A. **channel lock pliers**

slipper chair Any short-legged chair with its seat close to the floor.

slope An incline, such as the pitch in a roof or the grade of property.

slop sink A low deep sink, such as used by janitors to empty pails of dirty water.

sludge Waste material in a liquefied form, produced from various manufacturing operations. A.K.A. **refuse, sewage**

slump In masonry, a measure of consistency of freshly mixed concrete, mortar, or stucco.

smoke The vaporous cloud of small particles (carbonaceous matter) in the air, resulting from the burning of organic material, such as wood or coal.

smoke alarm system See: **smoke detector**

smoke detector A device (photoelectric, ionization, or ultraviolet heat detector) used to sense the presence of smoke in a room or building. A.K.A. **smoke alarm system**

smokestack See: **chimney**

smoking room A room set aside for people who smoke. **2.** A small building used for smoking meats. A.K.A. **smoker**

smooth finish   A flat, nontextured surface.

snake   A tool in the form of a long, slender strip of flat wire *(tempered spring-steel)*, used by electricians to pull wires through conduit or through any inaccessible wall space.   2. A motor-driven plumber's tool with a long, flexible metal wire, that is rotated and fed through pipes to unblock or clear them.

snakewood *(Wood)*   A yellowish brown or reddish brown hardwood wood with dark spots and markings. Used for paneling and marquetry.

snow guard   Any device used to restrict or prevent snow from entering, collecting, or moving.

snow house   A temporary house made of snow.

soapstone   A soft gray-green sedimentary stone traditionally used for sink and countertops. *NOTE: Can be cut with ordinary power tools.*

socket   See: shoe

socket wrench   A ratcheted wrench with changeable sockets to fit over the heads of various-sized nuts and bolts.

sod   Long strips of pregrown grass, with soil, used to start a new lawn, rather than starting from seeds.

soda fountain   A commercial appliance made to dispense soda water (carbonated water), used in the creation of ice cream sodas, which were very popular in the late 18ᵗʰ to mid-19ᵗʰ centuries. More than just a dispenser of soda, many fountains were a self-contained factory for making all sorts of drinks and ice cream treats, that included refrigerators for the ice cream, a sink for cleaning up, and various compartments and contraptions for dispensing and storing toppings. *NOTE: Soda fountains are a part of Americana and were traditionally found in local drug stores.*

sod house   A house with a roof of logs covered with earth and sod, and/or walls constructed of layers of sod.

soffit   The exposed undersurface of any architectural element of a building, such as the underside of a balcony.

soft water   Water, treated to be free of magnesium or calcium salts.

softwood   Refers primarily to wood, usually evergreens, that are relatively soft and easy to cut and drive nails into.

soil compaction   Compacting the soil to the point that it will support the weight of a structure.

solar   The collection, conversion and utilization of heat from the sun as a source of usable energy.

solar collector   A device designed to absorb radiant heat from the sun (**energy**) and transform it into a fluid to transport that heat, as needed, to various parts of a building.

solar energy system   A built-in system that collects and converts solar energy into thermal energy for heating and/or cooling a building or to heat water.

solar heating and cooling system
An assembly of components designed into a house that capture and convert solar energy into thermal energy, specifically to heat or cool the building.

solarium
A sunny room with many windows, usually enclosed with one or more glass walls. Often on the top floor of a building. A.K.A. **sun room**

solar water heater
A device that uses the sun's heat specifically to heat water.

solder
A soft metal alloy used to join *(fuse)* metal parts, such as copper tubing or electronic connections. **soldering**

soldering gun
An electrically heated soldering iron, with a pistol grip, used to melt solder that connects electrical wires to various components. A.K.A. **soldering iron** *(without a pistol grip)*

soldier
A masonry term to describe a brick set vertically (on end) instead of horizontally.

soldier coarse
A coarse (layer) of bricks laid side-by-side on end.

soldier pile
A decorative grouping of vertically laid brick in a wall, often repeated.

solid-core door
A door of solid wood construction, as opposed to hollow-core construction.

solvent
A liquid chemical solution used to thin out or dissolve paint or other substances. A.K.A. paint thinner

Sorbonne
An old Paris school, particularly known for its prominence in the world of music.

sound
Vibrations (oscillation) in atmospheric pressure detectable by the human ear. A.K.A. **sound waves**

sound absorption
A property possessed by various materials and objects to absorb sound energy. **2.** A standard by which materials are tested and rated for their sound absorbing property, expressed in **sabins** or **metric sabins**.

sound barrier
Any obstacle that stops sound waves from traveling through it.

sounding board
A large surface with resonant attributes, so that the sound returns to its origin. **2.** A surface suspended above and in front of a speaker, to reflect and strengthen the sound.

soundness
The character of structural **stability**.

soundproofing
Any material used on or within the walls of a room that prohibits sound from escaping to other rooms, corridors, or buildings.

sound waves
See: **sound**

space
An area, indoors or out, and with or without boundaries. **2.** A blank or empty area: the spaces between words. **3.** An area provided for a particular purpose: a parking space.

space heater
A relatively

small, self-contained electric or liquid fuel heater with a powerful fan, used to heat the room or space in which it is placed.

spacer A small block of wood, a nail, or other material used to create a series of uniform spaces, as between the boards of a sun deck.

spade leg A traditional, square, tapered style of leg used in furniture. See: **furniture feet; club** A.K.A. **club foot, spade foot, thimble foot**

span The distance between two supporting elements that a beam or joist covers.

spandrel See: **stringer wall**

Spanish colonial *(1600-1900)* The architectural style of America's Southwest, characterized by the "enclosed household" of walled one- and two-story adobe construction, often with entry into an enclosed garden patio directly from the street. Its low-pitched or flat roofs featured hanging street balconies; galleries usually faced southeast to catch summer breezes and the warmth of the low summer sun. Unique to Spanish colonial / mission style were bell-shaped corner fireplaces. A.K.A. **mission style, Monterey style**

Spanish revival A stylistic rendition of Spanish colonial, featuring bell-shaped pediment walls and quatrefoil windows. Detailed and heavily influenced by the more sophisticated Moorish, Byzantine, and Renaissance styles, than the **Spanish colonial** style. A.K.A. **mission style**

Spanish tile A semicircular clay tile, typically used in Spanish or Southwestern style of architecture.

Spanish tile

spar A common rafter. **2.** A bar used to fasten a door or gate closed.

spare room A guest bedroom.

spark arrester A device, at the top of a chimney, used to prevent sparks, embers, or other ignited material from escaping into the atmosphere. A.K.A. **bonnet**

specifications A written description, in detail, of the scope of work, materials used, quality of workmanship, and method of installation, that is to be contractually performed. **2.** A written technical description of materials, systems, equipment, standards, construction, etc.

spectral colors The colors produced by a beam of white light refracted through a prism, as commonly seen in a rainbow.

sphinx A large, ancient mythical, animal-like statue with a human head, erected on the Egyptian desert.

spigot An exterior water faucet, threaded to connect to a garden hose. A.K.A. **sill cock**

spike A very large nail.

spillway   A channel designed to capture water overflowing a dam, lake, reservoir, or tank.

spindle   A slender rod or pin on which something turns. 2. In carpentry, a short turned part, such as a baluster.

spiral   A continuously wound cylindrical helix.

spiral stairs   A flight of stairs whose treads wind around a central newel. A.K.A. **caracole, circular staircase, cockle stair, corkscrew stair, spiral staircase**

spire   A tall, steep, pointed structure usually found atop a tower, cupola, or roof.

spired turret   A turret with a spire.

splash back   A board that provides protection to the wall against water splashes, as behind a sink.   See: **backsplash** A.K.A. **splashboard**

splay   An oblique sloping or beveled angle.   A.K.A. **beveled, cant, chamfered**

splice   To almost seamlessly connect, unite, or join two similar pieces of material to form one continuous piece of material.

splice plate   A metal plate used for fastening two or more members together.

spindle   See: **baluster**

splattering   A general artistic term used to describe the strategic placement of similar objects within a particular setting, as with the placement and utilization of plants, pictures, accent lighting, and other design elements. 2. A painting effect produced by flicking the bristles of a brush over the surface. A.K.A. spattering

spline joint

spline   A long, thin strip of wood or metal that is inserted in a slot formed by two members, each of which is grooved to receive the spline. A.K.A. **false tongue, feather, slip feather, slip tongue**

spline joint   Joinery utilizing a spline for added strength.

split   A separation *(break or crack)* in the surface of lumber. 2. A smooth tear, resulting from tensile stresses.

split

split-level   A type of house in which the floor levels vary in different parts or rooms of the house.

sponge float   A float used in the installation of tile and grout. See: **float**

sponge rubber   Synthetic foam rubber.

sponging   A painting technique that employs a sponge in the application of layers of paint or glaze.

spontaneous ignition   Combustion caused by a chemical reaction, in which heat is released.

spotlight   A floodlight equipped with a lens and one or more reflectors, that delivers a narrow beam of light to a specifically defined area.

spot-weld One of a series of small weld points placed strategically along a seam connecting two pieces of metal. Often used as a temporary hold, to make sure the piece is properly positioned before applying a stronger, more permanent weld.

spout To gush forth in a rapid stream or in spurts. **2.** A tube or pipe through which liquid is released or discharged. **3.** The burst of spray from the blowhole of a whale. See: **rain spout, gargoyle**

spray booth Originally, a simple enclosed or semienclosed area used to confine the color over spray associated with a paint spray gun. Today, they contain exhaust systems to quickly eliminate the chemical particles and fumes in the air the spraying of paint and solvents creates. A.K.A. **paint spray booth**

spray gun A tool, powered by compressed air or fluid pressure, that expels paint, mortar, stucco, etc., through a small orifice, onto the surface being coated.

spray painting The quick application of paint by means of a spray gun, which produces a uniform, even coat.

spray gum

spreader A brace between two walls to maintain a specific distance. **2.** A mechanical device for spreading various materials over a given area.

spring An elastic device, often a wound steel coil, used to maintain tension on a line or between two points.

spring clamp A clamp that holds material together with pressure supplied by a spring in the handles of the clamp.

spring hinge A hinge containing one or more springs, so that the door, to which it is attached, closes automatically. *NOTE: A hinge that swings both ways, as a swinging door, is known as a bomber hinge.*

spring line A theoretical, imaginary horizontal line above which an arch is formed. See: **chord**

spring lock A lock that automatically engages, because of the use of a spring to operate the through-bolt, when the door or lid is moved to the closed position.

sprinkler A device *(a nozzle)* designed to control the quantity and direction of water delivered to a designated area *(zone)*, within which it operates. A.K.A. **sprinkler head**

sprinkler system A system (often automatic) of a network of pipes *(or tubing)*, sprinkler heads, and switches in a building or garden designed for dispersing water over a specific area, at preset times or for specific reasons.

spruce *(Wood)* A strong whitish to light yellow straight-grained, low-density softwood. A variety of pine, closely related to the fir, native to North America and many other parts of the world. Used for general interior and exterior construction. A.K.A.

white deal, white fir, Norwegian spruce fir

spur Small pieces of ornamental foliage on the corners of a rectangular surface. **2.** A diagonal brace between a post and beam or rafter. **3.** Anything that resembles a cowboy spur.

square Any rectangle with four equal sides. **2.** See: **framing square** A.K.A. **carpenter's square**

square end The end of a board that is cut 90° to its edge.

square foot An area or object whose dimensions are 12" wide by 12" deep by 12" high.

square up To plane a timber, so that all four sides of a piece of wood are all 90° to one another. A.K.A. **S4S**

stability The ability of a material or structure to resist or withstand lateral stress or buckling. **stable**

stabilizer Any device or substance used to increase the stability of something.

stable A large building used to house and/or feed domestic animals, usually horses, and store grain and supplies. **2.** See: **stability**

stack Any vertical pipe of material or objects, such as a stack of books. **2.** A vertical air duct or structure containing a flue or flues for the discharge of gases. A.K.A. **chimney stack 3.** The various tiers of bookshelves in a library.

stackroom A room in a library, not generally open to the public, that is reserved for reference books.

stadium A large **arena** where various games of sport are played and viewed, many are designed for a particular sport, such as football, baseball, or tennis.

staff A plastering term used to define molded ornamental objects. **casting 2.** An employee, committee, or group member.

stage A raised floor or platform where entertainers (singers, comedians, etc.) or actors perform dramatic or musical plays.

stage door An exterior door leading to the backstage of a theatre, primarily used by theatre personnel.

stage left Stage directions indicating the left side of the stage from the point of view of the performer facing an audience.

stage right Stage directions indicating the right side of the stage from the point of view of the performer facing an audience.

stagger To arrange in alternate order, as if on alternating sides of a centerline, or offset, as rows of theatre seats, for clear viewing.

staggered Descriptive of a nailing, riveting, or screwing pattern for fastening one object to another, that usually involves two or more rows of offset aligned nails. A.K.A. **zig zag pattern**

staging The preparation involved in preparing a stage for a particular performance or event. **2.** A temporary platform for

STAIRCASE DETAILS

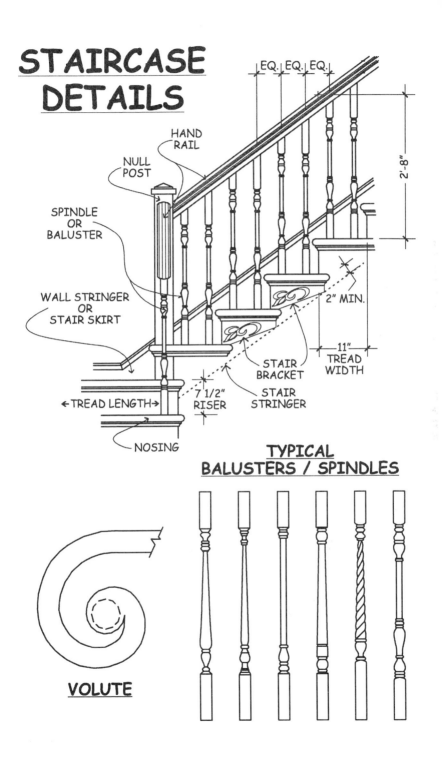

EQ. EQ. EQ.

HAND RAIL

NULL POST

2'-8"

SPINDLE OR BALUSTER

WALL STRINGER OR STAIR SKIRT

2" MIN.

11" TREAD WIDTH

STAIR BRACKET

STAIR STRINGER

7 1/2" RISER

←TREAD LENGTH→

NOSING

VOLUTE

TYPICAL BALUSTERS / SPINDLES

workers and the materials, erected on the exterior of a building or structure. A.K.A. **scaffolding**

stain A transparently dye that leaves the grain of wood visible, as opposed to paint that covers with an opaque substance. *NOTE: Most stains are actually paint diluted with paint thinner, which allows it to penetrate the wood.*

stained glass Glass to which a transparent color has been added, during its molten state, or applied to its surface after forming.

stained-glass window A general term for an artistic arrangement of different shapes, types, and colors of glass that are held together by thin, flexible lead channels soldered into place, and glazed into the sash of a window.

stainless steel A strong steel, chromium, and nickel alloy that is highly resistant to corrosion and rust, commonly used for all kinds of silverware.

stair A step, or series of steps, that connects two levels of floor.

stair bracket A decorative bracket affixed to the side of each step of an open *(visible)* staircase.

staircase A flight(s) of stairs connecting the various floors of a building, including supports, handrails, and framework. A.K.A. **stairway**

stair rail The handrail on a staircase.

stairway A.K.A. **staircase**

stairwell The vertical shaft within which a staircase is erected. A.K.A. **wellhole, open stairwell** NOTE: Refers to an open area between flights of stairs providing an unobstructed view of the ground floor from the top floor. WARNING: Stairwells over 2-stories are considered a fire hazard and not permitted under most local **building codes** today.

stake A sharpened wooden stick driven into the ground to act as a boundary marker or to support or hold something.

stake out To mark the boundaries of a proposed building or the property with stakes driven into the ground.

stall A sectioned-off room or compartment, such as a horse stall, or a toilet stall in a public restroom.

stamping The process of shaping and cutting sheet metal parts using a large machine known as a punch press, a special dies for each of the various parts, to be made.

stanchion Any upright post or column used as a support.

stand A temporary retail booth, such as at a fair.

standard A flag or banner symbolizing a nation, chief of state, city, military unit, company, etc. 2. An acknowledged measure of comparison for quantitative or qualitative value or a yardstick by which something is compared. 3. Acceptable but of less than top quality or having no special or unusual features, i.e., ordinary.

standard wire A group of individually wrapped small wires, encased within a single covering, that conforms to a specific use or falls within a common standard.

stands Slang for **grandstand seating**, as found at most indoor and outdoor exhibition or sports event. See: **grandstand**

staple A small, U-shaped, metal wire fastener with pointed ends, similar to an ordinary (desktop) paper stapler, but the staples are much longer, of a heavier gauge, and the stapler is pneumatically powered. Used extensively in all kinds of construction to fasten materials together.

staple gun A tool, usually pneumatic, for driving wire staples into wood, used in construction to fasten materials together. Same as a pneumatic nail gun, except that it is made to be used with staples rather than nails. A.K.A. **stapler**

stapler A device or tool *(manual or powered)* that implants a staple. A.K.A. **staple gun, staple dispenser**

state house The primary or ceremonial building housing a state legislature and officials.

station The place, usually a building or facilities, from which specific services are provided or operations are directed, such as a **railroad station, police station, bus station, radio station,** etc. **2.** One of a series of manned posts, such as a gate guard.

statuary A form of sculpture that deals with figures.

statute of limitations A period of time, established by the law, within which legal action must be brought for alleged damage or injury. Varies from state to state and situation by situation.

stay Anything that stiffens or braces another object.   A.K.A. **brace, stiffener**

steam heat Heat that is furnished by steam.

steam pipe Any pipe used to transport steam from one point to another.

steel A very strong iron and carbon alloy, used extensively in the construction of large buildings and structures.

steel sheet See: **sheet steel**

steeple A tall, ornamental tower that diminishes in size as it rises, topped by a small cupola or spire.

stenciling The process of using a cut-out pattern(s), made as a guide for paint, used to repeat a pattern, as typically found running *(chased)* around the top of the walls of a room. A.K.A. **stencil work**

step One of the stairs of a flight of stairs, consisting of one tread and one riser.

step flashing Rectangular pieces of sheet metal material, galvanized metal or lead, bent to a 90° angle. Used at the intersection of a roof and a skylight or chimney, and interwoven into asphalt tiles to prevent water from getting into the structure. **stepped flashing**

stepladder A small, self-supported ladder having flat steps or treads instead of rungs.

sterling A silver content standard (92½%) in silverware.

stick Any long, slender piece of wood.

sticker machine A large wood-milling machine, with several cutting heads, used to mass-produce moldings. A.K.A. **sticker molder**

stick style architecture

stick framing See: framing A.K.A. **platform framing, stick construction**

Stickley, Gustav (1848-1942) Furniture maker, designer, and publisher "Craftsman Magazine" (1901-1916) and a leading advocate and proponent of the **Craftsman style** of architecture. See: **Craftsman style**

stick style architecture A picturesque Victorian architectural style reminiscent of a gingerbread ornamented resort or chalet, *circa 1860s*, featuring narrow boards nailed to exterior walls *(stickwork)* simulating a post-and-beam skeletal structure of the building. Similar to the country half-timber cottages of Normandy and rustic English Tudor homes, with large overhanging porches and balconies built of decorative cross-timbers. A.K.A. **eastern stick**

stickwork See: **stick style architecture**

stiffener A.K.A. **brace, stay**

stile The outer, upright structural members of a frame, door, or window sash. In a door, the outer structural members from which the door is hung or the door lock is installed. **2.** The vertical strips in paneling and wainscoting. *NOTE: Horizontal elements are called rails.*

still life A picture, paintings, or drawings of motionless, inanimate objects.

stilted arch An arch that rests, or appears to rest, on stiles rather than as one continuous piece, so as to appear to be separate elements.

stilted arch

stipple A decorative effect achieved by applying very small dots *(flicking brush bristles)*, points, etc., to a painted or plastered surface. A.K.A. **stippling**

stippled finish A dotted or pebbly textured finish, produced from the bristles of a

stock

brush over semi dried paint or plaster. See: **stipple**

stock Readily available material, parts, or supplies purchased for near future use. **2.** The principal part, supporting or holding other parts, such as screwdriver bits stored in the handle of a screwdriver.

stockade A fortified enclosure of logs driven into the ground. **2.** A military prison.

stock brick The standard brick produced by the local brick foundry.

stock sizes Popular sizes that are normally in stock and readily available.

stone Any aggregate of mineral matter; the material rocks are composed of.

stone dressing Decorative stone that has had its finished surfaces milled to conform to a standard pattern. A.K.A. **dressed stone**

Stonehenge The most imposing example, still existing, of a prehistoric megalithic monument, located near Salisbury, England, in Wilshire.

stoneware A hard, vitrified, ceramic ware, used for a variety of products including sanitary fixtures and pipes. A.K.A. **earthenware**

stonework See: masonry A.K.A. **stone masonry**

stool The flat piece

stool

which a double-hung window closes, similar to a door sill. **2.** A narrow shelf fitted across the lower part of a window opening *(butting against the sill)*. **3.** A chair without a back, used at counters and workbenches.

stoop A platform or small porch, usually several steps above grade, at the entrance or back door of a building.

stop Molding *(trim)* on the jamb face of a door or window, against which the door closes or within which the window sash moves. **2.** A backing for an ornament into which a figure or molding ends.

storage A compartment or room used to store personal property for an extended period of time.

store A retail establishment specializing in a particular kind of merchandise, e.g., clothing, bakery, jeweler, grocery, general merchandise, etc. **2.** A place where materials and supplies are accumulated and kept for future use.

storefront The front of a store or shop at street level, usually having one or more windows for the display of goods or wares. A.K.A. **shop front**

storehouse See: **warehouse**

storm cellar A cellar used for shelter during violent storms, cyclones, tornadoes, or hurricanes.

storm door An insulated-glass, exterior auxiliary door, in the same jamb as an entrance door to a house, that provides additional protection against cold air infiltration. A.K.A. **weather door**

storm drain An inlet to the city water-drainage system used for conveying rain and floodwater to a point of disposal.

storm window An exterior auxiliary window of insulated glass, used as additional protection against severe weather. A.K.A. **storm sash**

story Refers to one of many floors of a building, (e.g., the 35th floor) or the number of floors in a building (e.g., 35 stories). A.K.A. **floor**

storyboard A series of drawings that tell a story. *NOTE: Often used in advertising and the film and television industry to illustrate the various requirements of a particular commercial or scene.*

story pole A pole marked or cut to indicate the height of something, such as the height at which a picture mold is to be attached to a wall. A.K.A. **height board, storyboard**

stove An appliance for cooking that usually contains an **oven** and **range top**.

stove top A gas or electric cooking surface. A.K.A. **range top**

straightedge A rigid, straight piece of wood or metal used as a guide for a knife, pencil, or a power hand tool, such as a **circular saw**.

straight flight

staircase Refers to a typical single flight of stairs from one landing to the next.

straight-grained Descriptive of wood in which the grain is more or less parallel to the sawn edges.

strain A change to the form or shape of material or objects when subjected to an external force.

strap A flat, pliable material used to secure something to something else. **strapping 2.** A metal plate placed across and bolted or screwed to two or more timbers.

strap hinge

straphanger A straplike device used to hang metal supports, such as used in a suspended ceiling.

strap hinge A surface-mounted hinge with long flaps of metal on each side, by which it is secured to a door and an adjacent post or wall. A.K.A. **surface hinge**

stratified rock Layers of sediment deposits solidified by compaction. A.K.A. **sedimentary rock**

street A public thoroughfare, usually paved, including the sidewalks, trees, street lights, etc.

streetlight A large, tall light standard designed specifically to light up the roadways and sidewalks. A.K.A. **lamppost, light standard**

stress The external forces against a material, structure, or

stretcher

object, expressed in terms of pounds per square inch or kilograms per square millimeter.

stretcher　　The horizontal support connecting the legs of a chair, table, or other furniture.

strike　　To hit something. **2.** Demolition. **3.** To take apart for storage or disposal, as *strike* a theatrical set. *NOTE: Often referred to as a* **dead strike**, *meaning everything is to be demolished and disposed of.*

strike plate　The metal plate on a door-jamb that holds the through-bolt of a spring lock.

stringcourse　　A projecting row of bricks on the exterior side of a masonry wall.

stringer　　A supportive element in framing, such as stair stringers that support the steps. **2.** A horizontal timber connecting upright posts. A.K.A. **stringer board, stringboard**

stringer wall　The triangular wall below an open staircase, which follows the stringer line. A.K.A. **wall stringer, spandrel**

strip　　A long, narrow piece of any material. **2.** To remove a layer of material from a surface, such as stripping the shingles from a roof.

striped ebony　　*(Wood)* Refers specifically to Macassar ebony See: **Macassar ebony** A.K.A. **coromandel, calamander, coromandel ebony**

strip lighting　　A series of small lamps (bulbs) equally spaced and enclosed in a plastic conduit, used as decorative or accent

lighting, such as to accent an aisle in a darkened theatre.

strip mall　　A small group of stores, restaurant, etc., with parking, that cater to the needs of the local community. **2.** A row of shops along a highway that cater to the needs of the commuting or traveling public.

stripped　　Damage to the threads of a nut or bolt. **2.** Having removed the plastic insulation around electrical wiring to expose and connect the wires.

stripper　　A chemical liquid designed to remove coats of paint.

stripping　Removing old paint, wallpaper, distemper, etc., by the use of a blowtorch, paint remover, steam stripping appliance, stripping knife, or other scraping tools.

strongback　　A device *(T-profile)* made of boards and attached to the back of a framed wall or concrete form to stiffen or reinforce it. Similar in function to a **whaler**. See: **whaler**

structural damage　　Any damage to a structure. **2.** Damage to a structure that negatively affects its stability or creates a distortion.

structural engineering The branch of engineering specializing in the stability and ability of a building or structure to withstand physical force.

structural failure　　The loss of stability. **2.** The rupture, collapse, deformation, or failure of an essential component of the structure.

structural lumber

structural lumber The large posts, columns, beams, stringers, etc., used in stick framing, usually (timbers) larger than 4x material.

structural steel Refers primarily to the large steel I-beams used in the construction of multistoried buildings. **2.** Any steel object or material (beams, angles, bars, plates, sheets, strips, etc.) fabricated and used as a structural element in construction.

structure Any building or object (**bridge, dam, monument,** etc.). **2.** The connection of various elements to achieve a rigid form.

strut A brace or any piece of a framing *(upright, diagonal, or horizontal)*, positioned to resist movement or the weight of whatever it is supporting.

stucco A rough-textured, *plasterlike* exterior finish, applied to provide a uniform surface on a building, usually sprayed onto the surface with a gun-and-hopper combination made specifically for that purpose.

stud In stick framing, one of a series of vertical structural members within a wall or partition. A.K.A. **studded wall, stud wall**

studio A workshop, space, or factory where works of art are created. Studios adapt to the unique needs of a particular artistic endeavor and vary in size from a small portrait studio to very large film and television studios.

studio apartment An apartment dwelling with one large multifunctional room *(living room, dining room, bedroom, and kitchen facilities)* and a separate bathroom. **2.** An apartment, with large high windows and ceilings, used as an artist's studio.

study A room or alcove of a house or apartment used as a place for reading or writing, and furnished with the comforts and conveniences of an office or library. **2.** A preliminary sketch or drawing done in the early stages of developing a design concept.

stuff Slang for a mass of material or a variety of materials.

style Character. **2.** Individual preferences. **3.** Having merit. **4.** A theme, as in Egyptian or modern styles. A.K.A. **design, motif**

subcontractor A general term used to describe the licensed individuals or companies *(of the construction trades)*, with special skills or equipment, hired by the prime contractor to perform a portion of the work at a construction site, such as a drywall contractor, electrician, painter, plumber, etc.

subdivision A tract of land, improved with roads, water, sewers, and other utilities, sectioned off into individual residential lots.

subfloor Any underlayment or flooring material *(including the plywood sheeting attached to the joists)* below the finished flooring material. **subflooring** A.K.A. **underlayment**

sublease A lease by a tenant to a subtenant of residential or commercial property by the tenant under a preexisting lease.

submersible pump A type of water pump designed to operate underwater, as used in a pool of water to recirculate the water to supply an artificial waterfall.

subparagraph Part of the subdivided arrangement of a lengthy contractual agreement, which allows easy reference to descriptive clauses addressing or relevant to particular issues already agreed to. Subdivided paragraphs are identified by reference number, such as 3.9.3 or 8.7.2.

subrail The rail in a bannister or railing that the bottom of the balustrades die into, instead of dying into the individual steps *(treads)*.

subterranean Below ground level. A.K.A. **below grade**

suburb A residential community on the outskirts (in or near the boundary limits) of a nearby city.

subway An urban, underground commuter railway system.

suction The act or process of sucking. **2.** The sucking action of a vacuum that causes fluids or solids to be drawn into a container. A.K.A. **vacuum cleaner 3.** A process used, for example, to move sheets of paper through a printing press. **suctioned, suctioning**

suction pump A pump that draws water through a pipe by producing a vacuum.

sugar pine *(Wood)* A widely used, very fine *(almost invisible)*, durable, straight, even-grained

softwood, almost white in color. Easily machined, a favorite for milled structural and finished pieces, often used for moldings, sash, and door frames, especially if it is being painted. A.K.A. **white pine, soft pine**

sugi finish A Japanese technique of charring (burning) and wire brushing a surface.

suite A separate section or grouping of rooms designed to accommodate the needs of a single tenant.

Sullivan, Louis Henry *(1856 - 1924)* American architect of the Chicago school, a pioneer in the design of the steel-framed skyscraper.

summer house A home in the country or along the water used as a summer residence. **2.** A garden house of light airy design used to protect plants from the heat of the sun. See: **greenhouse**

sump A receptacle (**pit, basin,** or **tank**) where sewage or liquid waste is collected. See: **cesspool 2.** The funnel at the top of a rainwater gutter drainpipe that the water drops into.

sump pump A pump used to remove the accumulated waste in a sump.

sunburst An ornamental woodwork theme (**gingerbread**) resembling the rays of the sun, found particularly at the top of a steeply pitched gable roof end; a prevalent decorative theme found in Victorian architecture.

sunburst light A fixed window over a door or window

resembling a sunburst. A.K.A. **fanlight**

sundeck A flat roof area, balcony, open porch, etc., that is exposed to the sun.

sundial An ancient device for telling the time of day using a shadow cast from a projecting surface.

sunk Below an expected level or grade, such as a **sunken livingroom**.

sunken living room A living room a step or two below the level of adjoining rooms or corridors.

sun room See: **solarium**

superintendent The person designated by the contractor as their primary representative at a construction site, responsible directly to the contractor for continuous field supervision, coordination, completion of the work by construction foremen or subcontractors, along with site safety and accident prevention.

supermarket A large, self-service, grocery and general merchandise *(household and personal product)* retailer, usually one of a chain of supermarkets operated by the same company.

superstructure That portion of a building or structure above the foundation or ground upon which it sits. 2. Any structure that depends on another structure for a stable foundation.

supervision The assigning, overseeing, and inspection of work performed by a representative of the contractor.

supplier A person or company who supplies materials or equipment needed to accomplish authorized work, including subcontractors fabricating various elements off site. A.K.A. **vendor, retailer**

surcharge A fee charged for doing something, such as a transaction charge a bank might impose for handling a financial transaction.

surety bond A legal instrument financially obligating a third party (**the insurer**) for the timely competition of work being contracted to complete. The bond protects the owner/developer in the event the contractor fails to perform the contractual agreement A.K.A. **performance bond**

surface bolt A manually operated locking device with a metal rod or bolt designed to be mounted on the surface of a door, rather than mortised into the stile of the door.

surfaced four sides See: **dressed lumber** A.K.A. **s4s**

surfaced lumber See: **S4S, dressed lumber**

surface hinge A hinge, often ornamental, applied to the surface of a door and wall or cabinet face frame, instead of between the doorjamb and the narrow edge of a door stile. See: **strap hinge**

surface latch A latch *(no lock)* usually applied to the interior surface of a door.

surface plane The broad, relatively flat part of any surface.

surface planer A wood milling machine with a wide cutting head that, in small increments, levels the surface of boards, and sizes them to a uniform thickness.

surface texture The degree of roughness of a finished surface.

surform tool A coarse filelike tool of various shapes and sizes used to cut, shape, and trim various materials *(wood, foam, plaster, etc.)*.

surge A sudden thrust of voltage or current through an electrical wire or system, that can damage sensitive electrical equipment. See: **surge arrester**

surge arrester A electrical device that limits, *by shutting itself off*, and protects whatever electrical equipment to which it is attached from damage. A.K.A. **surge protector**

surge protector See: surge arrester

surround An encircling border or decorative frame, such as the tile or marble casing surrounding a fireplace or similar opening.

surveillance and observation A design concept that creates environmental space that is well lighted and easily visible and meant to subliminally discourage vandalism and other criminal activities. *NOTE: surveillance and observation is one of a series of design considerations meant to passively discourage vandalism and unauthorized entry.* See: **access control, territorial reinforcement**

survey Documentation, establishing a legal description of property, that includes maps, scaled diagrams, and a written description of the size, shape and exact location of the property or area. A.K.A. **boundary survey 2.** An analysis of the use of space in a building. **3.** An investigation and report of required data for a project.

surveying A branch of engineering concerned with the features of the earth's surface in relation to each other, and its position and size relative to other identifiable points on a map.

surveyor One whose education and occupation is surveying.

suspended ceiling system A nonstructural ceiling system of suspended metal struts designed to support acoustical tiles, lighting fixtures and air vents. A.K.A. **dropped ceiling, drop ceiling, suspension ceiling**

swag A festoon of festively draped cloth, or anything resembling it. **2.** A type of hanging lamp with a long cord interwoven in a decorative chain that hangs between the lamp and a nearby wall, and down to an electrical outlet. **3.** A tool or die used to shape metal.

swatch A representative patch or sample of a material or color, such as a sample of fabric, paint chip, veneer, or a small piece of carpet, for comparison.

sway brace A type of diagonal brace used to resist any lateral force, such as wind. See: **brace**

sweathouse An American Indian structure used for therapeutic or ritual sweating, from heat and steam produced by pouring water on hot stones. A.K.A. **sweat lodge** 2. A structure used to sweat tobacco.

sweating The joining of metal surfaces and tubing by heating and then soldering them together. **2.** The collecting of moisture (**condensation**) on a surface. **3.** The development of a glossy spot on a dull or matte finish, caused by rubbing (polishing).

sweep A characteristic of any large, curving form, mass, or shape, such as a curved wall or the *(wide)* sweeping view through a wall of clear glass.

swelling A raised area caused by moisture or chemical changes in the surface.

swimming pool Any basin or tank containing an artificial body of water of sufficient depth for swimming.

swing The action of a casement window or door's movement.

Swiss colonial See: **German colonial**

switch A device used to open or close an electric circuit or to change the connection of a circuit.

switch plate A flush plate for an electric switch.

sycamore *(Wood)* See: **harewood**

symbol A simple drawing that in the mind of the viewer represents something, as seen on handicapped or no-smoking signs

symbology The art and study of determining the significance and recognition value of a symbol.

symmetrical balance Artistically, equal mass and detail on both sides of a central object, such as having columns or sidelights on either side of a entrance door..

synagogue A building designated as a place of religious worship by a Jewish congregation.

- T -

T&G *Abbr.* **tongue-and-groove** See: **tongue-and-groove**

tabernacle A niche, recess or covered altar or shrine. **2.** A portable sanctuary.

table A multipurpose piece of furniture with a flat horizontal surface usually supported by four vertical legs, used for dining, a work surface, playing games, to study, etc. **2.** The setting of a table with objects laid out for a meal. **3.** Architecturally, a raised or sunken rectangular panel on a wall, or a raised horizontal surface. **4.** A plateau or flat facet cut across the top of a precious stone. **5.** An orderly arrangement of data, often in columns and rows. A.K.A. **tabulate 6.** As a matter of parliamentary procedure, acknowledging the proposal currently being discussed (**on the table**) or (**tabled**) to postpone discussion and consideration to a later date.

table saw A circular saw set below the surface of a table,

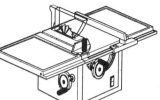

tablet 237

through which the blade protrudes. A.K.A. **ripsaw**

tablet A small slab or panel applied to a wall with an inscription or dedication.

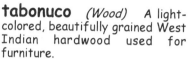

tabonuco *(Wood)* A light-colored, beautifully grained West Indian hardwood used for furniture.

tack A short, sharp-pointed nail. 2. To glue, staple, nail, weld, or otherwise fasten in spots rather than in a continuous line.

tack cloth A soft rag treated to pick up small particles and dust.

tackless strip A narrow wooden strip with rows of short angled nails protruding through it, which is installed close to the edge of a room, to hold, in place *(from beneath)* wall-to-wall carpeting that is stretched over it.

tacky The property of an adhesive to form a strong bond.

tails The ends of boards or sheet goods that hang beyond a desired point, and are cut off.

Taj Mahal A 17th century Moslem palace in Agra, India, of great size and elegance. *Said to have been built by an Indian prince for the love of a particular woman.*

tambour *(Fr)* Narrow strips of wood glued to canvas and used, for example, as the sliding front of a rolltop desk. 2. Architecturally, a wall of a circular building surrounded with columns. **tambouring, tamboured** 3. A

drum-shaped musical instrument.

tamp To pound an area of ground with a weight to compress and harden it for a foundation or floor.

tangent Touching, but not intersecting, a point on a line or circle. 2. A sudden digression or change of course, such as going off on a tangent during an argument.

tank A large vessel used to store liquids, often water.

tanker A vehicle (truck, boat, or airplane) used to transport liquid substances.

tap A faucet. See: faucet A.K.A. **spigot, sill cock**

tape measure A convenient spring-loaded device with a thin steel ribbon accurately graduated in feet and inches, commonly used to measure things. A.K.A. **tapeline**

taper A reduction of size, such as the narrowing of a spire or the diminishing width of the shaft of a column.

tapestry A decorative handwoven wall hanging depicting an event *(picture),* or having a unique design.

tapping screw See: **sheet-metal screw**

tar A dark, oily, viscous material, consisting mainly of hydrocarbons, distilled from organic substances such as **wood, peat, or coal.** A.K.A. **pitch**

tar-and-gravel roof A

tar paper

type of exterior roof finish utilizing a heavy coating of tar, covered with a thin layer of gravel, to seal the roof and protect the building from water damage.

tar paper A heavy paper, impregnated with a tarlike w a t e r p r o o f i n g substance, often used as an underlayment on roofs and exterior walls. See: **felt paper** A.K.A. **construction paper, building paper**

tarpaulin A large sheet of heavy-grade, waterproof canvas, used to cover and protect exposed materials from the weather.

task lighting Lighting located to illuminate a particular area or work surface.

tavern An inn for travelers, usually licensed to sell alcoholic beverages consumed on the premises.

tax abatement The reduction of real estate taxes on a property accomplished by a reduction in its assessed value.

tax exemption The release of an obligation to pay a particular tax, such as a property (real estate) tax.

teepee

taxpayer A person that pays applicable taxes.

T-bar An extruded metal flange that supports the

acoustical ceiling tiles, lights, etc., of a suspended ceiling system.

T-cushion A style of cushion that is cut around the recessed arm of an upholstered chair or sofa.

T-nut A flush mounted, metal machine screw fastener that in cross section resembles the letter T, with vertical treads, which is placed in a hole so the flat top of the T acts as a stop.

teahouse A Japanese garden house used for the tea ceremony.

teak *(Wood)* A dark yellow to brown, coarse-grained, high-density hardwood, often with fine black streaks. Native to parts of Asia, India, and Burma. More durable than oak. Used for shipbuilding, paneling, and fine furniture. A.K.A. **Indian oak**

tease In theatre, the short horizontal drape that runs across the top of a stage to hide rigging, lighting, and other equipment from the audience. Along with the leg drops, the tease frames the stage. **teaser** See: **theatrical curtains** A.K.A. **border**

tee A common pipe or tube connection that allows a perpendicular branch to flow off an existing straight line.

teepee A portable house, of long sticks and animal skins, once used by migrating Native American tribes. A.K.A. **tipi**

teeth Anything resembling teeth, such as the teeth of a saw blade, gear, or dentil.

telecommunications Voice, pictures, and data transmitted and received by satellite or over electrical wire, cable, or optical fiber.

telephone booth An enclosure for a telephone in a public area. *NOTE: Telephone booths have given way to smaller telephone partitions or shells, rather than walk-in **booths** with a **bifold door**.*

temper To increase the hardness and durability of a material (**steel**, **glass**, etc.) by applying heat followed by rapid cooling, which compresses the molecules on the material's surface layer. **tempered**

tempera A rapidly drying water-soluble paint containing egg whites (or a whites and yoke mixture) along with gum, pigment, and water. A.K.A. **watercolor**

tempered glass Glass that is five times stronger than ordinary glass as a result of being prestressed by heat and then suddenly quenched in cool water. See: **temper**

tempered steel Steel that has been strengthened by tempering. See: **temper**

template A pattern used as a guide for duplicating a part. A.K.A. **templet, fixture, jig**

temple A term used by several religions and sects to describe a building dedicated to worship. **2.** A Jewish synagogue.

3. A term applied to the building that houses the local lodge of a fraternal organization.

tenancy Occupation by a tenant, under a lease or rental agreement, of property owned by someone else.

tenant The person(s) or company occupying a building under a lease or rental agreement.

tender offer An offer made to purchase an item or to do specific work for a fixed amount.

tenement Denotes a low-rent apartment building that is not well maintained. A.K.A. **tenement house**

tennis court An area of appropriate size with high fences, where the game of tennis is played.

tenon A projecting end of a piece of wood, or other material, that has been reduced in width and depth to fit snugly into a corresponding cavity *(mortise)* in another part, in order to form a secure, stable joint.

tenon-and-mortise See: **mortise-and-tenon joint**

tensile strength The capability of a material to resist a force tending to tear it apart, measured by the maximum amount of tension the material can withstand without tearing.

tensile stress The amount of pressure, per square inch, exerted on a measured *(sq. ft., sq. yd.)* example of a sheet of material before it begins to buckle or elongate.

tension The act or condition of being stretched or pulled tight *(taut)* by force. **2**. The interplay of conflicting elements, such as a strained relationship on the brink of all out-hostilities. **3**. A mental, emotional, or nervous strain between people or groups.

tension bar A metal bar to which a tensile strain is applied or resisted.

tension rod A rod that runs between two trusslike structures held apart by a horizontal stretcher to prevent them from spreading. A.K.A. **tie rod**

tepidarium A warm room in a Roman bath.

terminal One of a number of computer monitors, with keyboard, attached to a network, and through which data or information can be added or retrieved. **2**. An ornamental figure or object placed at the end of a larger structure. A.K.A. **finial** **3**. In electrical circuit, a device where a connection is normally established or broken. **4**. A passive conductor or station positioned to facilitate a connection, such as a train or subway station. **5**. Medically, the inevitable demise of a patient suffering an incurable disease or illness.

terminate To end or stop.

terrace An embankment with a level top, or a flat roof, that is paved, planted, and decorated for leisure use.

terrace house A house or row of houses, situated on a terracelike site.

terrace roof See: **cut roof**

terra-cotta Hard-baked *(fired)* clay, glazed or unglazed, fine-grained, often handmade into tiles, commonly used as roof and flooring materials, especially in Mediterranean, Southwestern, and Spanish architecture.

terrazzo Cast concrete slabs of marble aggregate, ground smooth and used to decorate floor and wall surfaces. A.K.A. **terrazzo concrete**

territorial reinforcement A design concept that defines property or space -- through the use of vegetation, fences, doors with locks, etc., -- as privately owned. It is meant to send a subliminal message that intruders will be challenged. *NOTE: Territorial reinforcement is one of a series of design considerations meant to passively discourage vandalism and unauthorized entry.* See: **surveillance and observation, access control**

tertiary colors A color formed by the combination of a primary and a secondary color. See: **color wheel**

test To ascertain the qualities of a material and equipment by trial.

tester A canopy, over a throne, pulpit, or bed.

tester bed A four-poster bed topped with a fabric-covered canopy frame. *NOTE: Originally used to hold a fine light netting to protect against insects.*

tester bed

tetrastyle   A portico with four columns.

texture   The look or feel of a surface, other than smooth.

thatch   Straw, reed, large leaves, or similar materials, fastened together to shed water or provide thermal insulation, used to cover a roof, and sometimes the walls of a building. *NOTE: Still widely popular in tropical climates.*

theater   See: **theatre**

theatre   A building or outdoor structure providing a stage and audience seating where theatrical performances are presented. **theater**

theatre-in-the-round
A theatre with a stage in the middle of the audience, as in an arena. A.K.A. **arena theatre**

theatre seating   Offset rows of seats, in sections, and with aisles for easy access and egress by members of the audience. A.K.A. **auditorium seating**

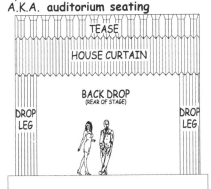

THEATRICAL CURTAINS

theatrical curtains All of the component parts (house curtain, tease, leg drops, and backdrop) of a curtain system traditionally used on theatre stages.

thermal barrier   A thin layer of low heat-conductivity material that is wrapped around the walls of a house or building, used in the manufacture of thermal glass to reduce the amount of heat that is able to escape.

thermal conductor   A material that readily transmits heat by means of thermal conduction.

thermal unit   A measured unit of heat energy, as defined by the **British thermal unit (Btu)** metric standard.

thermal window   A window insulated with a thermal material.

thermometer   A device for measuring the temperature.

thermostat   An instrument that controls a heater and/or air-conditioner unit and utilizes a **thermometer** to automatically adjust to changes in temperature, to maintain a desired temperature.

thickness   The property of depth. 2. To bring to a specified, uniform, and constant thickness.

thimble foot See: **spade leg**

thinner See: **paint thinner**

thread   The uniform ridges protruding from the internal or external surface of a cylinder, typically found on a screw or nut. *NOTE: A tap-and-die set is used to thread holes and pipes.*

threshold   The sill of an

exterior door. **2.** A strip of wood or metal fastened to the floor beneath a door, to cover the joint between two different flooring materials or to provide weather protection on an exterior door sill. A.K.A. **door saddle**

throat A shaft or channel through which something is collected and emitted, such as the passage from a firebox to the flue in a chimney.

throne An elaborate chair of state, in the court of a monarch, and from which they rule.

throne room The chief formal room of state, containing a throne on a raised and canopied dais, and an area for the members of court.

through-bolt A bolt, in a lock, that passes through the catch (**strike plate**) on the jamb to close and secure a door.

through stone A stone or series of stones wide enough to pass-through a wall and protrude slightly on both sides.

throw The maximum distance a bolt projects when fully extended.

thrust To forcefully shove or push. The amount of punch or force exerted by or on a structure. **2.** In an arch, the resultant force normal to any cross section of the arch. **3.** Architecturally, the gravitational force of weight resting on a support, such as an arch.

thumbscrew A screw designed to be turned with the thumb and fingers.

thumb tack A fastening device with a short, sharp pin and a large, flat head, used to tack something in place, and affixed by pressure applied by the human thumb. A.K.A. **thumb pin**

thuya *(Wood)* An ancient dark red-brown hardwood from North Africa, known to the early Chinese and Greeks. Similar properties to *Arbor vitae (same genus)*. Predominately used for highly polished cabinetry and contemporary furniture.

ticking A tightly woven, striped cotton or linen fabric once commonly used for mattress covers.

tieback drape

tie In framing, any structural member used to hold together or maintain a relationship between two component parts, such as a collar tie that strengthens and maintains the relationship of the roof rafters.

tieback A ribbon, braid, or other object used to tie open a drape.

tie beam In framing, a large horizontal beam that runs from wall to wall. **2.** The lowest horizontal stretcher in a truss. A.K.A. **cord**

tier A row, or a group of rows placed one above the other, such as in a **pigeonhole** or **egg-crate** mail or message boxes. See: **egg-crate**

tiered curtains

tiered curtains Two or more overlapping layers.

tie rod See: **tension rod**

tile One of a number of like, usually flat, ceramic squares, used to cover a floor, counter, or roof surface. The term also applies to tiles made of asphalt, cork, and wood, and also includes rounded terra-cotta roofing tiles.

tileboard Refers to a nonporous wallboard, *usually 1/4" Masonite*, that has been scored to simulate a grouted tile surface.

tilt top See: **drop-lid**

tilt-up construction A type of construction that employs a series of concrete wall panels, usually cast horizontally on site and simply tilted up (vertically) and secured into position when hardened.

timber Uncut trees or logs suitable for conversion to dimensioned lumber. **2.** Heavy beams and posts, usually larger than 4x4s.

timber framing A framing style that utilizes large timbers, 6x6 and above, for the structural stability of a building. The space between these timbers is filled in with nonstructural wall.

tin A soft, malleable sheet metal, used for many building applications, particularly as roof covering *(because it is relatively unaffected by exposure to air)*, and as ornately stamped ceiling decoration. A.K.A. **tin plate**

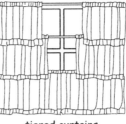

tiered curtains

tin ceiling A ceiling covered with sheets of ornately decorated tin. A.K.A. **metal coffering, metal ceiling**

tin-clad fire door A solid-core door covered with galvanized steel sheets to prevent the spread of a fire.

tinfoil Very thin sheets of tin, now mostly replaced by aluminum foil.

tin snips Heavy-duty, scissorlike hand tool used to cut thin sheet metal and wire mesh. A.K.A. **shears**

tint Varying amounts of white mixed with pure color.

tinted glass A process applied to window and auto glass to filter out the glare and heat of the sun.

tipi See: **teepee**

title A legal document establishing ownership of real property.

title insurance Insurance, offered by a company, guaranteeing that title to property is free and clear of all leans, debts, or other incumbrance that could negatively affect the value of the property.

title search An inquiry into the historical ownership records of a particular piece of real property to ascertain true ownership and possible existence of liens or easements on the

toe joint

property that could negatively affect its value.

toe joint A carpentry joint to support an inclined section with a notched horizontal section.

toe kick In cabinetry, an accommodation *(overhang)*, at the bottom of most cabinet pieces *(built-in and furniture)* made for the human foot, especially on kitchen cabinets where people are often barefoot. **2.** A kickplate on the bottom rail of a door. A.K.A. **kickplate**

toe joint

toenail To drive a nail or spike at an oblique angle. **2.** To fasten or secure with obliquely driven nails or spikes.

toggle bolt A long machine screw with a spring-activated winged flange that, after being inserted into the cavity of a wall through a hole, opens to anchor whatever the bolt is holding.

toilet A bathroom plumbing fixture consisting of a bowl, a flushing apparatus, a hinged seat, water supply, and waste pipe. A.K.A. **privy, lavatory, water closet**

tole A style of elaborately painted *(lacquered or enameled)*, and gilded metalwork or jewelry.

tollbooth A booth near a tollgate of a highway or bridge, serving as the shelter for the attendant. A.K.A. **tollhouse**

tollhouse The offices serving

several tollbooths on a multilane highway. **2.** Formally, a residence for a toll collector at a distant bridge.

tomb Architecturally, a memorial structure or marker over or alongside a grave.

tonal value A characteristic of color, which addresses its relative strength in contrast to black or white. A.K.A. **tone, value**

tongue Any projecting element, either a continuous ridge along the edge of a board or an extension (like a tendon), such as found on tongue and groove flooring or paneling, intended to fit into a corresponding groove or open to form a joint. **2.** Anything that resembles a tongue.

tongue-and-groove
Dressed-and-matched boards that have a groove milled on one edge and a corresponding tongue on the other, so that when laid side-by-side a tongue and grove interlock.

tongue-and-groove joint A joint formed by the insertion of a tongue element into a corresponding groove of an adjoining piece. A.K.A. **T&G joint**

tongue & groove

tool room A room where tools are kept, maintained, and issued from.

tools The various instruments *(hammers, drills, saws, etc., both manual and powered)* carpenter's, craftsmen, and mechanics use to accomplish their work.

topcoat The final coat of paint applied to a surface. A.K.A. **finish coat**

top out To finish the top of anything, such as the cap of a chimney.

topsoil The upper layer of soil, containing organic matter and nutrients, as distinct from the subsoil. A.K.A. **loam**

torch A source of light, such as a flashlight.

torque The force applied to a rotating object, such as that applied to a nut or bolt. A.K.A. **pressure**

torque wrench A wrench with a gauge that indicates exactly how much torque or pressure is being applied to a nut or bolt.

torso The body, excluding the limbs and head.

torus A donut-shaped object. 2. A large, convex molding at the base of a column.

to-the-trade See: **wholesale showroom**

to-the-weather A term used to describe which side of a material is to be used as the exterior face.

town planning See: **city planning**

tower A tall, often circular, structure originally designed for observation, communication, and defense.

tower crane A type of crane with a fixed vertical mast topped by a rotating boom and winch, used to hoist and move materials from one location to another, within the diameter of the boom.

Tower of London An ancient London castle tower on the North bank of the Thames, historically known as **the Tower**, today, a museum and safe storage for the British crown jewels and other valuable national treasures.

townhouse A house in town, as opposed to a house in the country. 2. A small house, usually attached, with a common wall, to one or more other small, single-family housing units, in or near a city.

trabeated construction Post and lintel construction, as opposed to arches.

tracery Lacy integrate ornamental work of interlaced and branching lines.

tracing paper A transparent paper artists use to trace or make original drawings.

track To follow a path. 2. A strip of metal that supports and/or guides something along a path.

track lighting Lighting fixtures designed for easy positioning at any point along a fixed lighting track.

tractor A powerful engine-driven vehicle, on wheels or on tracks, used for pushing and pulling a trailer, equipment, or tools.

trade A person's profession or craft, usually involving artistic or manual skills. 2. One of the many specialist or skilled professionals *(masonry, carpentry, plastering, etc.)* involved in construction. A.K.A. **the trades**

traditional style   See: Regency style

trammel points   See: bar compass

transformer   A device used to transfer electric energy from one circuit to another

transit   A surveying instrument, employing a telescope and cross-hairs, used to measure and lay out horizontal and vertical angles, distances, directions, and differences in elevation.

transitional style
A general term describing a style between or incorporating two major design motifs, particularly that between the Romanesque and Gothic periods *(late 12th - early 13th centuries)*.

translucent   A material that transmits and diffuses light, so that only silhouetted images can be seen through it.

transom   See: transom window

transom bar   A horizontal crossbar separating a door or window from a transom window or fanlight window above.   2. A horizontal element separating a door from a window, panel, or louver above.

transom light   The glass pane of a transom window.

transom window   A small hinged window above a door or another window, that can be opened for ventilation.   2. A fanlight or sunburst window over the front door. See: **door styles** A.K.A. **transom, transom light**

transportation   Moving people and materials from one location to another and the associated costs.

trap   Various sewer devices to filter out or catch gasses, air, odors, and other debris.

trapdoor   A door set into a floor, ceiling, or roof. Suggests an attempt to hide or appear inconspicuous.

trapezoid   A 4-sided nonsquare figure with two parallel sides.

trapezoid

trash   A.K.A. garbage, refuse, rubbish

trash chute   A vertical shaft in a multistory building used to transmit trash from the upper floors to a large trash bin at the bottom end of the shaft.   2. A temporary shaft for the quick removal of debris collected during the demolition phase of a multistory building rehabilitation project.   A.K.A. **refuse chute**

travel   The distance an object moves from one end of a track to the other. See: **track**

travel rise   A technical term referring to the vertical distance between the bottom terminal landing and the top terminal landing of an elevator, escalator, etc.

traverse   A screen, railing, or other barrier that crosses an opening to allow passage from one place to another.

travertine   A coarse *(marblelike)* limestone commonly used as wall covering and flooring.

travertine rod   A curtain rod with cords and pulleys to open and close curtains and drapes.

tread The horizontal part of a step, includes the **nosing**, upon which the foot rests. See: **staircase details**

tread length   The width of a staircase length; width of a tread, measured perpendicular to the normal line of travel *(left and right)*, or the width of the staircase. See: **staircase details**

tread width The dimensional width of a tread, measured along the normal line of travel of the stair *(toe to heal, including the nosing)*.

trefoil *(Fr)*   A 3-lobed ornament resembling a clover.

trellis   An open grating or latticework frame used in a garden to support vines and climbing plants. **treillage** See: **arbor**

trench   A deep, long, narrow furrow, or ditch. **2.** A long, steep-sided valley on the ocean floor.

trestle   The framework consisting of vertical, slanted supports and horizontal crosspieces supporting a bridge.

trestle table   A tabletop supported by a trestle.

triangle A manual drafting instrument in the form of a right-angled triangle made of metal or plastic, that rests against a T-square to make vertical lines.

triangulation   A

method of surveying in which **base lines** are derived by computation from points *(the vertices of a chain or network of triangles)* measured by sophisticated instruments, to establish a precise measurement on the ground.

tribunal See: **tribune**

tribune   A raised platform or dais from which a speaker addresses an assembly.   A.K.A. **dais, tribunal**

trim Artistically, anything that adds character, authenticity, or creates a decorative or festive effect. **2.** Refers to the various decorative moldings *(**window and door casing, crown, base, picture mold, chair rail, sills, etc.**)* that are permanently affixed to bare walls. **trimmer, trimmings 3.** Any visual element, such as hardware flanges, that covers or protects joints, edges, or ends of another material, including faucets, spigots, exposed traps. A.K.A. **fitting 4.** A rigging term for an adjustment in the vertical positioning of scenery or equipment.

trimmer   In framing, a **sistered** stud that supports one side of a header.   **2.** A short horizontal beam, between three or more floor joists to create an opening in the floor for a staircase or fireplace. **3.** See: **trim**

triplet A group of three.

tripod   A 3-legged instrument

trestle table

triptych

support or table, for surveying equipment, telescopes, camera, and other instruments.

triptych Any picture or artistic design made on three panels and hinged to fold, for easy transport.

tri-square An instrument (a **square**) a carpenter uses with both a 90° and 45° permanently set angle, along with an adjustable blade for marking a parallel line and a water bubble to check for level and plumb.

tri-square

tristyle A portico with three columns.

triumphal arch A large arch historically erected to celebrate, a significant event, a military victory or national hero, as the Arc de Triomphe erected in Paris between 1806-1835. See: **memorial arch**

triumphal column A large column erected to celebrate a national hero or a military victory, exemplified by many such columns in Rome, *circa AD 100-200*.

trolley beam Any beam established to carry the weight of something that travels along its length, such as the beams on an **overhead crane** (A.K.A. **trolley crane**) travels along.

trompe l'oeil *(Fr)* Means, to "fool or deceive the eye."

trowel A flat hand tool with a broad steel blade, used to spread and smooth concrete, plaster, or mortar.

trowel

truck house A building to house a hook-and-ladder and other types of fire engines. A.K.A. **fire station**

true To check for level and plumb, either by eye or by means of instruments.

true north The direction from an observer's point of view to the geographic north pole.

trumpet leg A turned furniture leg that takes the shape of the cone of a trumpet *(musical instrument)*.

trundle bed A bed on wheels that is rolled out from beneath a larger bed when needed. A.K.A. **day bed**

trunk line A large or principal conductor of air, grain, information, etc.

truss To tie up or bind tightly. **2.** Architecturally, the flat, rigid raftered framework that rests on the sidewalls, shaping the roof and stabilizing the walls of a structure. *NOTE: Trusses are generally used to create an unobstructed spans of more than 20 ft. from wall to wall.* **truss beam, trussed beam** See: **roof truss details**

T square An instrument, shaped like the letter *T*, used to mark a perpendicular line off a straight edge. **2.** A drafting tool with which a draftsman, *working in pen or pencil* establishes a horizontal line, using the side

T square

edge of the table as a guide. **tee square**

tubular A tubelike shape.

Tudor arch A bluntly pointed arch. A.K.A. **blunt arch** See: **arches**

Tudor architecture The final stage of Perpendicular style of medieval English Gothic architecture *(1485-1560)*, during the reigns of Henry VII and Henry VIII *(the Tudor kings of England)*, and preceding the Elizabethan and Jacobean periods. Characterized by steeply pitched gabled roofs and entryways, masonry walls with half-timber trim, and narrow windows. A.K.A. **English Tudor**

Tudor revival *(Late 19th and early 20th centuries)* Reminiscent of Elizabethan and Jacobean period of 16th and 17th centuries England, with steeply pitched roofs and one or more decorative, rather than structural, intersecting gables. Also featured half-timber details over plaster walls, with long rows of casement windows. A.K.A. **English Tudor**

tufted carpet Carpet made with short pile yarn punched through a carpet-backing material, so that the *ends* of the fibers make up the surface pile of the carpet, as opposed to continuous loop carpet.

tulip column See: **lotus column**

tulipwood *(Wood)* A light yellow hardwood with red streaks, native to Brazil, often used in marquetry.

tumbler Part of the inner workings of a locking mechanism, that frees the bolt when a properly grooved key is engaged.

tungsten steel Steel made with a small percentage of tungsten, the strongest metal known.

tunnel A passage or corridor excavated through rock and dirt, at or below the surface.

turbine fan A rotating roof fan designed to pull hot air out of a building.

turf The upper layer of earth within which roots of grass and other small plants form a thick cover.

turnbuckle

turnbuckle A metal coupling device with either a right-hand or left-hand threaded hook at the end, so that when its elongated center is turned, *drawing in the hooks*, tension is applied to whatever the opposing hooks are attached.

turning Objects shaped on a rapidly rotating lathe. A.K.A. **turned wood ornaments**

turn-key operation A project in which the contractor completes all work and furnishings of a building so that it is ready for immediate use.

turn-of-the-century Refers to anything that took place or was made around 1900. NOTE: The popular phrase to recognize the beginning of the 21st century,

turnstile

and to distinguish it from the beginning of the 20th century, is **millennium** See: **millennium**

turnstile   A revolving partition that allows only one person at a time through a gate.

turnstile door   See: **revolving door**

turret   A superimposed, small slender tower emanating from the corner of a large building.

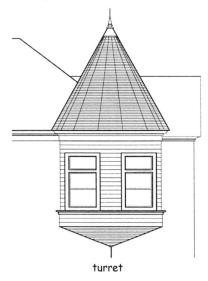

turret

turret steps   Triangular steps that form a spiral staircase in a turretlike structure.

Tuscan order   A simplified version of the classic Roman Doric order. A.K.A. **Etruscan order**

twist   A warp or spiral-like curl in a plank of lumber. Not on the same plane.

twist

twisted column   A column with a twisted or spiral appearance. A.K.A. **wreathed column**

two-family house See: **duplex**

tuxedo arm   A style of arm on upholstered sofas, chairs, or love seats that is as high as the back rest.

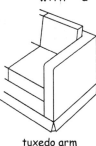

tuxedo arm

tympanum   The recessed triangular face in a pediment, surrounded by the sloping sides and horizontal base.

- U -

U-bolt   A U-shaped rod with threads on both ends for nuts, used to hold a pipe in place.

UL Label   An identification affixed to electrical and mechanical components, that have successfully passed the stringent laboratory testing of **Underwriters Laboratories, Inc.** (an insurance industries watchdog), which is considered an industry standard.   See: **Underwriters Laboratories, Inc.**

ultramarine   A blue pigment used in paint.

ultrasonic motion detector   A motion detector employing sound, used in switches to turn lights on and in alarm systems to detect intruders.

ultraviolet light Ultraviolet light radiation.

umber

umber A naturally occurring brown siliceous earth, used as a pigment in paint. A.K.A. **burnt umber**

unburnt Clay objects (pottery and tile) that are air dried, rather than baked or fired in a kiln.

uncoursed Masonry that is not laid up in uniform courses and layers.

undercoat A coat of paint applied on wood, over a primer, or over a previous coat of paint, to seal; serves as a adhesion base for the topcoat.

undercut The slightly narrow cut of a panel to easily fit within the frame. **2** In sculpture, the removal of material from behind, to add dimension, such as on a relief. See: **relief**

underfloor heating
Heating provided by hot water pipes or electric heating cables, installed beneath a finish floor.

underglaze Refers to a pattern or design applied to tile or pottery before the final glazing is applied.

underground Below grade or ground level.

underground structure
Anything built below ground level, such as a subway, fallout shelter, sewer system, a garden sprinkler system, etc.

underlayment Any material (plywood, hardwood, carpet padding, felt paper, etc.) placed on a subfloor to provide a smooth, even surface to which a finished surface is applied **underlay**

underpinning To support from below, as with props, girders, or masonry. **2.** A support or foundation, used to support a wall or structure. **underpinned, underpins**

Underwriters Laboratories, Inc. A
nonprofit organization sponsored by the National Board of Fire Underwriters that inspects and tests electric devices to assure their compliance with the National Electrical Code.

undressed lumber
Rough-sawn lumber that has not been planed.

unglazed tile Tile that derives its color and texture from the clay itself, rather than from a coating of colored, opaque, or transparent material, used to seal and decorate fire-hardened clay tiles.

unicorn A mythical animal, the symbol for chastity, often depicted in the art of the Middle Ages.

uniform load A load uniformly distributed over all or a portion of a floor or surface.

union A pipe fitting, connecting the ends of two pipes. A.K.A. **flange union**

unit price The price, on an invoice, of one unit of a quantity of the same item, which the total is based.

university An accredited institution of higher learning. A.K.A. **college**

unloader A type of forklift

that unloads trucks and places pallets of material wherever needed on the job site.

unstable soil Soil or contour conditions on property that would prohibit the construction of a building without additional support, such as would be furnished by a system of pylons and/or shoring.

uplight A light, in or on the floor, that casts a beam of light upward, as to wash a wall with light.

upright A vertical structural member.

upstage The back part of a stage, away from the audience.

upstairs An upper floor of a house or small building, above the main or entrance floor.

urban area An area within a city's limits or closely linked by common public utilities or services.

urban renewal The improvement and rehabilitation of relatively sound structures of a deteriorated, underutilized, or slum areas of a city.

urinal A sanitary fixture equipped with a water supply and drain for flushing away urine, used in men's public toilets.

urn A decorative receptacle for the ashes of the dead.

utility knife A cutting instrument with a replaceable razor blade.

utility pole A large pole installed by a telephone or electric utility

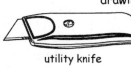
utility knife

company to support overhead electric and telephone lines and equipment.

- V -

valance Part of a window treatment, the horizontal detail, an **overdrape**, used to accentuate the top of a window.

valley The internal angle formed by the intersection of two inclined planes of a roof. See: **rafter details**

valley flashing The sheet metal (copper or lead) used to line the valley on a roof, so that rainwater will not seep through.

valley jack A.K.A. **jack rafter** See: **rafter details**

valuation An appraisal or estimate of the value of property, including any existing or proposed buildings or structures on it.

value Refers to the amount of black or white in a color.

valve A device that regulates or closes off the flow of a fluid. See: **faucet** A.K.A. **spigot, tap**

vanity

vane See: **weather vane**

vanishing point In perspective drawing, a point toward which a series of parallel lines seem to converge.

vanity A small make-up table, with mirror.

vapor lock A device that eliminates or minimizes the collection of vapor in a pipe.

variance Written authorization, from the responsible municipal agency, permitting construction in a manner that is not allowed by code or other regulations.

varnish A clear, unpigmented resinous liquid, that dries a thin, hard, smooth, transparent, glossy protective film when applied to a wood surface.

varnish remover A chemical that softens or dissolves varnish for easy removal.

vase A hollow decorative, glass or ceramic, container used to hold flowers or ornamentation.

vault A masonry roof or ceiling over an area, made using the principles of an arch. **2.** A walk-in safe, usually in a bank, where cash and safe-deposit boxes are kept. A.K.A. **vaulted, vaulted ceiling**

vaulted ceiling See: **vault**

vega The round peeled logs used as ceiling beams in the Southwest adobe style. See: **adobe**

vehicle A self-propelled mechanical device used to transport people and/or materials from one place to another. A.K.A. **motor vehicle 2.** A medium through which something is transmitted, communicated, expressed, or accomplished, such as a book, a play, etc. **3.** A technique or medium *(oils, watercolors, clay, theatre, dance, painting, etc.)* an artist chooses to express themselves.

Velcro A brand name for a 2-

VAULTED CEILINGS

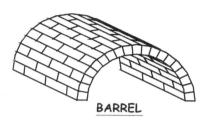

BARREL

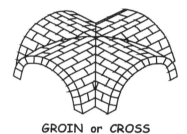

GROIN or CROSS

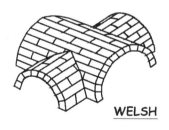

WELSH

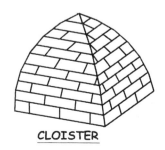

CLOISTER

part fabric fastener that adheres when pressed together.

vellum   A heavy grade of tracing paper used in drafting. *NOTE: Once applied to paper made of lambskin.*

vendor   An organization or person that furnishes materials or equipment.   A.K.A.   **supplier, distributor, retailer**

veneer   A thin material used as a finished surface. **2.** A thin sheet of wood sliced *(rotary-cut)* from a log, and applied as a finish surface, especially in furniture. **3.** Thin sheets of wood glued together to form plywood.

veneered door   A door to which a wood veneer face has been applied.

veneered plywood
Plywood faced on one side with a decorative wood veneer.

Venetian arch   A true semicircular arch.

venetian blind   A blind (for a window) made of evenly spaced, thin horizontal slats or louvers, connected with cord and webbing. When closed, they slightly overlap one another and when open, the thin slats almost disappear from view, allowing fresh air and light to enter.

Venetian furniture
Applied to the extravagantly carved and ornamented furniture of the Baroque and Rococo periods of the Italian Renaissance.

Venetian motif   See: Palladian architecture

Venetian window   See:

Palladian window   A.K.A.   **serlian window**

vent   An outlet through which fumes, liquids, gases, or steam are permitted to escape or are discharged. **ventilate, ventilator 2.** An outlet in a particular room that provides heat or filtered air from the building's heating and/or air-conditioner system. **ventilation 3.** To give, often foreful, expression or utterance to.

vent cap   A fitted cover that either directs the flow of the vented material to, or prevents foreign objects from falling into the vent. A.K.A. **vent cover**

vent cover   See: **vent cap**

ventilation   The process of supplying to or removing air (naturally or mechanically) from any space.

venting   The discharging of air, liquids, gases, or steam into a building's drain or waste disposal system.

vent pipe   An open outlet pipe installed in plumbing systems that prevents gas or liquid pressure from building up.

veranda   A covered porch or balcony, extending along the outside of a building.   A.K.A. **porch, portico, sun porch**

vertical-grained Straight wood grain that runs the length of a board.

vertical plane   Refers to a vertical wall surface, which is at a right angle to the horizontal floor.

vertical sliding window
A window with one or more sashes

that move vertically, such as a double-hung sash.

vestibule   An anteroom or small foyer *(a weather lock)* just inside an entry door.

V-groove   A small, pointed groove detail on a surface.

viaduct   A series of arches that carry a road, canal, or railroad over a valley, or flood or shallow water plane.

vibrating sander   See: oscillating sander

vibrator   A power-driven machine that agitates fresh concrete to eliminate voids and air bubbles, and ensures contact with form surfaces and embedded materials.

Victorian architecture
Typical of the Gothic Revival period of British Queen Victoria's reign, includes revived Queen Anne style.

Victorian architecture

vignette   A small, decorative setting, as if in a picture frame. **2.** A short, descriptive literary sketch, or a scene in a play or movie. **3.** To describe in a brief way.

villa *(Italian)*   An elaborate country estate of some pretension, often including outbuildings and gardens.

village   A small collection of houses forming part or a section of a town or city.   A.K.A. **community, neighborhood**

vinyl   A polymerized vinyl chloride thermoplastic compound, used for a variety of products, including flooring.

vinyl-asbestos tile   A resilient vinyl floor tile made with asbestos fibers. *NOTE: No longer an approved flooring material because of the health concerns associated with asbestos.*

vinyl flooring   Sheet or tile flooring made of vinyl.

viscosity   The property of a liquid to flow, spread, and/or cover.

vise A gripping tool with movable jaws used to firmly hold an object being worked on.

visibility
The state of being visible or perceivable by the eye. **2.** A   vise
clear unobstructed view **3.** The furthest distance, *depending on weather conditions*, an object can be seen.

visual field   See: **field of vision**

visual inspection
Inspection by examination, as opposed to using testing apparatus.

void   Areas in sheeting, concrete, mortar, etc., that are not filled, such as where a knot has fallen out of a board, spaces between stones not filled with concrete, or spaces caused by air bubbles.

volatile   Descriptive of a substance that quickly evaporates or vaporizes into a gas. Suggests a possible or potential danger.

volcanic rock   Stones of cooled molten lava, once spewed from an erupting volcano.

volt A unit of electronic force.

voltage   The force or magnitude of an electric circuit.

voltage regulator   An electrical device that maintains a constant voltage supply, even though the line voltage may vary

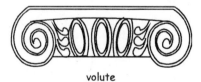

volute

volute A spiral scroll easement at the bottom end of a stair rail. See: **staircase details 2**. The classic spiral scroll found atop fundamentally Ionic columns, but also found on Corinthian and composite columns. See: **column details**

voussoir   The wedge-shaped stones that form the curved parts of an arch or a vaulted ceiling.

vulcanization   A chemical process by which the structural properties of rubber are made stronger, more resilient, and free of odor and stickiness.

- W -

wainscot   A traditional decorative and/or protective facing applied to the lower portion of an interior wall, either flat or wood paneled.

wainscot cap   The molding which finishes the upper edge of a wainscot.

wainscot chair   An early 17th century English chair with a wainscotlike back.

waiting room   A room, with seating, as found at a train station or airport, for people to wait for the arrival or departure of transportation, at a hospital or professional (doctor, lawyer, etc.) offices, or while awaiting the completion of any service (auto repair, car wash, etc.)   A.K.A. **reception room**

walk   A pedestrian path or passageway.

walk-in   An enclosure large enough for one or more people to enter into, such as a commercial refrigerator/freezer or a vault in a bank.   A.K.A. **walk-in box**

walk-up A walk-up, *as opposed to a drive-through*, service window at a fast-food restaurant. **2.** A multistory apartment or commercial building without an elevator.

wall A structure of any material serving to enclose a room, building, or other space. **2.** A division or partition between rooms.

wallboard See: **drywall**

wall cavity The space between the two surfaces of a wall, usually the width of the studs *(3 1/2" or 5 1/2")* and often filled with insulation.

wall dormer See: **dormer wall**

wall heater A self-contained vented furnace, permanently installed in a wall, to heat the surrounding space, on one or both sides of the wall. A.K.A. **wall furnace**

wall height The measured vertical dimension of a wall, from floor to ceiling.

wall-hung water closet A water closet attached to the wall, as opposed to resting on or part of the toilet itself.

wall line A line, in plan view, following the path of an interior or exterior wall.

wall opening Typically, a door or window opening in any wall, but also includes openings made for a **pass-through**, **chute**, etc.

wall outlet An electrical outlet in a wall (See: **duplex receptacle**), into which an electrical appliance or equipment is inserted to receive power.

wall painting Painting the surface of a wall with an ornamental design or mural. A.K.A. **mural**

wall panel A panel (sheeting, wainscoting, control box, etc.), decorative or practical, permanently or temporarily attached to a wall.

wallpaper Decorative wall covering of paper, or paperlike material, pasted to the walls of rooms. *NOTE: Wallpaper is distributed in (approx.) 18" to 24" wide rolls, depending on the pattern. HISTORIC NOTE: Decorative wallpaper was a popular substitute for plaster or paneled walls by the 1750s.*

wall plug An electrical outlet A.K.A. **electrical receptacle, wall plug, plug**

wall sheathing Sheets of plywood or composite materials applied to exterior stud wall-frame, ties the structure together, stiffens it, and provides a base for finished siding.

wall space Those parts of walls that are not encumbered by doors, windows, or other elements.

wall stringer A board that runs along the wall and extends slightly above a flight of stairs, as a kick rail or baseboard, to prevent damage to a wall. A.K.A. **stringer wall**

wall ties Metal strapping used to tie various elements of stick-framed buildings together, such as tying down the rafters of a roof to the walls, in areas where strong winds, tornados, and hurricanes are common.

wall vent An intake or outlet

vent on the wall of a room. A.K.A. **vent, vent cover**

wall unit   Shelving and cabinets attached to the walls.

wall wash A type of spotlight that washes a wall with ambient light. **wall washing**

walnut *(Wood)*   A strong hardwood, grown worldwide, varying from fine-to-coarse open grain and from light brown to very dark brown *(almost black)*. Walnut rarely splits and it can be polished to a high gloss. Used primarily for furniture, cabinet faces, and moldings. Similar in character to **hickory, butternut, black walnut**

ward   A division of a city or town, particularly by electoral district. **2.** A room or wing in a hospital for the care of a particular group of patients, such as a maternity ward or a large room in a security ward holding several patients, as opposed to a private or semiprivate room. **3.** Legally, custody of a minor guardianship (A.K.A. **ward of the state**), or the confinement of an individual for the protection of others. **4.** To try to avert or prevent, as in **warding off** a colds by taking vitamins.

wardrobe   A small room large piece of furniture used for hanging and storing garments.

warehouse   A building designed for the temporary storage of merchandise. A.K.A. **storehouse**

warm colors   Red, and the secondary and tertiary colors surrounding it. See: **color wheel**

warp   A distortion or deviation in shape of a parallel surface, usually resulting from a change in moisture content in wood. **2.** The fine grid material carpeting fibers are woven into.   **warped 3.** In weaving, the treads that run lengthwise on a loom.

warranty   See: **guarantee**

wash   A technique for applying paint and watercolor to a surface. **2.** A natural path that water drains or follows.

washable   Capable of being washed repeatedly without significant erosion or change in its appearance or functional characteristics.

washbasin See: **sink** A.K.A. **lavatory**

washboard   Baseboard or tile installed to protect the wall from the normal mopping of a kitchen or bathroom floor. A.K.A. **baseboard**

wash coat   An undercoating, establishing a color, much of which is removed by cloth, and over which a glaze coat is usually applied, to produce a less formal, almost rustic, finish to cabinets. See: **pickle finish**

washed finish   A less formal rustic finish, using the **pickled** or **wash coat** technique.

washer   An appliance used to wash household linens and clothing, or a dish washer. **2.** A thin flat ring *(metal, rubber, or other materials)* used in various applications, as a spacer or to form a seal to prevent leakage between parts or pipes.

wash fountain A large, round, factory-size sink, around which several people can wash their hands and face, that often dispenses the water in jet streams, like a fountain.

washroom A room providing public facilities for washing. A.K.A. **men's room, rest room, lavatory, toilet**, etc.

washtub See: **bathtub**

waste See: **garbage** A.K.A. **refuse rubbish, trash**

waste disposal unit An electric-motor-driven device, attached to a drain in a kitchen sink, to grind waste food into very small pieces to easily wash through a drain pipe.

waste pipe A drainpipe for waterborne discharge, other than sewage *(fecal matter)*.

watch house The office(s) the on-duty security force uses.

watchtower A tall tower from which the landscape can be observed. **2.** A tower built to hold a large clock.

water absorption The absorption properties of a material expressed *(from tests)* as a percentage of its increased weight, after immersion in water for a specified time, compared to its dry weight.

water closet That part of a toilet that stores water for the next flush. *Abbr.* **WC 2.** A room containing a toilet.

watercolors See: **tempera**

water cooler A container or vessel, often ceramic pottery, with

a spigot that keeps water cool without refrigeration.

water filtration system A device, installed under a kitchen sink and attached to the plumbing, that filters incoming water and delivers clean drinking water to a special spout.

water fountain Artificially created stream(s) or jet(s) of water, as found in a water sculpture, drinking fountain, or washing fountain.

water heater A device, gas or electric, attached to the plumbing system of a house or building, that heats and stores hot water for domestic use, usually supplied at temperatures between 120-140°F *(approx. 50-60°C)*.

water level A device used to establish a level line at various points around a room using a transparent, water-filled, flexible hose.

waterline The height at which standing water finds its own level. **2.** A line established by a manufacturer to indicate the level to which a vessel should be filled with water.

water main The water supply pipe, provided by the city, which is tapped into in order to establish a water supply for a residence or building.

water meter A mechanical device, *usually installed at or near the connection to the water main*, to measure the volume of water a building uses, which is then used as a bases for billing.

waterproof Any material

waterproofing

made of or coated with rubber, plastic, or other sealing agent or membrane that is impervious to water.

waterproofing Applying or covering with a waterproof material to prevent the penetration of water.

water repellent Said of a surface or treatment that resists water penetration, but that is not impervious to water.

water retentivity The property of a material, *like a sponge*, to retain water. 2. The ability of a material to prevent the rapid loss of water through absorption.

watershed A region draining into a river or other body of water. 2. A term used to describe the natural drainage or movement of water, such as a **wash** or **water table**. 3. A critical turning point that marks a division or a change of course.

water softener An apparatus that chemically removes calcium and magnesium salts from a water supply.

waterspout A pipe or duct to carry rainwater from a roof gutter to the ground or into a drain.

water supply Clean water, for human consumption, made available through a city's water system.

water table A sloping, horizontal projecting ledge, molding, or stringcourse along an exterior wall, designed to throw off rainwater. A.K.A. **drip mold, canting strip** 2. The level below which the ground is completely saturated with water. A.K.A. **groundwater level, water level**

watertight A barrier or enclosure that is impenetrable by water or moisture. 2. A surface that is impervious to water.

water works A facility to expedite the distribution of water through the city's water system.

watt An internationally recognized unit of electric power.

watt-hour The use of a watt of power for one hour.

wavelength The distance between two successive waves of light or sound. 2. The distance a light or sound wave travels in a specified period.

wax Beeswax. 2. Any of various natural, oily or greasy, heat-sensitive substances that are insoluble in water, but soluble in most organic solvents. Used in paste or liquid form as a protective coating or polish on wood surfaces. **waxing** 3. A material a sculptor uses to create an image or object that will become a casting, such as a bronze casting, using the hot metal wax replacement method. A.K.A. **lost wax method**

way A street, alley, or other thoroughfare or easement permanently established for the passage of persons or vehicles.

weather The atmospheric conditions at any given time or place, including temperature, moisture, wind velocity, and barometric pressure variables. 2. To age, deteriorate, discolor, or to otherwise be adversely affected by exposure to the elements. **weathered** 3. A roof sloped to shed water.

weather barrier An exterior layer that insulates and protects a building from weather damage or discomfort.

weatherboard See: **drip edge** A.K.A. **weather mold**

weathercock See: **weather vane**

weathered Descriptive of a surface *(particularly wood)* showing signs of long-term exposure to the elements. 2. To withstand the effects of weather.

weathering Changes *(natural or artificial)* in color, texture, strength, etc., due to the weather.

weather mold See: **drip edge** A.K.A. **weatherboard**

weatherproof Constructed so that exposure to the weather will not interfere with or negatively affect function or operation.

weather strip A strip of material applied to an exterior door or window to fill or seal spaces where rain, snow, cold air, etc., could enter or escape. **weather stripping**

weather tight Sealed against the intrusion of rain, snow, cold air, etc.

weather vane A rotating device put on the ridge of a roof that turns, depending on the wind, to indicate the speed and direction of the wind. Often ornamented with a rooster, or other decorative element. A.K.A. **weathercock**

weave To make cloth by interlacing the threads, strips, or strands of material. 2. To spin a tale. **weaving**

web A structure of delicate threadlike filaments, characteristically spun by spiders 2. A thin flat strip of strong woven fabric A.K.A. **webbing**

webbing See: **web**

welch cupboard A large, open dining room cupboard with wood shelves, often including a tongue-and-groove backing, over a cabinet base, used for the storage and display of silverware and china.

wedge A tapered piece of wood, metal, or other hard material, inserted under something to force it up or hold it in place.

weep hole A hole, such as near the bottom of a retaining wall, that allows water to drain to the outside of a wall and prevent a buildup of pressure behind it.

weft In weaving, the treads that run across the width of a loom. A.K.A. **woof**

weld A general term describing various methods of applying heat, at suitable temperature, to pieces of metals for the purpose of uniting them, with or without the use of filler metal. **welded joint**

welding The process of uniting two pieces of metal by heating, with a torch or electricity.

welding rod A filler metal, in the form of a wire or rod, used

well

in arc-welding, gas welding, and brazing that actually holds a weld together.

well A deep hole or shaft sunk into the earth to obtain water, oil, gas, etc. A.K.A. **wellhole 2**. An open space extending vertically through the floors of a building, such as for stairs or ventilation. **3**. An enclosed space for receiving and holding something, such as the wheels of an airplane when retracted.

well curb A parapet wall around a well.

welting See: **piping**

western hemlock *(Wood)* A white to yellowish brown, straight-grained, moderately low-density softwood native to North America, used for general construction and plywood. Similar in character and uses to **sugar pine**.

western larch *(Wood)* A strong, reddish brown, coarse-textured softwood, native to the western USA, used in general construction and flooring.

western red cedar
(Wood) A durable, low-density, straight-grained softwood, native to the western U.S., with color variations ranging from a decided red, *from the heart of the tree*, to almost white, *from the outer layers* **(sapwood)**, with the extremes of both colors often found in a single board. Used extensively for shingles and pencils, but chiefly used to line clothes closets and chests, as its pungent aromatic odor repels insects, particularly moths.

western stick See: **Craftsman style**

wet wall A term used by plumbers to indicate a wall meant for plumbing fixtures, such as the wall in a shower with all the control knobs.

whaler Two boards attached at right angle and used as a brace to strengthen a wall or concrete form. See: **strongback**

what-not shelving
Ornamented shelves used to hold brick-a-brac and china.

wheelbarrow A handcart with one front wheel and two supporting legs in back, used to transport materials short distances.

wheelbarrow

wheeling step
See: **winder stairs**

wheel window A large round window with radial mullions. A.K.A. **Catherine wheel window, rose window**

whispering gallery A large room with a dome or roof so shaped that its acoustical characteristics occasionally allow conversations in one area of a room to be heard as whispers at a particular point on the other side of the room. *NOTE: Usually created accidentally.*

white A surface that reflects light without changing its spectral attributes.

White House The official residence of the president of the United States.

The White House

white lauan See: lauan A.K.A. **Philippine mahogany**

white mahogany A creamy-colored mahogany native to Mexico. See: **mahogany** A.K.A. **primavera**

white walnut See: **butternut**

whitewash A mixture of lime and water, often containing whiting or glue, applied like paint to fences, walls, and structures, that dries to a white coating. **2.** To conceal or gloss over wrongdoing.

whitewood The trade name for **poplar** and **cottonwood**.

whiting Dried chalk ground to a fine powder and used in paint and whitewash.

wholesale showroom A **showroom** established by a manufacturer or distributor that services and sells only to industry professionals and companies engaged in the fields of construction or design. A.K.A. **for-the-trade**

wicker A flexible twig or branch, as from a willow, used in weaving baskets or making furniture.

wickiup A Native American dwelling round or oval in plan, with a rounded roof structure consisting of a bent pole framework covered by pressed branches, bark, or skins, as made by the Pai Ute and Algonquin tribes. A.K.A. **wigwam**

widow's walk A walkway or narrow platform with a view of the sea atop the roof of early New England homes.

wigwam See: **wickiup**

wilderness An uninhabited, potentially dangerous area.

wilton carpet A cut-pile wool carpet with a cotton backing.

windbreak Any structure erected as shelter from wind.

winder stairs The wedge-shaped treads of a staircase that makes a turn, but doesn't have a landing at the turn. A.K.A. **wheeling step** *NOTE: Utilized in applications where space is an issue.*

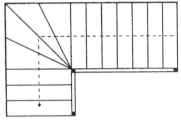

winder stairs

window A glazed opening in an exterior wall that provides an interior space with natural light and ventilation.

window frame The rough-framed opening for a window.

window guard A decorative security grille placed over a window.

window lead The lead channels used to hold small pieces of beveled or stained glass, as found in a **stained glass window**

window pane The glass in a window. A.K.A. **glazing, light**

window post An upright post separating a pair or series of windows.

window sash The framework within a window, movable or fixed.

windowsill The bottom of a window opening. See: **sill**

window stool The interior sill trim on a window.

window treatment The various elements *(casings, draperies, shutters, shades, valances, etc.)* that cover and/or decorate a window.

Windsor chair A style of chair. See: **chair styles**

wine cellar A cool dry room for storing wine. A.K.A. **wine vault**

wine vault See: **wine cellar**

wing An extension to an existing building, or part of a building that is distinctly different from the main structure.

wing-back chair

wing-back chair A high upholstered style of chair or sofa with wings at both sides of the back. Originally made to contain heat from a fireplace and/or protect against drafts.

wing wall A small low wall, usually meant to carry a structure, such as a bridge. **2.** Theatrically, a wall of scenery, moved into place, as needed, to cover various camera angles or hide something from the audience's view.

wire lath Wire mesh used as a backing for plaster and stucco to adhere to. *NOTE: Wire lath replaced the common use of wood strips known as lath. Today, most plaster is applied to drywall.*

wire nut A device used to connect the ends of electrical wires.

WINDOW STYLES

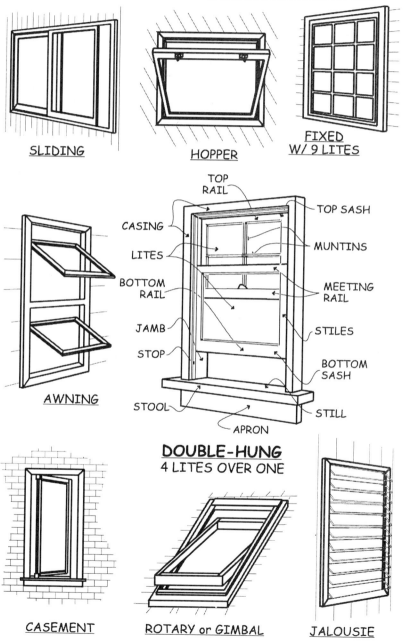

SLIDING

HOPPER

FIXED
W/ 9 LITES

AWNING

TOP RAIL

CASING

LITES

BOTTOM RAIL

JAMB

STOP

TOP SASH

MUNTINS

MEETING RAIL

STILES

BOTTOM SASH

STOOL

STILL

APRON

DOUBLE-HUNG
4 LITES OVER ONE

CASEMENT

ROTARY or GIMBAL

JALOUSIE

WINDOW STYLES

TYPICAL CONFIGURATIONS

WINDOW STYLES

TYPICAL CONFIGURATIONS

WINDOW STYLES
TYPICAL CONFIGURATIONS

witness line A line used as a reference. A.K.A. base line

wood The trunk of a tree that has been cut into usable boards. A.K.A. **timber** See: **lumber**

wood carving A sculpture in wood.

wood construction
Anything constructed of wood.

woodcut A design engraved on the surface of a wooden block, once used to print patterns on wallpaper and textiles.

wood flooring Hardwood and softwood boards or tiles, of various sizes and configurations, used to decorate a floor.

wood-frame construction Any building constructed of *(2x4, 2x6)* **dimensional lumber** and standard stud wall construction methods. A.K.A. **stick framing**

wood grain Descriptive of wood having wide-ringed, coarse, or grained annual rings, that show the growth of the tree. *NOTE: Wide rings denotes weaker structure than narrow-ringed wood.*

wood stain Various oils and finishes intended to protect and/or color visible and exposed wood surfaces; often paint with paint thinner added.

woodworking machinery Large saws, planers, shapers, sanders, drills,

etc., found in mills, manufacturing, or shops; used to make furniture, windows, stair railings, etc.

woof See: **weft**

workbench A counter-height bench where a craftsman works on small projects.

workbench

working drawings Scaled, measurable drawings (plans, elevations, and details), used to describe, estimate, and build whatever structure or object the drawings describe. A.K.A. **architectural drawings**

workmanship A craftsman's skills demonstrated in his work.

workshop A room or structure equipped to carry on some kind of work, often mechanical or artistic.

wreath An interwoven circular band or garland of leaves, fruit, flowers, etc.

wrecking bar See: **crowbar** A.K.A. **pry bar**, **pinch bar**

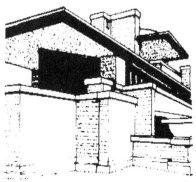

Robie House – Chicago
Frank Lloyd Wright

Wright, Frank Lloyd (1869-1959) Renowned and innovative American architect from the **Chicago school of architecture.** See: **prairie architecture**

X-brace Any braces which cross each other to form the letter *X*. **X-bracing** A.K.A. **cross-brace, scissor brace**

X-acto knife

X-acto knife An artists' knife with a replacable blade. X-acto is a trademark brand name.

yard Part of a lot or parcel of land, not occupied by a building, that is often landscaped. **2.** A term used to describe a quantity of **concrete**, expressed in **cubic yards. 3.** A area devoted to storing bricks, aggregates, and other materials.

yardage A term used to describe the amount of fabric required to upholster a sofa or chair.

yarn dyed Describes yarns dyed before being woven into fabric.

Y-branch A

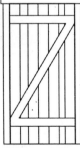
Z-braced door

connection that splits one line (electricity, air, phone, water, etc.) into two.

yellowing A brownish yellow coating that develops over time.

yellow ocher A yellow pigment used for paint. **yellow ochre**

yellow pine (Wood) The most commonly used light grade construction (softwood) lumber, with a pleasant yellow color. Often used for paint grade or stained interior trim and furniture. Native to Georgia and the Carolinas, with the common name **southern yellow pine.** See: **pine** A.K.A. **pine, hard pine**

yellow poplar (Wood) See: **poplar**

yelm A bundle of reeds or combed straw used as thatching material for a roof.

yew (Wood) A deep red-brown, close-grained hardwood. An evergreen native to England and parts of Europe. Frequently used in cabinetwork and paneling.

yoke A custom fit cross-bar support or binding beam made to hold another object in place.

Yorkshire chair A chair style of the **Jacobean** era. A.K.A. **Jacobean chair**

Z-brace A Z-shaped brace (backing) on a batten door.

zebrawood (Wood) A moderately dense, light golden-yellow hardwood with pronounced dark brown stripes. Native to central and western Africa. Used for plywood veneers and decorative applications. A.K.A. **zebrano**

zigzag A traditional ornamental pattern used in molding and fabrics. A.K.A. **dancette**

zigzag rule A folding ruler whose sections pivot to form a long stiff ruler when fully opened. A precursor to the modern tape measure.

zinc A hard, bluish white metal, not subject to corrosion, used for galvanizing sheet steel and iron, and as an oxide for white paint pigment.

zinc chromate A bright yellow pigment used in paints. A.K.A. **buttercup yellow, zinc yellow**

zinc coating See: galvanized

zone In air-conditioning or heating systems, a space (or group of spaces), whose temperature (or humidity) is regulated by a single control. **2.** A branch or subdivision of a water supply system or sprinkler.

zoning A system of controlling the use of land and buildings by the local municipality, established through the adoption of a municipal ordinance, including population density, open space, setbacks from the street, parking requirements, etc. The principal instrument in implementing a master plan.

zoning permit A permit issued by appropriate municipal authority authorizing land to be used for a specific purpose.

zoological garden A park designed to house and exhibit wild, often large, animals.

APPENDIX

WOODS
Quick Reference

acacia *(Hardwood)*

aceitillo *(Hardwood)*
   Similar to **satinwood**

alder *(Hardwood)*
   Similar to **birch**

amaranth *(Hardwood)*

amboyna *(Hardwood)*

apple *(Hardwood)*

arbor-vitae *(Hardwood)*
   Similar to **thuya**

ash *(Hardwood)*

avodire *(Hardwood)*

bamboo *(Softwood)*

baywood *(Softwood)*
   A.K.A. **Honduras mahogany**

beech *(Hardwood)*
   Similar to **maple** and **birch**

birch *(Hardwood)*
   Similar to **beech** and **maple**

black walnut *(Hardwood)*
   Similar to **butternut**

boxwood *(Hardwood)*

butternut *(Hardwood)*
   Similar to **black walnut**
      (except for color)
   A.K.A. **white walnut**

cedar *(Softwood)*
   Similar to **Persian cedar**
                  (nanmu)

cherry *(Hardwood)*
   Similar to **mahogany**
      (in appearance)

chestnut *(Hardwood)*
   (coarse-grained **oak**)
   Related to **beech**

circassian walnut
                  (Hardwood)
   (very curly grain)
   Similar in color to **red gum**

cocobolo *(Hardwood)*

coromandel *(Hardwood)*
   See: **Macassar ebony**
   A.K.A. **calamander, striped ebony**

cottonwood *(Softwood)*
   See: **poplar**

cypress *(Hardwood)*

Douglas fir *(Softwood)*

ebony *(Hardwood)*
   Also dark red, green, and
   coffee-brown with black
   streaks (**Macassar ebony**)

elm *(Hardwood)*

English sycamore
                  (Hardwood)
   See: **harewood**

eucalyptus
   A.K.A. **gumwood**
          oriental wood,
          oriental walnut

fir *(Softwood)*
   See: **Douglas fir**
   A.K.A. **white fir**
          silver fir
          balsam fir

French burl *(Hardwood)*

gum wood *(Hardwood)*
   (white to gray-green in color)
   Similar to **red gum**

harewood *(Hardwood)*
   A.K.A. **Sycamore,**
          English sycamore

hemlock *(Softwood)*
  Similar to **sugar pine**
  See: **western hemlock**
  A.K.A. **hemlock**

hickory *(Hardwood)*
  Similar to **oak**

holly *(Softwood)*

Honduras mahogany
                      (Softwood)
  A.K.A. **baywood**

jacaranda *(Hardwood)*
  See: **rosewood**
  A.K.A. **Brazilian**
         rosewood

korina *(Hardwood)*
  Similar to **primavera**

laurel *(Hardwood)*

Macassar ebony
                  (Hardwood)
  A.K.A. **coromandel**
         striped ebony

mahogany *(Hardwood)*
  A.K.A. **Spanish mahogany,**
         primavera, korina
  See: **white mahogany**

maple *(Hardwood)*
  Varieties: **curly, bird's eye**
  Similar to **beech** and **birch**

myrtle

nanmu *(Softwood)*
  A.K.A. **Persian cedar**

oak *(Hardwood)*
  See: **hickory**

olive

palisander *(Hardwood)*

pearwood *(Hardwood)*

Persian cedar
  See: **nanmu**

pine *(Softwood)*
  Soft pine: **sugar pine**
  Hard pine: **yellow pine**

poplar *(Softwood)*
  Similar to **cottonwood**
  A.K.A. **yellow poplar**

primavera *(Hardwood)*
  Similar to **korina**
  A.K.A. **white mahogany**

red cedar *(Softwood)*
  See: **western red cedar**

red gum *(Hardwood)*
  See: **gum wood**
  Similar in color to
         circassian walnut

redwood *(Softwood)*

rosewood *(Hardwood)*
  A.K.A. **Brazilian rosewood**
         jacaranda
         bubinga

satinwood *(Hardwood)*
  Similar to **aceitillo**

snakewood *(Hardwood)*

spruce *(Softwood)*
  Similar to **yellow pine**
  A.K.A. **Norwegian spruce,**
         fir, white deal, and
         white fir

striped ebony *(Hardwood)*
  See: **Macassar ebony**
  A.K.A. **coromandel ebony,**
  coromandel, and **calamander**

sugar pine *(Softwood)*
  A.K.A. **white pine,**
         soft pine

sycamore *(Hardwood)*
  See: **harewood**

tabonuco *(Hardwood)*

teak *(Hardwood)*
  (Stronger than oak)
  A.K.A. **Indian oak**

thuya *(Hardwood)*
  Similar to **arbor-vitae**
                (same genus)

tulipwood *(Hardwood)*

walnut *(Hardwood)*
 Similar to **hickory, butternut,**
  and **black walnut**

western hemlock
    (Softwood)
 Similar to **sugar pine**.

western larch *(Softwood)*

western red cedar
    (Softwood)
 A.K.A. **red cedar**

white mahogany
    (Hardwood)
 A.K.A. **primavera**

white walnut *(Hardwood)*
 See: **butternut**

whitewood *(Softwood)*
 Trade name for **poplar**
  and **cottonwood**

yellow pine *(Softwood)*
 A.K.A. **hard pine, pine,**
  southern yellow pine

yellow poplar *(Softwood)*
 Similar to **cottonwood**

yew *(Hardwood)*

zebrawood *(Hardwood)*
 A.K.A. **zebrano**

STANDARD YARDAGE
ESTIMATE CHART

54" wide fabric

Description	Railroaded		Vertical Run	
	No Skirt	Skirt	No Skirt	Skirt
Standard Ottoman (22" X 22")	2	3	2	3
Oversized Ottoman (27" X 27")	3	4	3	4
Upholstered Side Chair *(Back & Seat)*	3	4	3	4
Fully Upholstered Arm Chair *(Reversible Seat)*	6	7	6	8
Fully Upholstered Arm Chair *(Reversible Seat & Back)*	7	9	8	9
High Back Wing-Back Chair *(Reversible Seat)*	7	8	7	9

Chaise Longue - No Cushions
    Removable Deck Cushion
    Removable Seat & Back
	8
	9
	11
		9
		11
		13
			8
			11
			12
				10
				12
				14

Seat Cushions Only
    Love Seat   -
    6'-7' Sofa
    8' Sofa
Add one (1) yard for 3 cushions
	10
	14
	15
		12
		16
		17
			12
			17
			17
				13
				17
				18

Pillow Back
    Love Seat
    6' - 7' Sofa
    8' Sofa
Add two (2) yards for 6 cushions
	14
	16
	19
		16
		18
		22
			15
			17
			19
				17
				19
				22

Three-Piece Pillow-Back Sectional 10' X 10' w/ large ottoman	32	35	34	37

BIBLIOGRAPHY

Architecture & Ornament: A visual guide, Author: Antony White and Bruce Robertson, Publisher: Design Press (McGraw Hill) 1990.

Guide to Residential Carpentry, Author: John L Feirer Publisher: Collier Books (Macmillan Publishing) 1983.

Dictionary of Architecture & Construction (Second Edition), Author: Cyril M. Harris, Publisher: McGraw Hill 1993.

Elements of Interior Design and Decoration, Author: Sherrill Whiton, Publisher: Lippincott Company 1963.

Old House Dictionary, Author: Steven J. Phillips, Publisher: The Preservation Press 1994.

The Visual Dictionary of American Domestic Architecture, Author: Rachel Carley, Publisher: Roundtable Press 1994.

Sturgis Illustrated Dictionary of Architecture and Building (Three Volume, Unabridged reprint of the 1901-02 Edition), Publisher: Dover Publications 1989.

Webster's New World Dictionary of the American Language, Publisher: The World Publishing Company 1959.

Webster's Third New International Dictionary (Unabridged), Publisher: G. & C. Merriam Company, Publisher 1981.

Better Homes & Gardens New Decoration Book 1990.

The Decorating Book, Author: Mary Gilliatt, Publisher: Darling Kindersley.

The Complete Home Decorating Book, Author: Nicholas Barnard, Publisher: Dorling Kindersley.

The Field Guide to American Houses, Author: Virginia and Lee McAlester, Publisher: Alfred A. Knopf, 1984

Simon and Shuster's Pocket Guide to Architecture, Author: Patrick Nuttgens, Publisher: Simon & Schuster Inc., Fireside Book 1980